'In a world in which we are all living longer, *Changing Gear* helps us to think deeply about how best to use this extra time. Jan and Jon draw on their immense experience to guide you through the transition from a full-on career to a rich and fulfilling life.'

Camilla Cavendish, author of *Extra Time*

'Ever since I was young, I was amazed how bad people seemed at changing gear. Now I've driven into changing-gear land myself, I can only marvel at this book, which is full of practical wisdom. The gears can indeed be changed, without creaks and groans, but with a nice sweet glide.' **Sir Anthony Seldon**, author of *Beyond Happiness*

'At a time of great inflection, many are asking big questions about "what next" in their careers and lives. *Changing Gear* offers a practical and powerful roadmap for the route ahead, drawing on rich case studies and the deep experience of the authors.'

Henry Timms, Co-Founder of Giving Tuesday and President and CEO of Lincoln Center for the Performing Arts

'How to prepare for life after an intense career. In *Changing Gear* . . . authors Jan Hall and Jon Stokes set out how this next life – or "third age" – might be approached.' ***Financial Times***

'In their new book, *Changing Gear*, Jan Hall, a former headhunter, and Jon Stokes, a psychologist, discuss the strategies that people can follow when approaching the "third stage" of life, after their childhood and their careers . . . This is a critical issue. Think of all the time people spend deciding which university they would like to attend, which course they would like to study and which career they would wish to follow. Deciding on their post-career lifestyle is just as important. They may have decades left to enjoy . . . [They] must work out who they have been, who they are now and who they would like to become. [*Changing Gear*] presents a series of case studies of people who have been through this kind of upheaval, some a lot more successfully than others . . . readers will discover that the individual stories are instructive and the questions posed by the authors are important.'

Jan Hall and Jon Stokes

Changing Gear

Creating the Life You Want
After a Full-On Career

First published in 2021 by HEADLINE HOME
an imprint of HEADLINE PUBLISHING GROUP

First published in paperback in 2022 by HEADLINE HOME
an imprint of HEADLINE PUBLISHING GROUP

1

Cataloguing in Publication Data is available from the British Library

ISBN 978 1 4722 7703 9
eISBN 978 1 4722 7701 5

Publishing Director: Lindsey Evans
Copy Editor: Tara O'Sullivan
Proofreader: Anna Herve
Indexer: Caroline Wilding
Diagrams: Jason Cox

Typeset by EM&EN
Printed and bound in Great Britain by Clays Ltd, Elcograf S.p.A.

HEADLINE PUBLISHING GROUP
An Hachette UK Company
Carmelite House
50 Victoria Embankment
London EC4Y 0DZ

www.headline.co.uk
www.hachette.co.uk

With love and thanks to our families

'To exist is to change, to change is to mature, to mature is to go on creating oneself endlessly.'

– Henri Bergson, French philosopher

Contents

Introduction

Changing gear

Who this book is for

'To be what we are, and to become what we are capable of becoming, is the only end in life.'

– Robert Louis Stevenson

At some point after passing the age of fifty, many people begin to feel a lack of certainty about how the world will work out for us, as well as for our families, friends and communities.

All of this, of course, is set in the context of a world continuing to face enormous upheaval. The ever faster evolution of and use of new technology, data and digital is bringing massive and relentless change to our organisations, jobs and lives. The only certainty is that each of us are and will continue to be affected in multiple different ways. The futurologist Alvin Toffler has suggested that 'The illiterate of the 21st century will not be those who cannot read and write, but those who cannot learn, unlearn, and relearn.'

The pandemic has also caused both individuals and organisations to re-think. It has served to accelerate the trends around the speed of uptake of new technologies and the shift to a more digital and virtual world, and at the same time has alerted us to our vulnerabilities. The consequent opportunities and threats for individuals navigating their futures have also been accelerated and brought into sharper focus.

While wider societal change is not the focus of this book, it is relevant to the sense of unease many people are feeling. This sense of unease is inevitable when people start to face up to the fact that their old certainties are gone and their future is uncertain and fast changing in both positive and negative ways.

Changing Gear speaks to this new uncertainty and anxiety. In particular, it speaks to those who have broadly loved their jobs and, to a great extent, have been defined by what they do. This work persona or sense of identity can become who they are, both to those around them and, even more so, to themselves. When questions about stepping away from this role begin to appear in their minds, for whatever reason, it can raise real questions of identity.

We are all living longer. Average life expectancy in developed countries has increased by almost 30 years since 1900; in the UK, it has gone from 51 to 79 for men, and from 55 to 83 for women. However, these are only average figures. Many more of us within the age range that is the primary focus of this book – five to ten years either side of 60 – are likely to live until our late eighties, and even well into our nineties. But we don't necessarily know what to do with the gift of this extra time, and nor does society. The idea of 'retirement' no longer holds the appeal it once did; we want to be active, contributing and valued. Much of what we have to say will also have relevance for those younger than this who want to 'downsize' or make significant changes to their lifestyles.

Working and being part of an organisation provides us with a sense of purpose, value and community: a feeling of belonging, achievement and influence. Losing that, particularly for people who have invested perhaps too much of themselves in work, can be a challenge.

Stages of life

Many religions and life philosophies describe life in terms of stages and their various challenges. In the West, we tend to view life in terms of progressing through these stages, based on the Christian tradition of moral progress culminating in an afterlife in Heaven or Hell, as described by John Bunyan in his 17th-century allegory *The Pilgrim's Progress*.

Many theories and models have been proposed to describe and explain life stages in this sort of linear progression. However, evidence to support such a formulation is controversial. Some subscribe to the idea of a crisis in the middle of life, as Dante described in *The Divine Comedy: Inferno*: 'Midway upon the journey of life, I found myself within a forest dark, for the straightforward pathway had been lost.'

Our movement through each life stage can be characterised in terms of a series of 'crises', which can offer both danger and opportunity. Each life 'crisis' gives us an opportunity to adapt previous attitudes and behaviours, retaining some or all, or modifying some to suit the challenges of the new stage. Our progress through life will be affected by the choices we make, and whether we accept or deny the changed reality, both through internal transitions and external changes. Typically, each stage begins with a feeling of being somehow 'out of sync'. What was once held together begins to fall apart, bringing a fear of disintegration.

Hindu philosophy provides a useful framework in which life is seen as a developmental path through four life stages (*Ashramas*), which are combined with four life goals.

- The first, from birth up to the age of 25, is the scholar (*Brahmacharya*), focused on learning, finding one's identity and leaving home.

- The second, from ages 25 to 55, is the householder (*Grihastha*), focused on earning a living, building a family and worldly achievement.

- The third stage, from ages 55 to 75, is a period of retreat or retirement (*Vanaprastha*), described as going into the forest to contemplate life and its meaning. The focus moves away from the family to society more broadly, and from personal gain to the creation of a better world and the welfare of the community. This entails extracting oneself from a devotion to the material world and moving towards an emphasis on spiritual pursuits. In the Western sense, we might describe it as 'self-development'. In this book, we refer to this stage as the Third Life.

- The fourth and final stage, from age 75 onwards, is a time of preparing for death (*Sannyasa*), focused on passing on wisdom and the ultimate meaning of life (and everything!).

Each stage puts life in a steadily broadening frame, with the focus moving from the individual to the family, to society and finally to the universe and the meaning of existence.

It is leaving the second and entering the third stage of life that we are primarily concerned with in this book. This is a point at which we may feel the need to make a change due to a sense of boredom or repetition, or of losing vitality and meaning in our work and life. It can often result in us redoubling our efforts to try to preserve the life that seems to be falling apart. This is a defensive and vain attempt to reassert 'normality', and can result in overworking, stress and, often, damage to relationships.

It is normal for people to feel isolated in such uncertain times. Accepting this sense of being out in the wilderness is part of accepting the upheaval of change. Using it purposefully and thinking about what might be causing these feelings of isolation can help alleviate the sense of helplessness they can bring.

Our Western notion of 'retirement' has not traditionally captured these third and fourth phases. It was more a complete shift to the fourth and last phase, with a focus on leisure and pleasure – as captured in the advertisements for pension schemes – or, more sadly, simply a slow decline.

The realisation that one is entering a different life, our Third Life, inevitably leads to some reflection: an opportunity, as Friedrich Nietzsche puts it, to 'become who you are'. However, unlike more ancient traditions, our civilisation lacks an appropriate rite of passage. There are no rituals and expectations to help us adjust to and find a new balance in the third phase.

Leaving the second stage of life

Many people see work as a means to an end. For this group, their sense of purpose is fulfilled outside the work environment through their relationships and hobbies or other activities. However, for those who see work as a key part of their purpose, being faced with reconsidering or expanding their sense of self outside their work role (or in new roles that are less demanding or carry less kudos) can be very daunting. Not only does this mean losing their day-to-day routine, it also brings into question their 'status' in their particular community: their 'power', their sense of being needed, their relevance and their legacy.

This book is intended to be a guide to a phase of life for which our society has yet to develop its own norms and structures: a phase where happiness can be achieved in a variety of different ways. For some, it will include some work, be it paid or unpaid, perhaps using the valuable experience and skills they have learned over the span of a career, or perhaps in a completely new area. There is no universal formula. Everyone will find a different answer for themselves. Of course, this makes it harder, in some ways, than the transition from being a student to embarking on a career, as for many there was already a well-trodden path to follow as they moved from their first to second stage of life.

The book begins by exploring why work, particularly a successful career, can be such an important part of a person's identity.

Chapter 1 shares life stories showing examples of people who have been through this process. After each individual story, we shine a light on its underlying, and sometimes unconscious, psychological and social dynamics.

Chapters 2, 3, 4 and 5 highlight the factors at play in order to help you understand more deeply the drivers of this sometimes tumultuous phase of life. These chapters offer a sound psychological underpinning to the whole process of undergoing a work–life transition. A number of relevant theories and frameworks are explored to give you some intellectual context and content for what you might be feeling and experiencing.

Chapter 6 introduces the Eight-step Transition Process that will serve as a guide to moving from the second to the third phase of life.

Much of this tumult is a result of the challenge of finding a new set of values, new purpose and meaning, and new goals and ways of achieving them. Chapter 7 provides a practical toolkit for helping you make change happen in your life, with helpful questions and exercises to enable you to explore how you can become 'the best you can be', both during and after your transition.

Finally, Chapter 8 briefly highlights those all-important practical necessities and issues that must be faced and attended to. Taking time to get these prerequisites right is an essential element of making a successful transition and creating the life you want.

As you work your way through the book, you might find it useful to keep a notebook with you, so that you can make notes and carry out some of the exercises.

Entering the third stage of life

The change involved in moving into the third stage of life is not the same as the traditional midlife crisis, which is more about a fear of losing one's youth. After 40 – and especially after 50 – only those capable of total denial still think they are young! However, they also rarely think of themselves as *old*. So, what are they? And, indeed, who are they? Answering these questions now really matters for the many who, hopefully, happily, have a long life ahead!

In our parents' generation, you had a childhood, an adulthood and then you retired. For this generation aged 50-plus, there are some who relish the opportunity to retire and leave the world of full-time work far behind. Assuming they are financially secure enough for the life they are happy to lead in retirement, then this is a blessing – but this book is not for them. This book is for those who recoil from the R-word and are still thinking through how they want their lives to be, either while they are still working, or within a year or two (or more) of having left full-time work. This is a process that takes some time and, for some, one that can be iterative over a few years.

Changing Gear is about recognising that, as one's role as an 'important' person at work shifts and comes to an end, it is accompanied by premonitions of mental and physical vulnerability, and ultimately frailty. Fears that can either be allowed to take over, or can be accepted as part of recognising one's mortality. (And no amount of worldly success or wealth can make *that* go away.)

This time of life often coincides with 'empty nesting', when children leave home and take with them that parental sense of being needed. No longer being needed at home or at work can be an extremely uncomfortable realisation. For some, it can feel like an exciting adventure; for others, it can seem an unwelcome torture. But for all in this position, it represents a big change to their status quo. Our brains are not always helpful companions on this journey. Two helpful concepts illustrate why this can be the case: the 'brain as an organ' and the 'elephant rider'.

THE BRAIN AS AN ORGAN

Our bodies have five vital organs: the heart, lungs, liver, kidney and brain. These organs mostly function without our knowledge, and each play different roles in keeping us alive and healthy. One function common to them all is to keep us in equilibrium, and therefore to keep our internal environment stable. This is where the brain can be unhelpful to our pursuit of change, by heightening our fear of *externally* imposed change. While we might *consciously* embrace the idea of change, the brain's task is also to alert us to danger, which impending change may provoke. Often this function is essential, but it can hold us back when we are trying to make changes to our lives.

THE ELEPHANT RIDER

And now to the elephant rider. This is a tale of the reasoning rider and the emotional elephant. It is a metaphor to describe the relationship between two very differently sized parts of our minds: the smaller conscious reasoning part and the larger, sometimes unconscious, emotional part. The reasoning rider perches precariously on the emotional elephant, and when the two disagree on direction, guess which one wins?! We explain this in more detail in Chapter 2.

These two concepts, which both highlight our inability to 'control' our brains, simply serve to illustrate that the change is not necessarily going to be straightforward or happen quickly. It will require some considerable personal effort and perseverance.

THE THIRD LIFE

Entering the Third Life necessarily raises many questions. These include:

— Who am I now?

— What would I like to define me in the future?

— What might my options and choices be?

— How will I get from here to there?

— What will the impact be on those around me?

— How can I be the 'best me' in this next phase of my life?

— How do I begin to answer all the questions above?

These are questions most people would do well to ask themselves either side of 60, unless they are in a happy state of denial, or among the lucky few who have already found the answers.

Some might well be reflecting on what they have missed out on, how they can build on what they have already done, what they would still love to do, and many similar questions. Some will desire to spend their new-found free time tackling the issues dividing society or the problems threatening the planet. Others will look to find meaning in other ways.

This book is here for everyone who wants to make the most of this time they will 'win'. It is a time of real opportunity for review and renewal: an opportunity the authors are both trying to grasp too.

It is difficult to prepare for this shift, but there will come a moment when it needs to be confronted. There could be many different triggers, including significant changes at work or at home, or a sense of wanting a life with greater purpose or a better balance.

For some, the choice to leave a role is theirs to make, while for others, factors beyond their control make the choice for them. The reasons why people find themselves facing change differ widely but the challenges that they then face, and the ways in which they can deal successfully (or not) with making their transitions, are much more similar.

The traditional midlife crisis in your early forties typically entails accepting who you are, that your personality, strengths and weaknesses are unlikely to change very significantly, and that some of your aspirations simply won't be fulfilled. The solution is to make the best of what you have, rather than continuing to dream about what you might be capable of. It is a very different place from the sense of crisis that can come with entering the Third Life. It is a period that often throws up some challenging self-reflection. It necessarily has to involve changing who you are, having already achieved (or settled for) your assets and status. It is not going to be just about you, but also about the community in which you participate: it will mean redefining your role in your work community and exploring new roles in other communities. Moving to the position of 'work elder' might postpone the change – but, one day, having to accept the situation is likely to become inevitable.

Work can seem straightforward because it is so familiar, but many may not have considered what it has shielded them from. For some, work has provided an escape from the intimacy of domestic relationships, which can now seem threatening. For others, it may have prevented the development of a broader hinterland of friendships and hobbies, which now have to be discovered.

The problem with a life built on achievement is that the alternative may feel like failure, and so to change course feels an impossibility. But status and achievement can be separated: worldly success and successful relationships are very different. In addition, work has, for some, served as a formal escape from engaging in the domestic routines of day-to-day living, so that a life without work can feel daunting. If one has built up an enviable status at work, then one can easily assume its loss will provoke denigration and feelings of humiliation, exposing the fact that being dependent on the opinions of others is a fragile ship to sail in.

The psychologist William Bridges makes a distinction between change and transition: things change, but people transition. By this, he meant that a mechanical model of simply replacing one thing with another, like deleting an app and installing a new one, is a very long way from accurately describing what happens in human beings, or indeed animals in general. We need time to explore and investigate the new, then return to the familiar, like a child to its mother, before venturing out again, only gradually feeling that the new something is safe enough to commit to. He distinguished three phases of transition – first letting go, then being in the zone of uncertainty, and finally new beginnings.[1] This book takes a deeper dive into these phases with the creation of the eight-stage transition process in order to help the reader identify where they are in the journey, and how to make the process a more productive one.

We hope that this book will serve as a guide for managing successful transitions during this age of anxiety and longer lives. It will provide insight and advice to help you successfully confront issues and make better decisions, while taking account of your individual, domestic and professional make-up. It will provide the tools and understanding to help you find your transition mindset and create a roadmap to plan what might be waiting ahead.

Both of us have seen many people make transitions in their work and home lives, and we have also experienced this same disruption ourselves. Our goal and purpose in writing this book is to provide a much-needed route map for helping you to change gear and create your own 'transition mindset', enabling you to make the most of the huge gift of maybe twenty extra years between giving up full-time, full-on work and the inevitable slowing down that comes in the fourth phase of life. In the past, retirement was more synonymous with slowing down, and all too often illness and death, as life expectancy was shorter. *Changing Gear* recognises the possibilities of a Third Life, and how to make it just as fulfilling as the second phase – if not more so.

1

Approaching a gear change – everyone is different

Changes occur all the time. They can be identifiable and dramatic, or they can emerge imperceptibly, creeping up on you until one day you realise your foundations are less solid than you imagined. Whatever the trigger, your response will shape your future.

Before we look at how to manage your own transition process successfully, we are going to explore a number of different scenarios for how people might begin to experience their change of gear. In this chapter, through individual stories presented with a psychologist's perspective on each, we show what might trigger the desire or need for a change of gear, and explore what some of the psychological drivers might be.

No two life stories and no two people are the same, and although no one else's story is likely to exactly match yours, we hope that there will be some element of relevance for everyone.

We hope this will help to open up your own thinking about the process you will need to go through to change your gear and find what will work best for you for the next stage of your life.

Handing over the reins

Our first scenario looks at Daniel, who made the decision to step down from being CEO, but found it less straightforward than he anticipated.

Letting go has never been easy. As Shakespeare reminds us in *Richard II*, when the king hands over his crown to Boling-broke: 'You may my glories and my state depose but not my griefs; still am I king of those.' As a leader, you may relinquish your power and position, but your griefs and emotions are not transferable. Your emotional life stays with you and can, if not attended to, wreak havoc.

When planning for your succession, the psychological impact of the change is easy to ignore. As with death, people tend to focus on the practical arrangements (financial planning, communications, etc.). This is necessary and understandable. Equally important for a successful transfer of power, though, are the 'softer' issues relating to your own identity: coming to terms with a loss of status and the fact that you are replaceable and mortal. Inevitably, this leads to changes in your priorities and relationships. These so-called 'soft issues' become the ones that matter most.

Daniel's story covers some of the issues that arise when a leader or founder finds themselves facing the end of their reign. Although some people are able to thrive as they hand over the reins and are genuinely able to move forwards into a new life, the vast majority find this transition more challenging than they anticipate. Our story describes how Daniel plans his own succession with a logical approach for both himself and his people. However, despite his impeccable logic, he finds his own emotions less easy to manage. While his head is saying one thing, his heart is experiencing another. Over time, Daniel charts a course to where his head was taking him and ultimately where his heart is happy to be.

DANIEL'S STORY
The CEO of a high-profile business

Daniel came from a relatively humble background. He was the first person in his family to go to university and, although he acquired the trappings of a successful businessman, he remembered his roots. He was hard working, loyal and committed to his work.

When he was appointed to the top job in his company, he was over the moon to get the recognition he had always worked so hard to achieve. Over the eight years, he achieved significant success and was universally regarded as having done a great job. OK, he wasn't perfect, and there were things he could have done or not done that might have made things even better, but on balance he had done pretty well!

As Daniel was nearing 60, he began to think about the next stage of his career. He assumed he would go on to become the chairman of a similarly successful company, as many of his peers had done.

The question was when to make the move. He loved being the CEO, but as he was approaching 60 and had had such a long run in the role, he felt that the pressure to hand over the reins would begin to grow. Daniel was also quite tired, but the role constantly provided stimulation and congratulations, so he pushed to one side the reality that he was becoming more tired than he would like to be.

His wife was pretty supportive, but regularly complained that he was not at home enough for her or his daughters and their much-loved family dog. Quite recently, she had said to him that she wanted them to spend more time together before they were too old to enjoy the fruits of the financial success he had achieved.

He loved his wife and children, but also loved how much work needed him. For quite some time now, it had been easier to jump to the demands of his job rather than try to balance his work and home life – and while at work he was a hero, at home, although he was not a zero, he certainly wasn't top dog!

An honourable man who was basically comfortable in his own skin, he had been diligent in developing successors for his role. Although on paper there were several potential successors for the board to consider, Daniel had recognised two members of his top team whom he believed would be strong potential CEOs for the business. This made him feel he could make the decision to go with his head held high and with his legacy in good hands. This was hugely important to him.

Confident that things were in good shape, he talked to some trusted advisers and his wife and decided that he should begin the process of stepping down from his role as CEO. Then he talked to his board and briefed them on his views about who could best succeed him. They saw Daniel as a man in control who had made a calm, rational decision.

However, as soon as he had done so, Daniel realised that, somewhere deep inside, he had hoped they would say, 'Please stay for another two years, we need you.' (And two years seemed far enough away that the reality of leaving could be ignored for now!) Despite his taking the lead and his apparently clear decision, once he crossed the Rubicon, Daniel had a very serious wobble.

This was exacerbated by the fact that once he had shared his thinking, he suddenly found that others were beginning to drive the agenda of his leaving. He had absolutely made the decision to go himself, but suddenly he felt out of control and unwanted.

This did not bring out the best in him. Rather than stepping back graciously, he began to pick up the reins more tightly and impose his views on his top team, who at this stage suspected, but did not know of, his decision. It was not extreme behaviour on his part but it was unfortunate, as it made everyone uncomfortable and slightly marred his last period as CEO.

He did not know how to share with others what was happening to him, as he had been the one to make the decision and he felt exposing himself in this way would make him feel worse.

The real issue for him was that he could not envisage how his life would be – and indeed who *he* would be – without the trappings of his CEO role. Not only not doing the job itself, but not having the respect – and, in truth, power – that it bestowed upon him, as well as all the other benefits it brought in terms of access to other leaders and influencers, and all the perks that he enjoyed.

However, the die was cast and he found himself with no choice but to go. How could it be that he felt he was being pushed out when he had chosen to go? He felt terrified. Desperate not to face the future, Daniel asked to have a long handover period, which would not have been easy for anyone, least of all him. In fact, his chairman persuaded him not to wait too long because there were plans afoot in the company that meant it made sense for a new CEO to be in the driving seat sooner rather than later. Daniel could see this was true, and so his rational self came in to play and he agreed.

On the one hand, with the benefit of hindsight, he wished he had more carefully thought through how to talk to his chairman so that he could have managed the process better and had more control himself. But on the other hand, he could now see that it was never going to be at all easy, and in a way the momentum that developed once he made his intentions clear did mean that the agony was not more prolonged.

Happily for him, in time, the possibility of other work roles did emerge, and Daniel began to feel his old sense of worth returning. He was given lots of advice by all sorts of well-meaning people. This included the advice to take time out to think about what he really wanted to do next. It was not advice he liked, as he felt a huge urge to replace his CEO stature with another role that would keep him 'safe' in the business world. In the end, a chairman role that was a great fit for Daniel appeared just before he left his CEO position, but it was not due to start for six months. This meant Daniel was able to take some time out while still secure about his next steps in the business world. Importantly, it also meant he was able to spend some time taking a couple of long holidays with his wife as she had requested.

During this period, he began to enjoy having more time at home with his family and, on rare occasions, he even felt there were moments where he was top dog. However, he also discovered that his wife, while wanting to spend more time with him *some* of the time, did not want to spend more time with him *all* of the time!

At times, he was left at something of a loose end – a very unusual state of affairs for him. Finding himself under-occupied, Daniel rather tentatively reached out to old friends and, happily, he started to rediscover some hobbies and passions that had been rather neglected during his corporate existence. He even began to wonder why he had not valued spending time outside work more in the past few years.

By the time Daniel took up his new chairman role, a number of other offers had arrived at his door. While he was, in his own mind, embracing his new, more balanced life, he kept feeling that he should accept. The sense of being recognised for who he was in the corporate world proved just too alluring. Needless to say, this left his wife rather exasperated!

A tale of reactions to the loss of power
A psychological perspective on Daniel's story

The quotation from *Richard II* cited earlier tells us of the almost inevitable depression that follows the loss of power and position. However, as gifted a psychologist as Shakespeare was, he was writing well before our now greater understanding of unconscious processes. We now know that, when faced with grief and negative emotions, our psychological defence mechanisms can repress them into the unconscious. The result can be that we either no longer feel these undesirable (and now repressed) emotions. We see the other person as suffering the feelings of loss, and consequently needing us not to leave, rather than facing our own mixed feelings about our departure. This is also played out in James's story (page 61), rather more tragically than in Daniel's. Although he acknowledges the need to go, Daniel finds it hard to accept that he is no longer needed. We learn that he secretly hoped that the board would ask him to stay on for another two years, a period of time long enough to push any fears he had about the future into the long grass of eternity. At the root of this is a difficulty coming to terms with the inevitable feelings of emptiness that any loss produces, particularly in a man with a high need for control who has chosen a job where he is literally on top of things. It is said that a career in politics always ends in failure, meaning that, in the end, most heads of state are pushed out rather than departing gracefully. Daniel almost falls victim to this, but fortunately avoids it due to his rational self.

We learn that he is a person to whom recognition from others is a significant motivation. We also learn that he came from a humble background, so social recognition in wider society may well have played an important part in his desire for the job of CEO, and may be making it even harder to let go. There may be an unconscious fear that, without this social recognition, he would not amount to very much. While all loss entails a feeling of emptiness, how this emptiness is experienced differs between people.

Like all CEOs, Daniel is a man who seeks and enjoys power. Typically, such people dislike, and are relatively intolerant of, feelings of vulnerability and helplessness. They are often unable to recognise it in themselves and see it only in others, usually with disapproval. However, once Daniel had made his decision and announced it, he felt vulnerable and was helpless to reverse the decision. The loss of power in organisations is frequently dramatic in reality as well as in feelings. New coalitions develop without you. Once you have announced your departure from an organisation, power and influence rapidly drain away: the so-called 'lame duck' phenomenon (the literal meaning of which is a duck who is unable to keep up with the rest of the flock and therefore becomes vulnerable to predators). While Daniel's colleagues seem to have been generally generous in their reactions, there are many organisations where this is not the case. As soon as someone announces their departure, others are eager for the benefits that are now up for grabs, and can show a cruel disregard for how this might feel to the person who is about to leave. It is not uncommon for an organisation to attempt to speed up the departure and want the whole process to be over quickly. The expression 'to cross the Rubicon' has its roots in a decision made by Julius Caesar in 49 BCE. When he accepted the role of governor of Gaul, he was required by the Senate to give up his power in Rome and, as a means of restricting his power, was expressly forbidden to bring his troops back to Italy. As he was about to cross the Rubicon river into Italy, Caesar reputedly said 'Let the die be cast'.

Humans are prone to anthropomorphism, the childish projection of human agency on to non-human things: the belief, for example, that thunder is the result of the gods being angry. It is not something we ever fully grow beyond. When under stress, we all tend to regress to these sorts of more primitive ways of thinking and feeling. We are prone to the assumption that organisations are there to look after us like a parent, ignoring the fact that organisations are driven by the logic and mechanics of marketplace survival, with limited capacity for human feeling. Indeed, one of the tasks of good leadership is to mitigate organisations being overly focused on the personal ambitions and needs of the senior people within them.

Characteristically for people who find vulnerability and not being in control difficult, Daniel appears to find intimate personal relationships more challenging than relationships at work. In all close relationships, a dramatic change to one party's life inevitably has repercussions for the other. This is why making plans for changing gear should always involve others: their lives will be affected as well as yours, and they need to be involved in decisions that will have consequences for them too.

Daniel is keen to have a good legacy. This is a term that is frequently used by those in positions of power, as if they could control what happens next and what their reputation will be, failing to realise that, although they can *influence* their reputation or legacy, it is not simply a matter of their choosing. Fairly or unfairly, Daniel's 'legacy' will be something others – and history – will decide.

We learn that, once Daniel declared his intended departure, he did not step back graciously, but began to pick up the reins more tightly and to impose his views on others, making them feel uncomfortable, which slightly marred his last period as CEO. To let go with good grace is indeed a difficult thing to do. We learn that Daniel wondered who he would be without the trappings of his role (the word 'trappings' has its origins in a kind of cloth or ornament placed on a special horse). If Daniel was not to be the horse that pulled the cart, what was he to do? We can learn from Daniel's observation that he wished he had managed the whole process better, and thereby achieved some control over or influence on events. Of course, this is easy to say and harder to achieve. It will usually mean reaching out to someone else – in Daniel's case, probably his chairman – a difficult thing to do for somebody who is likely to take great pride in his autonomy and independence, and apparent lack of need for others.

The challenges of a transition as great as this normally require a period of time for reflection of at least six months, if not one to two years. It was perhaps fortunate that his new role as chairman was not immediately available, giving Daniel time to reflect. Frequently, it is impossible to reflect on what's next until one has left a busy job. It is difficult to start thinking about a new relationship before the old one has come to an end, and to take action prematurely may mean taking on a new job that is not really quite the right fit. Happily for Daniel, it looks as though things will work out well for him even if the patterns in his marriage remain unaltered – some work on these will perhaps need to be done at a later stage.

Personal crisis

A personal trauma or tragedy may strike at any time, forcing you to take stock of your life and what matters to you most. Questions you may not have asked yourself since you set out on your career become central to planning your transition. What are your real priorities? What makes you fulfilled? What balance are you looking for between your working life and domestic life? How much do you need to live on? What are your hopes and fears for the next 20 years?

For most of us, the demands of our daily lives leave little room for introspection or reassessment. We stay focused on the goals, achievements and pressure of our professional lives. So when an event occurs out of the blue, such as a major illness or the loss of a partner, we are knocked off balance, unsure how best to respond.

Our story uses the example of a personal illness. Davinia was a full-on businesswoman who suddenly discovered she had an aggressive cancer, which required her to pull right back from her hectic work life. In her case, she had no choice about the actions she took, but having stepped back, she was able to take a different perspective on how she wanted to live her life after her recovery. Although having cancer can never be described as a gift, Davinia discovered there was a gift in the reappraisal her cancer demanded.

With the right approach to transition, what first appears as a setback can become a positive pivot providing a catalyst for a reinvented and happier life. Many people who have been through a transition of this kind ask themselves why they didn't make the changes in their lives sooner.

DAVINIA'S STORY
Successful entrepreneur and owner of a consulting business

Davinia seemed to have had a gilded life. Born into a family of successful entrepreneurs, she had a secure and pretty privileged childhood.

Her parents, while not academic themselves, were very ambitious for her, so there was pressure on Davinia to succeed academically and be the kind of daughter that her parents could 'show off' to their friends. She excelled at school and university and, in time, built her own very successful business in the field of energy consulting.

She married but did not have children, and much of her life was her business. She loved being an entrepreneur and building her own business, and also relished the intellectual challenges it brought, as well as the limelight her success shone on her. She had one or two old girlfriends, but did not really let others in close or spend a great deal of time with family and friends. Her persona to the world was her role at work.

In her early fifties, Davinia started to feel her energy was failing. She thought this was the first signs of 'old age': not something that she would countenance happening to her. This meant action needed to be taken! She redoubled her efforts to get to the gym and embarked upon a diet, as she felt this would help combat the tiredness. She also started working even harder and pushing herself to do more to drive her business forwards. Looking back, her husband and her colleagues had had a sense that something was not right, but as she had not shared with anyone that she was feeling less than invincible, they simply watched her drive herself ever harder.

Then, one weekend, she felt she could not get out of bed. Unable to deny the need to seek medical help, Davinia went to see a doctor. Her symptoms did not point to a clear diagnosis and it took several months to reveal that she had a rare form of blood cancer.

During this time, Davinia tried to carry on as normal. She had no choice but to tell her assistant, as she needed her help to schedule her hospital appointments – and also to ensure no one else knew what was going on or where she was going. When it came to her husband, Davinia felt she had to tell him, but she played it down and did not share with him just how bad she felt or how worried she was. Both her assistant and her husband supported her as much as they could – and as much as she would let them, which was not a lot!

After her diagnosis, she had to accept that the treatment she needed would mean pulling right back from her work. Although the doctors were crystal clear about this, it still took her some time to get her head around the fact that this was for real. The doctors were insistent that her treatment needed to start straight away, and that she absolutely could not continue to work during this time. Never one to give in, she fought back and came to an agreement with her doctors that she could do some work, explaining to them that many people relied upon her. Her colleagues were shocked when they found out about her diagnosis, but it did explain why she had seemed to be a bit less effective in recent months. They were incredibly supportive, but Davinia still initially found it almost unbearable to let go and accept help. But there was no other choice – and, by now, she was feeling beyond tired.

The treatment was pretty brutal and, after the first few weeks, she had to face reality and accept that she really did need to stop working completely: partly because she had no energy at all, and partly because she had now realised that it was her best chance of getting better. But it had been a long, hard journey to get to this point of acceptance. Her colleagues were, of course, incredibly concerned for her and worried about how the business would manage without her, but they were also relieved that there was now some clarity, and that they could get on and do what needed to be done while Davinia was away.

The unspoken worry for everyone, including Davinia, of course, was that she might not recover.

Fortunately, this was a situation no one had to confront, as the treatment went well. After a few months, the doctors were confident she would make a full recovery. They said she could begin to work again, but, by this time, without the need for the doctors to have another tussle with her, Davinia had come to the painful realisation that she could not go back to her old 'full-on' life, where she was in control of her own agenda and that of her business. The doctors' advice was to work part-time, but to make sure she had plenty of down time and always slept well.

So, after much struggling, Davinia had now accepted that her life would need to change. This meant working out how her life would now look, both at work and at home. Aware that she could not make this happen alone, she took a deep breath and, rather than just telling them what was going to happen, she consulted her husband, colleagues and clients, asking them what they thought might work best.

Now, she saw becoming 'old' not as something to run away from, but as a gift – as she now understood that the alternative really was unthinkable. The question was how to use this gift: this new, third phase of her life. When she stopped to reflect, she could see that many other people her age were struggling with the same question, but without having had the unavoidable 'push' that she had experienced. In a way, she felt that this, too, had been a gift: a very precious one.

In large part, her work colleagues were supportive, although a small number of them had enjoyed spreading their wings in Davinia's absence and guarded, rather fiercely, their newly formed client relationships. They agreed she would work three-day weeks and take more regular holidays.

Davinia and her husband decided not only to take more regular holidays and long weekends away (something they had never done before as work had always 'needed' her too much), but also to take at least one month-long holiday each year so she could completely switch off and relax. Once they had agreed upon the plan, she was surprised to see just how excited she was about what her new life might bring.

Of course, she also had to consider the future of her business. This had always been at the back of her mind, but like many entrepreneurs, she had previously put off thinking about what would happen when she decided to stop. She had already given some of her top team shares, although as a private company controlled by her, this required relatively little risk. The risk had been not having a motivated top team. Now, she was sure what she wanted to achieve personally, so when she visited her accountants to discuss this, she was able to give them a clear brief. They came up with a number of options and, ultimately, Davinia created a scheme that would enable her to gradually hand over the shares at a more than fair price. This meant she would be able to cope financially and achieve her goal of sharing the load and stepping back.

Davinia sometimes misses the adrenaline and adoration that came with her previous life, but she has found a new rhythm and a new sense of calm. By working part-time, she is still able to enjoy the intellectual challenges of her consulting work, although she now has to be part of the team rather than leading all the teams. However, she feels that this brings its own new rewards.

In weakness there is strength: achieving grace in changing gear

A psychological perspective on Davinia's story

Children are created by parents – not just physically, but also psychologically, emotionally and cognitively. At least at the start of life, a baby is a powerful focus for parental wishes and needs. A child is brought into the world psychologically through the imagination of its parents, who have to imagine how it feels, what it wants and who it might become. Parental hope takes the form of various other imaginings: who might this baby turn into? What might they do with their life? This is a necessary and healthy part of parenting, as long as the parents can remember at least some of the time that this is simply what they imagine, and as such will be a projection of their own needs. To an extent, all children bear the burden of their parents' needs for a certain sort of child. Often, this can take the form of ambitions that the parents have themselves not managed to achieve in their own lives – to be more successful, to achieve more, to be more musical, more athletic, or whatever. Again, this is quite normal: hopefulness about a child – and even idealisation, the feeling that one has the 'best' baby in the world – can be a necessary illusion. Likewise, small children naturally idealise their own parents, endowing them with godlike powers and abilities. Over time, however, parents are inevitably disappointing: they are neither heroes nor gods, which enables the child to take a more realistic view. If the child is to develop psychological independence and emotional maturity, both they and their parents need to move from this phase of idealisation and illusion through a process of disillusionment: of realising that love can be realistic, and satisfying rather than necessarily perfect. That a need for one's child to be 'the best' or 'the most successful' may be a healthy aspiration, providing its achievement is not too essential or believed in too strongly. For healthy development, there needs to be a containing space into which the child can grow without the impediments and burdens of their parents' idealistic needs. It is a common observation in the family therapy of wayward teenagers that, when some shocking incident is being discussed, close observation of one or other (or both) parents reveals an unacknowledged emotion of excitement at the young person's 'misdemeanours'. Unbeknown both to themselves and to their parents, the young person is acting out their parents' wishes to challenge social or family norms. To an extent, this is the normal role of all teenagers throughout history, and is a consequence of a healthy need to find their own identity rather than the one created for them by their parents or society.

We learn that Davinia's parents were ambitious for her and had a strong need for Davinia to be a successful student, one whom they might have enjoyed 'showing off' to their friends. This may have produced a blurring in Davinia's mind as to what her parents' needs were and what would make them happy, versus what her own sense of herself was, and what she wanted to do with her life.

A child's response to powerful parental needs about who they should be and how they should behave can produce either rebellion or conformity. It would seem Davinia took the latter route, as, indeed, many 'high achievers' do. However, this conformity came at a price. Her parents' need for her to be successful may have led to her cutting herself off from her own needs: for intimacy, to express vulnerability, to look after herself as well as others.

Generally, we have at least two selves: a private self, which we only show to friends and family, and a public self, which we express more widely, and especially in the workplace. Parents are commonly surprised and impressed by 'how grown-up they are' when they see their child in a public setting. We need to keep these two selves in some kind of balance in order to lead a balanced life, but, inevitably, where aspirations such as the need to achieve are high, the risk is that the public self gains ascendance over the private self. The private life and personal needs take second place to the potentially infinite demands of the workplace and career. This generally happens slowly, and largely unconsciously, so that the person themselves becomes confused between their more personal needs and their ambitions at work. Indeed, a high need for achievement, with large amounts of energy being devoted to work and career development, can be more easily satisfied than the complex needs of deep personal relationships, where messy emotions and loyalties have to be navigated. It is easier to sink one's major efforts into one's career, where success and failure are easily measured and very concretely rewarded. This is a source of work addiction for some: the temporary biochemical hit and adrenaline rush of the high-speed workplace develops into an ever-increasing desire for more satisfaction.

Davinia's idea of herself, her identity, would seem to have been heavily influenced by her work. A fear of vulnerability made her avoid the realities of her increasingly weakening physical condition. She 'protected' her husband from the facts until they were incontrovertible. She was reluctant to let her friends and husband support her, and she fought with her doctors rather than following their advice. Only when too weak to go on was she able to relinquish this form of defence against the reality of her condition. Most successful professionals who get satisfaction from being the strong, helpful one would share Davinia's problem.

Knowing the difference between bearable and unbearable levels of stress is a necessary condition for thriving in challenging professions. Davinia, very characteristically for someone with her personality structure, failed to pay attention to the weakest potential link in any business: what happens when the boss gets ill? There seems to have been no succession plan in place to cope with such an eventuality. This probably led to an overextended denial of her physical condition, not only by Davinia, but also by her colleagues when the evidence of her illness must have been there for all to see. Her high need for achievement made her continue to work even though she was unwell, and at the risk of making herself more so.

However, Davinia's saner self was eventually able to take charge and take better account of the reality. Her shift from a fear of becoming 'old' (perhaps, at an unconscious level, a desire not to fail her parents' need for her to always be 'successful' and 'strong') to seeing her illness and weakened condition as a gift is a moving one. Many civilisations share tales of wisdom about how apparent weakness and vulnerability is in fact a source of strength and vitality, and that to deny inevitable vulnerabilities can lead to tragic consequences.

Davinia's illness provided an unexpected but ultimately welcomed 'push' towards recognising that she had now changed gear, which many of her friends still seemed to be avoiding. It seems also to have spurred a new generosity in her, as she created schemes for a greater share of the value generated by the business among her employees. True gratitude requires acknowledging our dependence on and need for others. Davinia is able to acknowledge loss in her recognition of how much she misses the excitement, adrenaline and adoration that came with her previous life. Becoming more mindful of herself, her physical vulnerability and the need for relationships with others, including her husband, enabled her to take better care of herself and others. She appears to have been gifted a sense of grace in her third phase of life, and may potentially find it even more satisfactory than her second or first phases.

A slowly dawning reality

For many approaching a transition, there is no big moment when life seems to change or major decisions arise. Quite often, there are many very faint signals and tiny changes, which, together, create a growing feeling of the need for change or of a change approaching. For some individuals, this can give a sense of optimism that there is potential for something new and different ahead, whereas for others it can start to feel quite daunting, or as if the world is somehow leaving you behind.

Together, these imperceptible changes add up to a slowly dawning reality that life is not how you planned it – and, for many, this life change will seem to be very different to that experienced by previous generations.

Accepting that change is happening, or will happen, may be a gradual process but, at some point, a re-evaluation cannot be avoided without causing discontent or unhappiness.

Emily's story is one of a hugely committed and successful charity CEO who controls her own destiny in terms of moving towards change. However, having moved forwards, it is then not possible for her to control the events that this move catalyses. With a sense of purpose – and, at times, a gritting of her teeth – Emily does continue on her path and is able to remain sufficiently insightful on her journey, taking herself to a new place and identifying the new possibilities she believes could be there for her. Despite this, her journey was not all smooth or uneventful.

EMILY'S STORY
the CEO of a children's mental health charity

Emily grew up in a family for whom public service was a given. Her father was a GP and her mother a primary school teacher. She was a clever and driven child who was able to have her pick of universities and, when the time came, of jobs. A job without social purpose had never been on her list.

She had a successful career in the civil service and met her partner at work. In time, they had two wonderful children. Everyone, including Emily, felt her dreams had come true. So far, life had dealt her a very kind hand and there was no reason to believe things would change.

But things did begin to change for Emily after her youngest child was diagnosed with learning difficulties. She felt she needed to be at home for him more, and so decided to leave her secure and relatively well-paid job. She was instantly given consulting work by those who had seen her operating at work, and initially it seemed a good compromise.

However, her child began to struggle more and more at his local school, and Emily felt powerless to help him. So, when the school suggested a specialist boarding school would be best for their child, Emily and her partner reluctantly agreed.

This, of course, left Emily desperately upset and the feeling of helplessness overwhelmed her, especially as she now had more time on her hands to think. This was not something Emily had ever experienced before. Throughout her life so far, including her childhood, she had always woken every day and 'pressed the "go" button'.

So, she began to consider what she might do. When a friend pointed out an advert seeking someone to help a fledgling charity involved in helping children with mental health issues, she decided to explore whether this could be for her.

Over the next few years, she became an expert in the field. The more she learned, the more she felt the desperate need to do more for children struggling with a wide range of problems. After three years, she was asked to become the CEO (although this request was just a formality: she was, in practice, already doing the job).

Emily loved being able to make a difference for the kids and she also loved being a CEO, with all that went with it. Over time, the public understanding of just how important the work her charity was doing grew enormously, and so did the pressure on her to be an external champion as well as running the organisation day to day. Emily thrived on the challenge and the adrenaline, all the time knowing she was 'doing a good thing'. Also, she was very good at it, and so her internal feedback loop reinforced her sense of purpose and achievement.

As the years passed, Emily's time became less and less her own. Her partner and kids seemed fine, and her youngest had thrived at his boarding school. But, increasingly, she had a niggling feeling that time was slipping away and soon her children would leave home. Although she was helping many other families, she was perhaps not present enough in her own.

Despite having a great team at work, Emily was unequivocally the leader and little happened without her direction, input and say-so. This meant pulling back was not at all easy, especially as the demands on her charity grew by the day. Her sense of duty to her job and her sense of duty to her family put her between a rock and a hard place. The irony was that she had given up her more steady – and arguably more manageable – job to be at home more for her youngest son!

She struggled with this dilemma for quite a while, not really facing into it. There was always a reason why now was not the right time: she was too busy to spend any time thinking about it, let alone to make any real changes to what she did.

What changed this was spending a weekend with her parents, who had always been pretty robust and incredibly supportive of her. She had not been to see them in their own home for some time, and what became clear during this visit was that they were not coping as well as they had been, and that they were starting to seem a little frail. This realisation helped Emily say to herself: 'Enough is enough'.

However, this simply added to the pressure on her!

It was easy to decide that something needed to change, but incredibly hard to act upon. Emily felt deeply conflicted. She had enormous loyalty to her team and to all the children her charity was supporting. Equally, she felt her own children needed her – and, if she was honest, she needed them, too, before she 'lost' them to 'full adulthood'. Although her partner had never pressured her at any stage, she knew he was considering retiring and that he would love to have more of her time. And now, her parents needed more of her, too.

Then came the next challenge. However she looked at doing less work, Emily could not see how the organisation would not suffer if she were to pull back. She talked to her board, who appeared sympathetic but who, in practice, did not want her to work any less at all. When she protested that she really was serious, they asked her who could step up. Emily realised she had made herself indispensable. Her team were all very capable, but they were all 'number twos': hard-working, but very happy to sit under her wings. She had not planned at all for this day.

Then Emily had a further realisation: she did not know what 'this day' actually was. What did she really want? To move to a four-day week? Or three days? Or maybe even no days? Now she was seriously scared. She had never stopped to plan what she might want or how she might cope if other demands on her time raised their heads.

If she gave up her role, who would she be and what would be her purpose? From early childhood, the noble cause of helping others had been front and centre, non-negotiable, for her. Now the 'others' she wanted to help were her own family and, in truth, herself. She was truly caught between the 'soft' questions of values and purpose, which were so hardwired into her, and doing what it was now clear was right for her.

Finally, she grasped the nettle and took a long, hard look at how *she* wanted to spend her time, rather than allowing others to take it.

Once she began the journey in earnest – and it had been quite some time in the coming – Emily began to have a sense of the fog clearing. The time pressures created by her children being almost grown, her partner heading into retirement and her parents beginning to decline made it easier to keep her own feet to the fire – not that she didn't falter and stall on regular occasions!

In the end, she decided that the only way to ensure change happened was for her to leave the charity. This felt like a terrifying prospect – but now, the idea of doing nothing was slightly more terrifying. The balance had finally shifted, and Emily was ready to act.

After several tough conversations with her board, they accepted that she really was going to leave. Once they had done so, to her relief, they began to share – and, over time, to own – the problem of how to replace her. In the business world, it is not considered best practice to allow the current CEO to replace themselves, but in Emily's case avoiding this was simply not realistic. She knew so much more than her board about the needs of the organisation, the sector and the people who worked for her. So they worked together to develop a way forwards. In the end, this meant acknowledging that Emily had been doing far too much herself and that they needed to share her responsibilities more broadly to enable a new CEO to stand a chance of succeeding. Even Emily was surprised by just how much weight she had been carrying.

The act of sharing the burden was a huge relief. Once she was on a path to leaving, the 'old' Emily, the one who made things happen, reappeared – but this time, she was focused on the task of replacing herself, not of being indispensable. She wondered why she had made it so hard for herself in the past!

Finally, she could also begin to give some time to thinking about what she would do next in terms of using her expertise and skills. She came to the conclusion that doing nothing for a while and giving herself some time to decide was the best course of action. It had been a very long time since she had put non-work-related things on her to do list, let alone made them a priority.

Emily knew that this next phase would not last forever, and that, in time, she would feel the need to use her experience to help others again – but next time, it would not be in a full-time role, and she would act with the benefit of hindsight as well as with a sense of priority for her own 'others' and for herself.

A tale of how difficult it can be to ask for help

A psychological perspective on Emily's story

Being of service to others, particularly to those less fortunate than herself, was a strong moral value that Emily's parents would have upheld and she would have learned from childhood. Having such parents can be inspiring, but it can mean that one's own needs are not always recognised or met. One is reminded of the old joke about the son of a GP who, when asked what he wanted to be when he grew up, replied: 'A patient, so I could see more of my father!'

Such parents might tell their children that they are the most important things in their life – and mean it – but the child may have a different impression. The children of 'helpers' might try to overcome the frequently mixed set of feelings this causes by identifying with their parents' sense of mission at an early age, a defence that Freud's daughter Anna describes as 'identifying with the aggressor'. Although alternative identifications are possible, they may necessitate rebelling against what can feel like the suffocating virtues of the parents. The impact of a parent's choice of profession may have both conscious and unconscious consequences on a child. Children are generally eager to please their parents, and are often consciously well aware of their ideals, which they will often unconsciously internalise. And, as parents ourselves, we may cast long shadows. Take, for example, the three children of an MI6 officer: one is a speech therapist, the second a psychologist, and the third an actor and theatre director; arguably, all have a shared motivation to help people communicate what isn't being said.

Those in the 'helping' professions are notoriously poor at seeking help for themselves, with the medical profession being one of the worst. Emily will likely have internalised a strong sense of duty to others, so when life deals her a tough blow, she is knocked off balance. The resulting state of being cut off from one's own needs can create a precarious, though apparently strong, personality structure. The need to help or repair others often derives from a difficulty acknowledging one's own needs and the projection of them on to others, resulting in the desire to find an ultimately infinite set of needy individuals requiring one's professional counsel. The unconscious pressure on individuals with jobs requiring a heightened sense of responsibility can, when under stress, swing into an opposite alarmingly irresponsible set of behaviours.

Having a child with learning difficulties is never easy for a parent: the reality of your powerlessness to remedy your child's suffering is about as cruel as it can get for a parent. At first, Emily managed to bear her sense of powerlessness, but it is possible that one of the reasons for the school's recommendation of a boarding school for her child was that they could see Emily was not finding it easy to care for him at home.

Like many readers of this book, Emily is somebody who struggles with feelings of helplessness and not being in control, factors that have a very positive impact in terms of building a drive to achieve and be successful in career and worldly terms. However, they can be impediments in matters of intimacy and relationships. She would seem to be a woman with high energy who is described as pressing 'the "go" button' as soon as she wakes up. Is it simply chance that she chooses to work with a charity whose purpose is to help children with mental health issues? Is she possibly projecting her own need for mental health help on to others? Again, this is not necessarily a bad thing: indeed, many of the most successful mental health professionals have, and sometimes still do, struggle with mental health issues themselves. After all, how better to have a deep and real understanding of what mental health problems are really like? The important thing is not to not have problems, since that is unrealistic; instead, it is to be aware of your problems and the impact they may have on you, and the vulnerability this may cause in your work and relationships.

I am not saying that Emily's child suffered in any way because of her personality and needs: indeed, it is clear that the help and care he received greatly benefited him. It would seem that her family were just fine, but that she missed out in her relationship with them by being so busy with others. Realising that her own parents were becoming frail seems to have been a moment of truth, and led to her realisation that it was really she who needed her children as much as they needed her. But, as is common with the 'helper' personality, she also feels beset by a series of 'needy' others: her own parents, her husband and her children. Those with the 'helper' personality style often wish to disavow neediness in themselves, and so project this on to others, surrounding themselves with an apparently infinitely demanding world in which their own needs are seen not in themselves but in others who appear to desperately need them. This is one cause of burnout in many professionals, including doctors, nurses and psychologists, but also lawyers, accountants and advisers more generally: anyone whose *raison d'être* is the needs of others, and who goes on in denial to the point of exhaustion.

All credit to Emily, she faces squarely into the issues and decides to step down from her CEO role. She begins to have 'a sense of the fog clearing'. The idea of leaving her position of control and power is terrifying. Of what does this terror consist? Sigmund Freud called it 'the return of the repressed'. In other words, the emotions that one has repressed or projected on to others have been repressed for a reason: that they cause discomfort. When, for whatever reason, the individual is once again faced with these denied aspects of themselves, their first reaction is almost always one of panic, both at the emotion and at what to do about it.

Having shared the burden with her board, she feels an enormous amount of weight lift. The fact that others were not overwhelmed by the prospect of her stepping down would seem to have provided reassurance that the situation was not as impossible as it had appeared to Emily initially, with her sense that she was indispensable. This sense of indispensability is a common feature for people who have held positions of power and significance. Their organisation may have played a part in colluding with this, quite happy that someone appears willing to martyr themselves. Managing changes of this sort is challenging at the best of times; it's easier to keep things as they are, although, in the longer term, there is always a price to be paid.

Emily very sensibly decided that she would 'do nothing', although taking time out to reflect is certainly not 'doing nothing'. The 'nothing' is perhaps an unconscious reference to the feeling of emptiness that anyone giving up a busy career inevitably has to face, and will often avoid by finding other forms of being busy.

Full-time to less time

We all reach a stage when we have to make choices. At Harvard Business School, students are asked to outline their ambitions against three priorities: fame, fortune and family. It is a soul-searching moment that implies future sacrifice. Thirty years after having completed this exercise, one alumnus was horrified by the choices he had made: 'I realise I deprioritised the people I care most about – my wife, children, family and friends – and as a result of that, my own happiness.'

The real question is how can people who gradually become consumed by their work retain their perspective on their whole selves? Many may say they do not want to, but is this really true? When their worlds are sufficiently disrupted and they are forced or compelled to stop and reflect on their lives, is this still their response? For some, there may be a genuine financial necessity or an unswerving sense of calling to serve others in some way, but, for many of us, working in this manner is not something we are 'forced' to do. In the second phase of life, we may feel we have no choice other than to focus heavily on our careers, but as people approach their Third Life, denying themselves this choice can prove to be a very poor decision. It is a choice which, it could be said, too many of us fail to make with our eyes and our hearts open.

There are many reasons why senior people decide to reduce their work commitments. How should you go about it? This story looks at Vivek, who, having had a successful career as an academic, including sharing childcare when his family were young, then followed a well-trodden path taken by those whose jobs begin to define them.

While his later career was an enormous success, it also resulted in him losing the balance he had so successfully achieved until his mid-career. This meant that he had to face trying to square the circle of being a leader in his field together with giving time to his ageing parents, whose health could not be taken for granted; his wife, who had selflessly moved to part-time work to support him; and his son and daughter. These were the people, he realised – too late, in the case of his father – that he would like to spend more time with.

VIVEK'S STORY
A university professor

Vivek's father came to England in his early twenties. Here, he met Vivek's mother. They built a small chain of shops and expected Vivek to work in the family business and take over from them. Despite being a compliant child, Vivek became a teenager with his own mind. He was a talented artist whose teachers encouraged him to follow his heart and go to art school. His parents had no frame of reference for this, and were terrified by their son's life and prospects as an artist. Vivek was also extremely good at maths, and his parents felt that if he was not going to join the family business, he should go to university and then do accountancy. There was a period of significant pain for all three of them as they wrestled with what Vivek would do beyond school. His parents could not understand how he could want to risk throwing his life away after all they had done for him. Vivek did not want to hurt his parents – but he did want to be himself.

Supported by his art teacher, he applied to do a foundation course at art school and won a place. However, much to his surprise, he discovered that while he was really *good* at art, he was not *great*. At first, he thought he just needed to work harder, but over the year-long course, he began to wonder if he had made the right choice. Too proud to tell his parents, he quietly applied to do a maths degree. He won a place at a great university for the following autumn. Once it was all settled, he finally told his parents, who were extremely surprised but delighted.

At university, Vivek discovered that not only was he good at maths – he was seriously good! His tutors encouraged him to do a PhD, which had not been his plan at all. He had assumed he would 'give in' and become an accountant, given that following his heart rather than his parents' wishes had not worked out that well! But not only did he thrive when working on his PhD, he was also asked to stay on and become an academic. He learned that, in advanced maths, he could combine his creativity and his natural mathematical ability: a complete revelation to him, but a very happy one.

His academic career went well and he really enjoyed the esoteric area in which he had specialised. He met Sanita at the university. She, too, was a bright young academic, in the field of chemistry. They supported each other and, when they started a family, took it in turns to look after their two children. The academic life suited the whole family really well and they were both very happy in their careers.

Vivek enjoyed his research and loved attending the international conferences that had begun to take up an increasingly large part of his time. Then he was asked to run a part of the maths department in addition to doing his own research. He had always tried to avoid this, as he wanted to be an active father, and because it was 'the deal' he had made with Sanita. Doing research was one thing, but managing others and getting involved in university politics was quite another, both in terms of time commitment, and also the 'headspace' and emotional demands. However, the colleague who asked him to take over this role had a very tough personal health issue to contend with, and so it was incredibly hard to say no. Sanita could see how torn Vivek was and, after much discussion at home, they both agreed he should take on this additional management role.

His time working in his parents' business meant Vivek had some basic management skills to draw on, and very quickly he felt he was doing a pretty good job. His department were giving him good feedback and he was enjoying having a much broader remit. In parallel with this, his research was getting noticed by an ever-widening audience of academics around the world, and his team was growing at a faster rate than ever. Everything was going swimmingly.

For the next few years, his success continued. Sanita said she would work part-time as he was spending so much less time at home. This came as shock to Vivek, although the minute she suggested it, he could see that she was right. Rather selfishly, he had not noticed the toll his working such long hours had taken on her. They agreed it was the best thing for the family. He would later wonder if it was the best thing for Sanita, though.

Vivek continued to throw himself into his work and, unintentionally, paid less attention to his wife and children. He did not worry, because he felt reassured by the fact that Sanita had suggested the arrangement, plus his children were heading towards university age, so would soon be leaving home. Many of his colleagues were in the same situation, and he settled into what seemed a 'natural' rhythm. His research work gave him huge satisfaction, he was increasingly validated by his intellectual peers around the world, and he enjoyed the responsibility and success he was having in growing his department. What could go wrong?

Out of the blue, Vivek's father suddenly died. He had not been completely well, but had seemed fine, and because Vivek was so busy with his work, he had not been to visit him recently. Vivek's distressed mother admitted that his father had actually been less healthy than Vivek had been led to believe. He had insisted that he did not want to bother Vivek, who was so successful and – they knew from Sanita – so very busy. Vivek felt incredibly guilty, as well as experiencing a deep, deep sense of loss. How could this have happened when, in his heart, he valued his family more than anything in the world?

At first, he threw himself deeper into his work as a way of coping. He could not see this himself, but Sanita and his mother, who was now spending more time at their house, could see it. His children just thought that Dad had more important things to do than be at home.

However, Vivek started to feel tired and less excited about his work, which had never been the case before. He wondered if he was ill or was just getting older. One day, when they were out for a walk, he admitted to Sanita that he was feeling low. She gently asked him what he was feeling low about. When she posed the question, he found he did not have an easy answer, but the conversation sowed the seeds of a lot more thought.

The thoughts grew in his mind. What really mattered to him? Had he lost the man he used to be? What should he do now? He looked at many of his colleagues and could see that they were working so hard they had lost a balance in their lives. Now, he had to admit to himself that he had lost balance too. Did that mean he had to leave the university? What had seemed to be a wonderfully broad role encompassing research, travel and management began to look less and less appealing to him. The thought of leaving prompted him to start considering what he would miss.

At the heart of all that he did was his research, and he realised that, without it, none of the rest made sense or counted for very much. Yes, attending some conferences was essential, as this was where he shared leading-edge thinking with other specialists in his field. Without this, he would not develop his own thinking, and if he did not do that, his research would be significantly diminished and would, over time, lose its value. But when he really thought about it, many of the conferences he attended were about building and validating the university's reputation or, if he was brutally honest, his own reputation, and also satisfying his personal love of travel. When he considered his management role, he realised he had never before given it a huge amount of thought. It was not something he had actively sought, and people told him he was doing a good job, but now he was acknowledging to himself that he had come to enjoy the status of the role.

What about his family, who he had always told himself mattered to him more than anything else? He found himself contemplating his own mortality, and the more he did so, the more he realised he did not want to do to his wife and children what he felt he had done to his father. He told himself this was a bit melodramatic, but the thought niggled away. He also started to think that he had missed out on his children being teenagers more than he ever intended to. They all still loved each other and nothing was broken, but he gradually owned the reality that he had become much more of an absent father than now seemed right.

And Sanita? This was the hardest part to open up to himself about. He had behaved in a way that they had always said to each other would never happen. Their plans to both build their academic careers and share the child-rearing home duties had been lost. Yes, the same was true for many of their other friends, both in and out of the university, but was it fair on Sanita? Had she been diminished through making sacrifices for him and the children? He began to think about several of his female colleagues who had also moved to become part-time. If he was honest with himself about this too, he knew they often struggled to make the strides he had made comparatively effortlessly.

Where did all this leave him?

A plan began to shape in his mind. Why didn't he suggest to Sanita that he would become part-time and make it her turn to work full-time, supported by him. As the idea settled in his head, he began to feel more and more of his energy returning, and he started to get excited about what the change would mean – not just for his family, but for himself, too.

When he first suggested this to Sanita, she was taken aback. She had secretly hated giving up her full-time research position and really missed it, but equally, she had got used to having a bit more time for herself, especially as the kids had come to need less of her time. She did not know how to react. This left Vivek at a loss as he realised he had come up with this plan for her, but without actually asking her what she wanted! Over the next few weeks and months, they gradually opened up to each other and, instead of Vivek doing all the thinking in his own head, he began to think aloud with Sanita. In turn, she did the same with him. They gradually came to the now joint decision that she would ask to go back full-time and Vivek would ask to work part-time.

Sanita's department said yes straight away, which was a huge boost for her, and arguably was also helpful for Vivek, as his department were very reluctant to agree to him becoming part-time! He found their reluctance very flattering and even wondered if they could both work full-time again. But then the voice in his head spoke up loudly enough to remind him what it was that he had decided he wanted.

When they told their kids, Vivek got another wake-up call. He had not thought through how they might react, and he was rather shocked to discover they were worried about having less of their mother and more of him! This time, however, he was able to listen and realise that this simply served to reinforce why his decision had been the right one.

Over the next few years, everyone in the family thrived. The kids had to get used to having Vivek around more. It didn't always go well, but, on balance, it was fine, and he was able to build a stronger relationship with his kids before they finally left the nest, several years after they graduated. Sanita was able to spend several years focusing harder on her research, which yielded some very well-received papers and gave her enormous satisfaction.

Vivek felt he was the biggest winner. He had started by feeling it was time for him to give back to his family, but what he found was how much he won from the new arrangement. As well as spending more time with his kids, he was able to spend more time with his mother. He had initially felt this was the best he could do for his father, but it actually brought him huge rewards. How had he not seen how great his mother was until now? Getting closer to her was very special for him. On top of all this, he loved the new-found freedom and lack of time pressure on him to do his academic research, which he was sure contributed to him doing some of his best work ever. Also, he had escaped the tyranny of full retirement, which a number of his colleagues were now facing! He felt he could see many more happy years ahead, both at home and at work.

Listen first, then ask questions; provide solutions later, if at all

A psychological perspective on Vivek's story

Being the child of first-generation immigrants can be tough. If your parents have been successful, they will almost certainly have had to fight for it, and having found it, will know that it can easily be taken away. They are likely to have had experiences of a challenging, even hostile world. While wishing the best for their children, they are likely to emphasise caution, good sense and stability in any career suggestions they make. Vivek's parents naturally concluded that a child who was gifted in maths should sensibly choose accountancy, believing the world will always need accountants. Vivek was an only child, meaning this pressure and his concerns about causing parental anxiety couldn't be shared with other siblings. Making any choice other than accountancy was felt to 'risk throwing his life away after all they had done for him'. Being an only child can be a burden, and make one a little self-centred. Good for Vivek that he at least had a go at art school: if he hadn't, it might always have been a hankering desire that he had never explored. And, luckily, he was able to find another avenue for creativity in his research.

Not all mathematicians make great people managers, but Vivek is obviously an exception, and he was able to acknowledge and use the business talents he had learned from his parents. It also provided an avenue for the expression of his need for impact and influence over others, something an academic career often doesn't provide, leading to frustrations for those with relatively high-power needs. Tussles and worse among academics are legendary. Vivek obviously felt a degree of guilt in relation to Sanita's willingness to put her career second to their children's lives. But guilt is a painful emotion and we tend to want to put it out of our consciousness. Like many professionals, Vivek may have persuaded himself that his contributions to research and his university outweighed any guilt that he felt. Perhaps he needed to keep persuading himself of this and so focused evermore on his career, driven by a desire to evade feelings of guilt. And, of course, his work gave him great pleasure, as did the validation by his peers, thus reinforcing an unconscious pattern of behaviour. His father's death seems to have further fuelled this, and it is suggested overwork may have been Vivek's way of coping with both his grief and guilt. He begins to show symptoms of potential depression – sadness and loss of vigour – which Vivek sees as potentially a physical rather than mental illness. Perhaps the feelings of self-accusation were too painful to bear. The acknowledgement of mental illness in oneself can be excruciatingly painful and terrifying: it hits right at the heart of one's sense of self. Feeling oneself falling apart mentally is even harder to acknowledge than physical deterioration. Sanita's gentle questioning about how he was feeling seems to have prompted Vivek to be more reflective and thoughtful about his life; she served as a midwife to his thinking. Many might have become defensive at this exposure of feelings of vulnerability, but Vivek seems to have been able to internalise his wife's understanding and do some thinking for himself. When Vivek's father became ill, he didn't wish to burden his son with this information: perhaps this was a family where vulnerability was hard to acknowledge, which is unsurprising if their own early lives had been tough. These events seem to have prompted a useful crisis in Vivek. What was life about? What was really important? And rather than throwing himself evermore forcibly into work, Vivek was able to take a step back and review how his life was going.

Vivek's approach to life would seem to focus more on task achievement than relationship development. So, unlike Sanita's gentle questioning approach, he goes quickly into solution mode, solving his perception of 'The Problem' before even asking how she saw things, how she felt, and what she thought or would like. However, they obviously have a good marriage and could work things out between them. If Vivek had become stuck in his guilt, he might only have worked harder, feeling his partner to be his guilty conscience, resulting in imagined criticisms, further distancing and overwork, all in aid of 'supporting the family'. Sanita was lucky to have a department that welcomed her back to a full-time role. Feelings towards people who have gone part-time are not always so generous or welcoming.

The voice in Vivek's head that spoke up to remind him what it was that he wanted perhaps has its roots in his parents' determination to get what they wanted, albeit in very different circumstances.

When Vivek's children had distinctly mixed feelings about the changes in the family's childcare arrangements, he was able to take it on the chin and not retaliate. He was able to hear his children's views and also listen to their feelings. All in all, he now recognises he is a winner rather than a loser in the new lifestyle that he and his wife decided upon. His self-criticisms for not spending more time with his father are ameliorated by his determination not to repeat this pattern with his mother. He is pleasantly surprised that his more rounded life still enables him to do some of his best work ever. He anticipates a happy next phase of life and maybe he will have another go with his art, even if only as an amateur: an opportunity to bring to life again a so far unlived aspect of himself.

When the choice is made for you

Forced retirement or redundancy are sadly an all too familiar part of life. There are many reasons they can happen, but whatever the reason, the adjustment required in your domestic and professional life is huge. Inevitably, the change prompts questions about your identity and relationship with yourself, as well as with others. You are facing a new world with a new set of values, attitudes and possibilities.

On the face of it, such a change can seem too hard to bear when it happens. For many, the initial emotions are hard to cope with, ranging from reacting to a loss of control, to humiliation, to feelings of rejection and straightforward anger. However, this is only the very first step on a journey that many will take. Not having chosen your own timescale for the journey is tough, but once you begin, you are on the same road as many other travellers, despite how you initially started your journey.

James had a successful career running a business, but was not aware his time was running out. He was shocked and angry when he was asked to leave to make way for the next generation. It was something he was not prepared for and did not find easy to accept. Changing gear did not come naturally to James.

JAMES'S STORY
CEO of a medium-sized enterprise

James had been the CEO of an international services business. He had joined the company when it was relatively small and not very profitable. In the early years, they were a close-knit team who all worked incredibly hard with a shared vision for growing and changing the business. As the organisation grew, James grew with it, and for the last 10 years he had been the CEO.

He gave much of his life to this role and believed that he was doing the best for his family, who had moved out of London to the country when his children were small. Over time, the structure around him grew and a board was formed with an external chairman whom James helped to select. He felt secure and happy, if busy and stretched by the continued growth and internationalisation of the business.

There was a price to be paid in terms of less time with his family, but James loved the job and was not overly concerned about this. Over this period, he did not really stop to reflect on how his life was going other than having an overall sense that it was as it should be. His own father had been a fairly self-contained man, and it had mainly been his mother who brought up James and his sisters, so it seemed natural to James for his wife to do the same. Yes, she had said it would be nice if he was around more when they first moved out to the country, but after a while, he felt they had settled in to a comfortable arrangement: one which suited him very well and which he did not really think about very much.

However, his comfortable life was interrupted when he was in his mid-fifties. At the end of one of their regular catch-up meetings, his chairman suggested they start to focus more actively on succession planning. At first, James saw this as sensible, and went back to the chairman saying he would work to ensure one of several possible colleagues would be ready to take over from him in the next few years. In James's mind, this was the time-scale. Whenever succession planning had been discussed, he had always assured the board it was something he was working on. In practice, though, it wasn't something he ever considered very deeply. He felt he was a long way off retiring, and so there was no real need to look at it in an active or structured way.

To his complete shock, it soon became clear that the chair-man actually meant for him to leave within the next year. James knew he was the right leader for the business and that it would not be what it was today without him. He knew the company needed him. Or so he thought.

What James had not realised himself, but the chairman could increasingly see, was that, despite the business itself changing faster and facing even more rapid change, James had not adapted and evolved his style over the last couple of years. Also, he could see that James's top team were feeling increasingly frustrated at not having more freedom to change the way the company was going and how things were being done.

James's team respected him and understood that the busi-ness was still performing, but the growth was slowing and they felt more change was needed – and with more speed than James seemed willing to embrace. They had reached a point where, despite their shared history, they now wanted a new leader who would have a more inclusive and collaborative style, and who would not be so quick to tell them why things would not work. They had tried to say this to James over the course of the previous year, but somehow they felt unable to get through to him.

James was completely shocked to find himself under threat and felt he was being treated incredibly badly. He told the chairman this was a mistake and that they should look at a timescale for his departure of two to three years. The chair-man believed that the risk of losing one or both of the two key potential successors to James during this timeframe was too high to take. The conversation went back and forth, without James fully realising that he was not the decision-maker in this. He had run the company for so long that he just could not see how the company would thrive without him – or, indeed, as he was now starting to fear, what he would do without it.

After several painful months for both James and the chairman, with James simply not accepting the reality of the situation, the chairman felt he had no option but to tell James that they wanted him to step down as CEO at the year end – in six months' time. James was shocked once again. He had known that he could not stay forever, but he had just not accepted that the decision could be taken for him. He was angry, hurt and humiliated, and felt totally betrayed by the chairman.

By now, James was not sleeping very well. Rather than stepping back and looking at what was happening and how he personally was behaving, he simply kept pushing harder to prove the chairman was wrong. He did not share his feelings with his wife – or, indeed, anyone. He told himself he could sort it out: after all, he had won many battles in his career to date.

Although he had finally accepted that the chairman was not going to change his mind, James was still not convinced that this was the right decision. He felt that all he needed to do was to make the board as a whole see that he, James, was right. So, he decided to reach out to his top team to say that the chairman, who did not understand their business well enough, had suggested he step down, but he was sure that they did not want this. He was greeted with lots of compliments for all he had achieved and lots of 'thank yous' for all he had done for them, but not one of his key people said they would go to the chairman and tell him he was wrong.

James now felt betrayed by his team as well as the chairman. He did not know how to tell his wife, or anyone else in the outside world. Over the next few months, he put his head in the sand and carried on running the business as if nothing had changed, except that he became more adversarial and critical about everything around him.

Just before Christmas, the chairman told him that they had selected his colleague Susan to be the next CEO. James knew the decision about who would succeed him was coming but, in his mind, he had anticipated that the following six months would be spent with someone as the CEO designate, during which time James would then show them how to step up and ensure they understood what the CEO needed to do. However, when he explained to the chairman that this is how he saw it working, he was once again very surprised to learn that Susan would be taking over in the New Year.

James then accused the chairman of treating him beyond badly after all he had given to the company. The chairman was heavy-hearted as he could see how much James was struggling to let go – indeed, everyone around him could see that he was not OK. But James had not shared how he felt with his close colleagues, so they felt unable to support him emotionally, despite really wanting to.

His top team and the board were all conflicted in their feelings. On the one hand, James had done an incredible job as the CEO and had built the company very successfully, and they had also, by and large, enjoyed working with him. On the other hand, this was business, and they could not help being very disappointed at his behaviour over the last few months, which they felt to be too much about himself and his own position rather than about the company. Ultimately, it left them sad that such a talented and good person had allowed his inability to face his own departure spoil what should have been a proud and graceful handing over of the baton to Susan.

At home, James had now shared his story with his wife, who was very loyal. After hearing James's side of the story, without realising what she was doing, she made it worse by stoking his sense of injustice. They both focused on what was happening to James at work, because neither of them knew how they would cope with James not having his job. They were lucky that this was not a big financial blow, but they had, in effect, been living quite separate lives for a long time, and this would be a huge change for each of them.

Despite the way James had behaved, the chairman was still sympathetic and so, after some long rants from James, it was agreed that he could stay in the business for the following year to help with the customer relationships and to enable him to travel the world and say goodbye. James was just about all right with this, although in reality he had no choice.

This decision led to James telling himself that he had been proved right and they really did need to keep him for at least another year. Deep down inside, he thought they would come to realise they needed him around for longer.

The final humiliation, as he saw it, came at the start of January, when the office administrators arrived to move him out of his large corner office with the fabulous views. What? This was his office. How dare they suggest he move? But to add insult to injury, as he saw it, he was moved to a smaller office with one small window. Over the course of the following year, he felt increasingly diminished, but he hung on – or, probably more accurately, he *clung* on. In his mind, he simply had nowhere else to go. His home was in the country, fine for a weekly commute, but not a daily one. His city flat was tiny and, in truth, incredibly lonely. Finally, he disappeared from the business the following December. It was not until he had no options left that he began the painful process of really engaging with what he would do next.

Initially, there were some other harsh realities for James once he started to explore his options.

On the personal front, while his wife was trying to be supportive, they both needed to find a new way of being together. James had a new set of circumstances, whereas his wife's life was unchanged, apart from James no longer having his job. When James first became free, he suggested he and his wife go travelling together, something they had often discussed doing. However, he was to discover that she had a number of commitments and activities she did not want to disrupt by heading off around the world for a couple of months. She was not going to be there to help fill his days; indeed, she did not want him at home at all during the day, as she had her own routines and was reluctant to include him in them. This was not because she did not love him, but because she had needed to find a way to be happy when he was in the city all week and she was alone in the country. After a few years, she had created a life of her own: one she enjoyed.

On the work front, his skills were not as transferable as he hoped and, after visiting a number of headhunters, the advice James was getting was that he might not find it very easy to get an equivalent or bigger CEO role. His less-than-ideal behaviour over his last 18 months at his old company was not a secret, and although ex-colleagues did credit him with his many outstanding achievements, they also said that he struggled with facing into change, an attribute that was one of the top requirements for new CEO roles. James did not realise that there were some unhelpful views on him out in the marketplace and, because he had always presented such a confident and somewhat impregnable front, no one felt they could really tell him. So, not only had he buried his head in the sand inside his company, he had also not sought out feedback from outside.

CHANGING GEAR

In reality, James was also still struggling to come to terms with what had happened, and it really was not possible for him to make a realistic assessment of his situation. Because he had not found himself able to reflect on what had actually happened, when James started to explore what new roles might be open to him, he employed his default position of pushing too hard. This meant he went through a painful period where he presented his own version of events, failing to acknowledge that those people he was talking to might – and sometimes did – have information on his situation from other sources. He spent several months pushing ever harder to get a new CEO role, but, after a number of unsuccessful conversations and getting quite close to one offer, he began to realise that he might fail to get a bigger or equivalent role. He also felt a new kind of fear: that he might not have a 'long shelf life'.

Finally, James began to accept that his situation was far from what he had wanted and expected. He started to think that maybe he should take stock. Although for many years he had been happy 'keeping his own counsel', he was now feeling lonely. He started by admitting to his wife that he was struggling badly. She was hugely relieved when he shared this with her, as she could see the toll all this was taking on him, but knew that she had to wait for him to open up to her. If she had pressured him into telling her what the matter was, he would have been even less likely to share how he was feeling.

James felt some of the weight had been lifted off his shoulders by talking to his wife, and so, when she reminded him of a good friend of his who had also unexpectedly lost his job in his fifties, James decided he would risk a conversation and let his guard down a little. His friend was initially reluctant to have a 'sharing' conversation, but they saw each other a few times and, eventually, they opened up to each other enough to see that their experiences had a number of similarities, not least of which was how hurt, let down and shamed they had each felt – and, to differing extents, still did feel.

So, after a very painful year of flailing around, James began to discover that there was life after his company. His good experiences with his friend gave him the confidence to make an effort to seek out other old friends. He quickly discovered they were not very interested in what his job was or what had gone on: they were just happy to reconnect after a long time. The more James let his guard down with them and relaxed, the easier and more enjoyable the interactions with them became. The other hugely positive thing was that he and his wife began to spend a bit more time together and to his (and her) relief, they found they enjoyed being together more and started to rediscover the slightly dormant, but nonetheless still flickering attraction they felt for each other.

James found reaching out to his children harder. They were initially a bit cautious about being with him on their own. He had been a pretty absent dad for so long that they did not have the foundations to build on straight away. However, his wife played a key role in nudging both James and each of his children to spend more time together and helpfully gave him ideas of things she knew they would all enjoy doing together. Soon his life outside of work settled in to a happier place. This helped James to feel more at peace and, in time, he started to reflect on what had happened – and, most importantly, *why* it had happened.

He decided not to try for another CEO role, partly because he feared failing again, but also because it now seemed more possible to accept that he should let this desire go. In time, he began to explore other options. Having relaxed about what he felt fitted the status and the power he had had in his old job, James resolved to find other ways to use his experience. He started to explore places where he felt he could make a difference.

He had always had an interest in the delivery of healthcare, and so applied to sit on the board of a hospital trust. This was a serious learning curve, because it involved being interviewed by people who were either younger or less experienced than him – or both. However, he swallowed his pride, did his homework and tried his hardest to show them he could add value to the board. Happily, he was appointed. Soon after, a small charity who were providing services to the elderly approached him out of the blue to be their chairman as they felt his experience running a services business would be really helpful to them. He spent some time exploring it, but came to the conclusion that the CEO would not be open enough to his advice – the irony of which was slightly lost on him! However, it did make him decide to look out for a charity he believed he could help. He was also approached by an old colleague who was significantly younger and who had set up a services business quite similar to, but much smaller than, the company James had run. He asked James to be his chairman and, after a few conversations to clarify what the role would be and how they would work together, James accepted.

Although his new life and new emerging roles were not at all what he had imagined for himself when he first left his business, James found he did actually enjoy them and was able to take satisfaction in using his expertise to help others. He also came to realise something that he had always known, but had not been able to appreciate enough: namely, that he was extremely lucky to be financially secure. He could still find the anger inside himself around losing his job, but by now he had started to countenance, privately, in his quiet moments, that maybe he could have handled things better.

Gradually, he felt a growing sense of a new James emerging.

A tale of hubris, nemesis and humility

A psychological perspective on James's story

This is a classic case of failing to notice a slow but gathering process of disruption, as well as failing to make the necessary adaptations and transition in sufficient time. James was appointed as CEO in one context, with a close-knit team who needed his expertise. However, like the frog in the pot who does not notice that the water is gradually getting hotter, James did not notice that his staff were developing and becoming more capable, and that the work and the firm's customers were changing, and so he became unable to respond effectively. Not only was he unable to change gear for way too long – he failed to even see the bike!

Like many ambitious people, James's sense of who he was came in significant part from his work, and the power and status it brought. They say power goes to the head; power over others seems inexorably to lead to an inflated view of oneself. Person (who I am) easily becomes confused with Role (the authority and resources my role gives me access to). Those in power gradually become insulated from reality; they mistake the powers conferred by the role with their own personal powers, and develop an inflated sense of their own importance. This often leads to a denial of their actual dependence on others, and their vulnerability to events. James was to realise how limited his personal powers were once his role power was threatened and ultimately removed. This was not corruption of power in an ethical sense, but a corruption of James's ability to sense emotional realities and take effective action. In addition, those around people with power are often loathe, for reasons of self-interest, to take up the risk of challenging their boss directly about behaviour or attitudes, as seems to have been the case here.

Like many men and women who devote a large part of their lives to work, and particularly if success and status are important to them, other areas of James's life, such as family, friends and outside interests, suffered through a lack of attention. The sense of importance that work provides is seductive, and the relative predictability of command-and-control work relationships, compared to more intimate and exposing personal ones, can all become an addictive retreat from any sense of vulnerability. It would seem that James had lost touch with his dependency on his colleagues and his need for intimacy in his private life, and consequently had become blind to the vulnerability of his position. Command and control had come to dominate his leadership style, while greater collaboration might have helped maintain his colleagues' support.

James was probably unconsciously aware of his increasingly vulnerable position, both at work and outside. Unconscious emotional awareness continues even where consciously it is being repressed. It would seem that the more precarious his position became, the more he went into denial.

James was unable to hear the messages his chairman and colleagues were sending, just as they were in turn unable or unwilling to send those messages in a way that meant they could be heard. As so often happens, changes had taken place but not been noticed, and so the necessary psychological adaptations and transitions needed to respond to the change did not take place. Under pressure, James, like most of us, retreated into a world of his own, one of denial and inattention to his feelings. Neither his wife, nor his chairman, nor his colleagues, were able or prepared to break through the barriers and defences he had set up. James was managing three relationships: to his organisation, to his family and to himself. In the sense of survival, the latter took precedence, although, in his mind, James believed himself to be focused solely on the needs of his organisation.

His wife, as is almost always the case with a loyal partner, sprang to his defence as soon as she knew about his situation. Being the partner of someone facing challenges at work is tough. Often, a partner will not know or understand enough about the actual situation to offer much in the way of useful advice, and their natural inclination is to view criticism in the workplace as an attack on their loved one. This is the natural reaction, but not necessarily an entirely helpful one. Instead of taking sides, asking open-ended questions and supporting the partner in a problem-solving process could be more useful. However, this may be experienced as unsupportive, and may even be perceived as irritating and annoying – at least until this anger can be channelled towards a more constructive plan of action for the workplace situation. Not uncommonly, nobody was really prepared to face James with the truth. His chairman told him of decisions, but failed to help him respond more effectively as CEO earlier in the process, when a change of leadership style might have been possible. And it appears the headhunter was prepared to convey negative messages about James to others, but not to him directly. Professionals are often not better – and quite often are worse – at difficult conversations than anyone else. Again, there is nothing especially surprising or unusual or indeed reprehensible about this, but it will have reinforced the sense of isolation and confusion James was experiencing.

It sounds as if James has learned something through the whole process: that he was, in fact, more dependent on others than he had realised. He rediscovered how much he valued his marriage, his children and his friendships. He was lucky in having an understanding partner who was prepared to support him, and go on a journey with him as he finally embraced changing gear.

Public humiliation

This is perhaps one of the most difficult transitions. In some extreme cases, a scandal, often involving sex, drugs or financial issues of some sort, precipitates a dramatic fall from grace played out in the humiliating glare of publicity. Within 24 hours, a hero can become a pariah – or so it seems. For the main protagonist, it can feel like the end of the world. Happily, it usually isn't. However, many people experience far more minor humiliations, which, to them, do feel all-consuming at the time. How do you battle through the pain and the shame to reach your new (more liberated) existence?

The story of Tina is one very familiar to those who find themselves caught up with a colleague on a personal level. Tina's story is particularly tough as it involves losing her job, tarnishing her reputation and being personally rejected. However, the human spirit has the capacity to shine through at the times when it is most tested. Loyal previous colleagues and time enabled Tina to reach a resolution.

TINA'S STORY

A divisional managing director

Tina was a bundle of energy and drive: she was smart and brave, and she was loved by most. For reasons she didn't really understand (and maybe he didn't either), her husband had an affair and, after much heartache, he left her.

Their only daughter had joined a fast-growing tech company after graduating, and soon before Tina found out about the affair, their daughter had moved with her company to San Francisco.

So when Tina was offered a new role running the division of a bigger competitor, she felt it would be something of a fresh start. The downside was that it meant a hit to her pension, as she was now in her mid-fifties, but they had made her a good offer and, with a likely divorce, more cash now felt good. And most of all, she welcomed the sense of moving on.

Tina made a fantastic start, taking a fresh look at the business and spotting new ways to find growth for a business that was doing well but had stalled a bit. She worked closely with her top team, but also brought in external advisers to help chart their way forward. One of these was a strategy consultant, seconded to be the strategy director. Simon was very clever and ambitious, and had also had a failed marriage. Tina was captivated by him, and over time they grew closer and closer. Simon became her closest confidant and she really trusted him. The changes they had planned for the business together, and which she had executed, were all going incredibly well and Tina was getting great feedback from her boss and her team.

Then Simon suggested they explore making an acquisition that would further drive revenue and expand her role. Tina was unsure because, to date, all her successes had come from growing her businesses organically. However, Simon really pushed her hard to support his plan and, in truth, she was becoming scared to lose him – both professionally and personally. She had come to rely on him more than she ever meant to, and soon she was being a full-on advocate for pursuing the deal.

A number of her team expressed reservations about the target company and said they thought there may be better alternatives. Tina's boss was keen to show his support for her given the results she had delivered (which had also reflected very well on him), so although he was unsure, he did not dissuade her. So, despite her colleagues' misgivings, Tina let Simon run with the acquisition and take the lead on driving it forward. He assured her she could trust him and she felt she had to show him that she did. Also, this was not her area of expertise.

Over the next few months, she and Simon began to work together even more closely, and what had been a purely platonic relationship moved to being a physical one, too. The more her team put up obstacles, the more Simon reassured her that his expertise was greater than anyone else's in her business, and that she could absolutely rely on him. After all, he was doing this for her.

As the deal got closer, Tina's boss began to get more nervous, sensing from the team that there could be issues with the deal that were being overlooked – especially by Simon, who they felt had his own agenda. Also, the team found subtle – and, increasingly, not so subtle – ways to point out to the boss just how close they believed Tina and Simon had become. In time, her boss, who still wanted to give her the benefit of the doubt, shared these concerns with her.

Under pressure and tired from having to run the business by day and work on the acquisition in the evenings, Tina reacted defensively to her boss. She felt it was not her boss's call to say she was too close to Simon, and she believed that she had the situation under control. Deep inside, though, she knew that this was not true, and that Simon was able to influence her, both inside and outside work.

Over the next few weeks, the issues around the acquisition grew more complex and Tina, under pressure from Simon not to withdraw from the deal, grew even more defensive with those around her. Finally, her boss reached the view that the deal should not go ahead. Tina was so invested in both the deal and Simon by now, that she found it impossible to pull back.

Not wanting to lose Tina, but by now deeply concerned, her boss commissioned some fresh due diligence on the target company. The results of this research showed that Simon had missed some key facts. When Tina was shown the data, she confronted Simon, who made a strong defence of his work. He assured Tina that if the deal went ahead, she would prove everyone else wrong. After an agonising night, she went back to her boss and argued that the new facts were not as material as her boss thought, and said that they should continue to make the acquisition.

A few days later, her boss asked her to leave the company straight away, telling her it was because he felt she had lost her judgement on both the situation and on Simon.

Tina was in a state of complete shock, but when she went to Simon to seek his support and consolation, he reacted by attacking her for handling the situation with her boss badly. He shouted at her, saying that it was all her own fault and that she had let him down after all his incredibly hard work. He then added that he was happy that at least he would no longer have to work with her!

Tina was devastated. Far from a fresh start, this was a disastrous end. She was nearly 60 and, apart from her daughter in the US, she felt she had lost everything. She kept asking herself, how could she have been so stupid?

Fortunately, she was wrong – she had not lost her loyal friends. They rallied round and supported her, eventually being brave enough and good enough friends to tell her she had been a fool over Simon. What they would like to do to him!

Once she had recovered sufficiently to think things through, she realised that her financial situation meant that giving up work altogether was not a great option. Both her parents were still alive and going strong, so the likelihood of Tina living into her 90s was high. Also, she had sacrificed some of her pension by leaving her old company in the way she had. She wanted to hide away, but this was not an option if she also wanted to keep on earning.

Her first few meetings trying to find a new role did not go well. She was still too bruised – and too proud – to own what had happened. By chance, an old boss got in touch out of the blue, and when Tina had a drink with her, she opened up about what had happened. The old boss thought very highly of Tina and could see that she did not need to reinforce how foolish Tina had been. Instead, she reminded Tina of the skills and talents she had and encouraged her to be less defensive and take her search into new areas where her skills were still relevant, but where she would not feel so exposed.

This coincided with another piece of good advice from a friendly headhunter: namely to 'chill' for a bit. To stop rushing at what to do next until she was a bit calmer and a bit more in control. Although she could not see it, it was obvious to others that Tina was struggling to come to terms with what had happened, and that this is not a good look to potential recruiters!

Tina wisely took a three-month break. She went off to California to spend time with her daughter; she worked on getting fit and had some much-needed 'me time'. She loved walking and wine, so happily California presented the opportunity to enjoy both.

She returned looking relaxed and well and ready to get back into the fray. Her time away had also given her a chance to reflect, and she decided to explore roles where she could have more balance in her life. She reasoned that doing a bit less for a bit longer would be the best option for her and the life she now wanted to lead.

A tale of confusion in the transition zone

A psychological perspective on Tina's story

Her only daughter moving to California, followed shortly by her husband leaving her, must have been a double whammy for Tina, and left her reeling emotionally. It sounds like the new role and company gave her something to get stuck into, but at the same time, perhaps it provided too much of a retreat, leaving her open to what sounds like exploitation.

Workplace romances can be complicated; the confusion and combination of romantic partners and work dynamics can make a relationship complex. Are we relating as lovers or workers? Are the power dynamics in our relationship caused by our personalities or the hierarchy at work? While it is, of course, fine and natural that people find a partner in their workplace (where, after all, we generally spend more time than anywhere else), if things get more serious, it may be advisable for one party or the other to consider working elsewhere for the sake of the relationship.

These complications, combined with the inevitable lone-liness of Tina's situation, perhaps resulted in her not being as sharp in her judgement as she should have been. She had apparently 'come to rely on him more than she ever meant to' when she advocated Simon's recommendations. Was she doing so as the head of the division, or as his girlfriend? And it seems her boss was faced with the same problem. If he was at all sensitive to the situation, which it seems he was, then he might have been understandably reluctant to create tension for Tina and maybe hoped that her blossoming friendship might wither.

If you are a boss in this situation, the best advice would be to discuss the whole situation openly. But this is easier said than done! Regardless of their seniority, most human beings, unless they are a complete sociopath, have an aversion to interpersonal conflict, and this can get in the way of having the difficult conversation that may need to be had. It can be even harder with someone who seems a little fragile emotionally. These conversations also mean crossing boundaries into a staff member's private life, which, under normal conditions, would not be appropriate. This is why workplace romances are often no bed of roses. Your colleagues will have to tread carefully and will inevitably have mixed feelings about your relationship. The situation also risks creating a sense of injustice, whether fair or not, when the romantic partner is apparently favoured.

Organisations provide human beings with a container for the expression and working through of a range of emotions. In simple terms, people need their workplace to provide three very important needs: a sense of achievement, a sense of belonging and a sense of influence. When these are not met, employees typically feel a justifiable sense of frustration, which they may express in different ways. In order to permit their safe expression, organisations need to provide a space in which inevitable feelings of failure, occasional exclusion and vulnerability can be shared, handled and contained safely. Organisational life can sometimes feel like a gigantic soap opera, but then it is these very same emotions that account for why soap operas (whether of the TV or Royal Opera House variety) can have such an addictive hold on us. Adding a romance to the mix can become lethal to professional relationships, judgement, and everyone's sense of safety.

And all of this was going on in Tina's situation, where deals involving a large amount of money (and, inevitably, egos, competition, power plays and battles) were a daily diet. Tina reacted defensively when challenged by her boss, as she had been pulled in different directions by her conflicting loyalties. Perhaps her internal confusions about her life found a distraction and a home in external events. All credit to Tina that she challenged Simon about the results of the due diligence research; however, overnight she reneged, and allowed her personal feelings to once again get in the way of professional judgement. When she was asked to leave, Simon's true loyalty (to himself) was exposed. As is so often the case, instead of facing his own accountability and shared guilt for the situation, he blamed her, demonstrating his own confusion, or maybe deliberate selfishness, around managing responsibilities and boundaries.

Luckily, Tina has loyal friends who are able to tell her the truth as they see it. When we are confused, we often do what Tina calls 'stupid' things – but calling the behaviour 'stupid' is sometimes an easy way of dismissing painful emotions. 'Stupid' is a word that has had multiple meanings over time. It has moved from describing a 'lack of feeling or emotion' (1560s) to 'stupor', 'struck senseless', and 'numbness' (c.1600), to its present meaning: a lack of intelligence. Perhaps one of the causes of stupidity could be a desire to withdraw from unbearable feelings. An example, perhaps, of how, in our overly 'rational' Western culture, we struggle with emotion: our wilful delusion about the strength of the rider in relation to the elephant.

However, it seems that Tina regained her intelligence – and her saner self – and was able to take time out to reflect. As she

CHANGING GEAR

changes gear, she will face the challenge of bringing together her emotional and rational sides in a more integrated way. She may need to learn that the emotional intelligence of the elephant may sometimes be superior to the rational intelligence of the rider.

Wilful blindness

Wilful blindness is a legal term for a situation in which a person seeks to avoid civil or criminal liability for a wrongful act by intentionally keeping themselves unaware of facts that would render them liable or implicated. In her book *Wilful Blindness*, entrepreneur and writer Margaret Heffernan says that we ignore the obvious at our peril, arguing that the biggest threats and dangers we face are not the ones we *cannot* see but the ones we *choose not to* see, whether by keeping them secret or refusing to look.[2] In this way, we are wilfully blind.

This poses an interesting question about why so many of us can, apparently, be wilfully blind. Is wilful blindness a sign of neglect, of just not caring enough – or maybe even of caring too much? It can, of course, be caused by either – and other things, too.

In important areas of our lives, especially in times of difficulty or change, it becomes a necessity to scan our horizons for areas where we might be being unknowingly, but ultimately still wilfully, blind. Ideally, we would do this all the time, but we are human and often it requires more energy or discipline – and certainly inclination – than we can muster! However, we should aim to be proactive in looking for the potential causes of our situation.

Christopher's story is of a man who lets things carry on as they are for too long. His comfortable life and narrow focus made it too easy for him to ignore what was happening around him, with potentially tough consequences for himself and his family. Fortunately, his wife was able to come to the rescue and help him to open his eyes to his predicament. Without her insightful intervention, he may reasonably have been charged with wilful blindness.

CHRISTOPHER'S STORY

An accounting firm partner

Christopher was always a fairly intellectual child. At school, he had avoided the 'cool kids' and been very happy to have two close friends who were rather like him. They all loved reading and shared an interest in history. He went on to study history at university and, again, was contented with a small group of friends who also took their studies very seriously. He was never happier than when debating the finer points of a historical dispute. While he was very clever, he was not obviously clever enough to become a don, of which, even some years ago, there were increasingly few. Also, while his parents were not poor, he would not have an inheritance to rely upon. The careers service advised him to study accountancy or law and, being pragmatic about a greater intake and being paid more sooner, Christopher chose accountancy.

Once again, he was not at the heart of the party scene for the graduate trainees, but he found some allies among his quieter peers. Although the accounting itself seemed rather dull to him and he did not relish the client interface, he did enjoy the intellectual challenge found in the complexities of tax accounting and planning for international businesses. Christopher was hard working, reliable and extremely diligent – all three traits being essential in the tax area. While he did not push himself forwards, he was promoted quickly, as he could be relied upon by the firm to produce good work.

He met Priscilla at work just after he had qualified. She was more outgoing than him and, while she passed her accountancy exams first time, she preferred working on the client management side rather than rolling up her sleeves on the technical accounting side. They married and, after they had their second child, they decided to move out of the city. Priscilla gave up working full-time and, over time, gave up her career altogether to look after their now four children. She loved being a mother and was fully integrated into their local community, where she did charity work.

Christopher continued to be promoted and he began to specialise in the pharma sector, where there were lots of interesting tax issues, many of which meant working internationally.

The pharma team was also a good one, in that they had built a collegiate culture. Christopher enjoyed this as he was supported and respected by his fellow team members. He was able to continue to progress in the firm as a technical expert, not a client service person, which suited him very much. He worked really hard, but was able to be there for his kids most evenings, as he did not socialise with his colleagues after work and, if he needed to work late, he could do it from home. The same was true at weekends. Life seemed pretty good for Christopher, his wife and his kids.

Over time, he was given the most challenging tax assignments and, by and large, he was able to solve the problems that were given to him. On occasions, he had to take the lead and engage more deeply with clients on specific issues, but otherwise he was able to just get on with the technical problem-solving.

While Christopher was rising through the firm, the pharma area was growing fast and he was becoming ever more a specialist.

This did not trouble him, because he had been a beneficiary of this so far. The work just kept coming to him.

However, his firm then restructured and, although Christopher did not see it at all at the time, this was when he stopped being on solid ground. The restructure saw him become part of a tax group, not an industry group, and made him more responsible for generating revenues. This was something he had never had to do before. Initially, his colleagues from the pharma team passed him work as they had done before. He didn't spot some of his new younger colleagues in the tax group start to sell themselves internally to the industry groups. It took some time for Christopher to wake up to this, as the work from the pharma group's most long-standing clients kept coming to him. What he had not noticed was that one particular pharma client had been in a phase where they needed a great deal of his time, and that he was not being asked to work on business from new clients.

After a couple of years in the new structure, Christopher began, for the first time at work, to have time on his hands. The work from the big client that had dominated his time since the firm had restructured was coming to an end, apart from routine work. He could now see that his younger colleagues had formed relationships with all the industry groups, including his old pharma team. Although he felt cheated, they had not done anything wrong or taken work away from under his nose. Nonetheless, they had usurped his position as one of the key 'go-to' people in the firm.

Christopher had no repertoire for dealing with this. All his life, he had been able to operate on his own terms. He hadn't seen it this way because it had happened naturally for him, and he had never been given any feedback other than to be told he was a great tax accountant and a good, steady husband and father. He really struggled to see how such an unfair thing had happened. To add insult to injury, he was not given the support he felt he more than deserved from his team leader in the tax group, who simply told him to get more work from his internal clients in the firm or from the tax departments of the clients he had worked with. Christopher was outraged to be told this. He had never had to sell himself before, and he had no intention of starting to do so now. He did what he had always done and let the world come to him, on his terms – but, for the first time, it did not do so.

Christopher did not tell his wife what was happening. He hunkered down and waited for the situation to sort itself out. Not that he could see how that would happen, but what else was he to do? Over time, his wife realised that he was getting less and less busy at work. She began to wonder if it might affect his bonus, as they were planning an extension to their house: their kids were beginning the process of leaving home, and she had plans to make their house more suited to returning rather than resident children.

When Priscilla really pushed Christopher to talk about what was going on, he let out the anger he had been bottling up. How dare they treat him like this? They would soon realise the superior tax expertise he could bring, and which he knew clients appreciated. What he didn't see was that many of the younger partners were not so young any more and had also become strong tax partners.

Fortunately, once he had opened up to Priscilla, she could see what had happened – and also what might happen going forwards if Christopher continued to do nothing about it. He wasn't quite at retirement age yet, but he would be soon enough, and the firm might push him into earlier retirement than their family finances could easily bear.

Priscilla's natural empathy with clients and understanding of the firm meant she could, in effect, become his coach. The

CHANGING GEAR

solution was not complicated. Christopher had to do some networking, both internally and externally. She knew he could not go out and sell to strangers, but he was good at his job and respected in the firm for his technical skills. Together, they mapped out who he was comfortable reaching out to and how he might do this.

Christopher hated having to consciously build his relationships: doing it with clients felt bad enough, but having to do the same inside his own firm was against all his instincts. But, with Priscilla's help, he could see that he had two choices: to either get on with it, or to retire too early. He gritted his teeth and got going.

He was, of course, a perfectly nice man and the people did respond positively to him, so it was not long before he had enough work to make his bonus the following year.

However, this way of operating at work was a necessity rather than a pleasure for Christopher. Having shown Priscilla he was prepared to put his family first, he began to work out how soon he could retire and still support his kids until the youngest had finished at university. Priscilla was reluctant, but knew the situation was making Christopher unhappy, so she supported his wish to retire in two more years.

When he came to the end of the two years, Christopher felt good to be leaving on his own terms – but, more than that, he felt good to be leaving!

The joy of history was calling and there was a lifetime of reading to be done, alongside enjoying his retirement with Priscilla, visiting ruins of ancient civilisations and historical sites. Once again, however, Christopher had failed to take into account his environment, and had not asked Priscilla how she felt about this! Another example of how easy it is to fall victim to wilful blindness.

Wilful blindness caused by a just-world fallacy

A psychological perspective on Christopher's story

Christopher is an introvert with a preference for being in the world of ideas over being in the world of people and relationships. An extrovert gets energy by interacting with others, while the introvert's internal battery gradually runs down around other people, causing them to retreat in order to recharge in solitude. Typically for an introvert, Christopher prefers the company of a few close friends rather than a wider social circle. His seriousness is perhaps a defensive retreat into the belief that ideas can somehow keep the world under control. He seems to prefer to think about the past rather than the future, perhaps believing that the historical world makes more sense to him than the babble of contemporary life. Of course, if he had been able to travel back in time, he might have found rather more similarities: have human beings really changed that much? Whatever one believes about such a question, it's unlikely that it can actually be answered with much certainty. He might have enjoyed a career attempting to do so, but that was not to be. Christopher was also a pragmatist who wanted a certain style of life, and so a professional career it had to be, though partly, it would seem, through gritted teeth. He found interactions with clients unrewarding and dull in comparison to the intellectual challenges of tax planning. His choice of profession may have been one that reinforced his defences, and allowed for his preference for intellectual clarity over messy human relationships. We make choices about our careers for both conscious and unconscious reasons, and the relatively closed world of tax accountancy has some resemblance to our picture of history, where the world could be drawn in black and white. Not unusually, he chose to marry a woman with strengths he did not have (and which he was

CHANGING GEAR

never likely to have). Happily, that worked out well for both of them.

His approach to his career could be said to be based on the just-world fallacy. It is the belief, reminiscent of the classical world, that a person's actions will inherently bring them moral fairness and fitting consequences. If you behave badly, fate will punish you; if you behave well, the gods will reward you. The idea is that the universe is based on a fateful logic of moral justice, which requires that those who behave badly will eventually come to a sticky end. Sadly, the experience of our world, at least, would seem to disconfirm such a hypothesis. Bad things can and do happen to people, no matter how well they behave; and people who behave badly can, and arguably too often do, seem to do rather well out of it. Christopher behaved well and worked hard, but still came unstuck in his career progress. His just-world belief misled him into thinking that a good world would continue to be good, that good behaviour would be rewarded. His wilful blindness seems to be psychologically motivated. As an introvert, he had not developed particularly effective social skills when it came to selling his services. This is a common problem for professionals who grew up in a world in which the strength of the brand of their firm, and their own personal brand within it, meant that the phone always rang with another request for help. These days, the world has changed into a much more competitive place than it was, and expertise alone is insufficient, unless it is in extremely short supply. Christopher blinded himself to a recognition that clients may prefer to work with people who are fun to be with, provided they are also sufficiently clever to solve the client's problems. His overvaluation of thinking rather than relationship-building eventually led him up a cul-de-sac. To be fair, having a client that demanded all of one's time is a pretty attractive proposition, and most people would probably fall victim to the same error, as, indeed, whole companies often do. Unlike the attractions of an unchanging past world, the present world certainly changes rather faster than most of us would like.

Christopher was also naive about the fact that organisations – certainly large ones – are power structures, and playing power games certainly wasn't the way he wanted to spend his time. That's fair enough, but there are consequences. Many people complain that there is too much politics within their organisation, but what are they expecting? The idea of a just world in which power is distributed fairly is a fallacy. Christopher also probably underestimated the degree to which his success was dependent upon how his organisation was structured. With little interest in management issues, he seems to have been blind to the importance of influencing his world, which he preferred to believe would remain static.

Many professionals have a distaste for 'selling'. Indeed, professional ethics are a complex subject, but this distaste is also a convenient attitude for those who find spending time with clients uncomfortable – and even perhaps a little beneath them. The ivory tower is no defence these days. Christopher failed to realise that the rules of the game he was in have changed. His picture of professional practice could be said to be based on the idea of a finite game: that is, a game with rules, beginnings and endings, winners and losers. But in a world where structures are continuously changing, such a view is wilful blindness. We live in a world of infinite games, games with constantly changing rules, no endings and only temporary winners or losers. The aim is not to win or lose but to stay in the game. Without Priscilla's help, Christopher would surely have been a loser. She helped him overcome his inherent introversion and force himself into more extrovert behaviour: something all introverts who want to be successful in large organisations probably have to come to terms with

CHANGING GEAR

doing, unless they are exceptionally able and lucky. You may not be able to change your personality, but you can change your behaviour.

Christopher is now looking forwards to returning to his love of history. We are told that he is looking forwards to visiting historical sites too, but has his wilful blindness got the better of him again? He hasn't asked Priscilla how she feels about this. When you are planning how to change gear, you might want to make sure you consult your partner about your plans as well.

Letting life take its course

In his novel *Survivor*, Chuck Palahniuk wrote: 'You realise that our mistrust of the future makes it hard to give up the past.' Humans don't always 'do' change very well and this quote beautifully captures one of the reasons for this!

For the vast majority of us, our lives have not been 'too awful' so far – so why are we so fearful of what is to come? Why do we all too often consider the future as a half-empty glass, rather than one half-full – or even just full?

Imagining the future or potential futures requires doing a number of things that are not compatible with busy lives and, arguably, do not come naturally to most people. Among these things are finding the time and space to really think and consider questions such as 'Where am I now?', 'Where do I want to be?', and 'Where have I come from?' It is entirely possible that we have lived our whole lives without really considering these questions. But the insights they provide will help create a road map to our future.

In order to embrace the future, there is a necessary acceptance of letting go of the present. This does not mean not living in the present, but it does mean taking some time in the present to think about your own past as well as future.

Helen had lived her life pretty much to the full, following her dream of becoming a doctor and caring for others. She saw herself as lucky in having had a pretty straightforward life, a wonderful partner, healthy and happy children and a fulfilling career. Her challenge came in how and when to embrace a new future. She was surprised to find this much harder than she had anticipated, and to discover just how much time and energy it would require, as well as how scary opening this 'box' would feel.

HELEN'S STORY
An NHS doctor

Helen had wanted to be a doctor for as long as she could remember. Well, that was not strictly true – initially, she wanted to be a nurse, because they were the role models for caring when she was a small girl. When it became clear that she was going to do well at school, her teachers suggested she might like to think about being a doctor. There were no doctors within her own family and she had to find her own way, not always helped by her parents, who simply did not have the experience to guide her. They did not really actively support her, but equally they did not stand in her way, unlike the parents of some of her other more ambitious female friends at the time.

So, from a relatively early age, Helen learned to be her own champion, an approach that served her very well as she embarked upon her career as a doctor. While at university she met Tom, who was similarly set on a clear path, as he loved the theatre and knew he wanted to work in that world. Over the next few years, they juggled their sometimes competing ambitions and careers and gradually, over time, they could not imagine not staying together. It also became clear that Helen was going to be the main breadwinner: unless Tom struck lucky, his would be a rather more hand-to-mouth existence. Helen was fine with this, as neither of them was particularly money orientated and, as an

NHS doctor, she was likely to have a stable income and, when the time came, pension.

'As a younger woman, Helen had had a clear sense of purpose as a doctor and her horizons beyond this were not only unclear, but also unimportant to her. As she underwent her training, she always had a sense of where she might be able to make a difference, and this led her to explore geriatric care and in particular geriatric psychiatry. It was an 'unloved' field of medicine and certainly not one pursued by most of her mainly male and often competitive fellow young doctors.

For many years, she honed her expertise. However, in time, she began to despair at the lack of priority old people with mental health problems were given in the NHS. Outside the NHS, there was very little expertise in geriatric psychiatry, as it was not an area that attracted those who wished to make a name for themselves in private medicine and it was seen as very 'unsexy'. Helen's focus on just being the best doctor she could be remained, but little by little she started to see that more needed to done on the policy and management side to drive much-needed change for patients.

Initially, she started to try to change the way things were done at her own hospital. It was tough, but people really respected her and the staff in her unit could also see how inadequate much of the patient care was. The hospital manager was focused on hitting her targets, and paid virtually no attention to psychiatry at all, let alone geriatric psychiatry. It became clear to Helen that it was going to be hard to drive any significant change as this required an acceptance of both the need itself and a reallocation of some budgets. However, undeterred, she did what she could and made small changes. While they were a long way from meeting the patients' needs, these changes did help more patients for more of the time. Her tireless work on this was noticed by her colleagues and also, to her surprise, by the hospital manager, which led to her being promoted to head of her department.

Then there was a moment where some light shone in. The hospital manager was promoted and a new manager arrived. His father had been diagnosed with Alzheimer's, and the new manager was struggling to come to terms with how to help manage his father's dementia, and in particular how to help his mother, who was now a full-time carer.

Helen now had a 'comrade in arms' and, after years of frustration, decided not to waste a moment. She and her new manager agreed to develop a plan for improving patient care, both for outpatients and for those on the ward. They then championed this within the hospital and won the support of their colleagues, who could see the improvements that were beginning to come through. The health service was beginning to worry about the increasing cost of treating the fast-growing number of elderly patients with various forms of dementia, and when they learned of the success being achieved by Helen and her team, they asked her to join a group to explore how the NHS could improve its approach to geriatric psychiatry.

Although she did not see it clearly at the time, this was when it became clear that Helen's sense of purpose had changed. Being a good doctor herself was no longer her goal: she wanted to enable all the doctors like her to do more to support their patients. Over time, Helen became a very visible champion for a wide range of issues in her area. She continued to see patients, but much of her time became focused on changing the system itself. What she did not see was how much she enjoyed this broader remit, and how much energy she drew from it. She was never one to seek the limelight, but she did thrive on the visibility she now had and really valued the respect she was given by her peers.

Alongside her career, she and Tom had had a family. Their children, while now technically grown-up, were not financially independent. Tom had also been working hard and had carved out a niche in the rapidly growing area of performance art. He never made much money, but was nonetheless successful in his field and continued to enjoy what he did. He had no plans to stop what he was doing. His work was his hobby and his hobby was his passion. He felt himself to be a very lucky man.

It was only when Helen realised she was approaching what could be her retirement age that she spent any time at all thinking about her future. The family depended on her income and, from a pension's perspective, retiring was a wise decision, but the idea of 'retirement' filled her with dread. Tom was going to work 'forever' and Helen had become accustomed to doing things that mattered. Without realising it, she had also become used to 'mattering' to others. Her children needed her, as children always do, but no more than that. Grandchildren were not about to beckon, but even if they did, although she would enjoy them immensely, she did not want to be a full-time grandmother.

So what to do? There was no imminent pressure on her to retire other than securing her pension, so after consulting with Tom, they decided she should retire in two years' time. The plan was for her to develop new areas of interest that would help to compensate for stepping down from her much-loved job. A year went by and Helen had changed nothing: if anything, she was working even harder! Dementia was becoming more and more of an issue for society and she felt more and more needed. When Helen and Tom talked seriously about things again, she found herself somewhat shocked to find that, unless she changed her mind, she was now only a year away from stopping. This made her decision feel real – and more than a little terrifying!

It gave her serious pause for thought, making her ask herself what she really wanted. In truth, she did not know, but she did know that at some point the need to formally retire would come. She feared leaving her career, but she also feared leaving it too late. If she was to have another set of interests and do more in the future, then, in theory, getting on with it was the right thing to do. It was just that the theory felt considerably easier than the practice. The pressure to change was ultimately going to have to come from her: Tom would not push her, and her kids did not know the state of the family finances. Even if they did, she knew they would say, 'Mum, you must do whatever you want and whatever is best for you.'

Taking the bull by the horns, Helen told her manager that she was going to retire the following summer: the deed was done! Now all she had to do was keep her nerve and focus on her own needs – something she had never consciously done before.

Unlike the previous year, where she had continued in a state of denial, now that Helen knew what she wanted, she pursued it diligently. She decided to take herself away for a few days to think. She and Tom had a little cottage in the country and this was the perfect place to go, as it would give her time to reflect and plan. Also, one of her great friends, who had recently been through similar changes, lived nearby, and Helen could use her as a 'safe' sounding board.

Helen came to the conclusion that she did not want to leave all that she had learned behind, and that she needed to find a new way to use her expertise and continue to play a part, albeit a different part, in helping advance the care for old people with mental health issues. By now, her focus was primarily, but not exclusively, the dementia diseases. Her plan was to talk to her colleagues about how she might play a part in training new doctors and healthcare professionals to deal more effectively and sensitively with patients who were displaying problematic behaviours. Although she did not know how she might best do this, she did know that the need was massive and that she had the capacity to help make a very real difference over the next five to ten years, even working on a part-time or project basis.

On a personal level, she decided several things. She needed to build more exercise into her life and wanted to see more of her friends, so she would start planning walking trips, which would be wonderful and have the added benefit of forcing her to train in advance! She had always also harboured a desire to learn Italian, so she would sign herself up for a course at a local college. And, last but not least, she would plan some holidays for her and Tom: going away together was something they had rarely done in the past and, with her new-found language skills, Italy would beckon. Helen loved Tom very much and knew he would love this as much as she would.

She also wanted to make her last year at work a very fulfilling one, but not in the way it had been in the past. Rather than leading from the front, she shifted her focus to enabling others and supporting them from behind. It would require some serious adjustment and discipline on her part, but she was now up for the challenge of letting go both as intentionally – and also as gracefully – as she possibly could!

Our Third Life offers opportunities to rework and find new solutions to old issues

A psychological perspective on Helen's story

We are told that Helen learned to be her 'own champion'. It appears that her parents were not fully in tune with her and her wishes, seemingly less ambitious for her than Helen was for herself. Such children may have to parent themselves, reversing the 'normal' relationship, and learn from an early age how to tune in to the needs of others. She would have experienced her own parents as putting a lower value on ambition than she did. This mismatch can be a cause of impostor syndrome (see Chapter 5), which can be seen in children with a higher desire for impact and power than their parents, whose ambitions might be seen as 'unacceptable'. The desire for power in British society is generally regarded by most people with ambivalence, although, of course, 'power' itself is a neutral word and can be used in a positive as well as a negative way. Like many professionals, Helen would probably regard herself as having a desire for impact, but would be uncomfortable calling this a desire for power. This is one reason why it is often difficult to find anyone in the professions (e.g. doctors, academics, lawyers, accountants) to take up leadership roles. Such roles are regarded with deep ambivalence and any individual seeking them is looked at with suspicion, and often with an implication that they must be second-rate at the professional task in some way – 'Why else would they be so motivated?' By contrast, the culture within most corporations is encouraging of the wish to lead: indeed it is seen as a central and healthy desire.

Helen's early experience of feeling somewhat misunderstood is a common foundation for the choice of a helping profession in adult life: becoming the metaphorical 'parent' to others. And she chose as a partner somebody who was also ambitious in his own way. However, we also learn that she is uninterested in and even disapproving of competitiveness. The distinction between ambitiousness and competitiveness is a fine line: finding the right balance between getting ahead and getting along with others is something everyone has to deal with in the workplace. It would be interesting to know more about Helen's family and whether or not she had brothers and sisters, and how she managed her relationships with them as a child. There is, of course, no 'solution' to these issues; they are value dilemmas and choices inherent in the human condition. How we each resolve these, and our own definitions of and attitudes to 'success', may need to be re-examined as we begin to change gear.

Helen chose one of the most challenging, poorly understood, most vulnerable and 'least loved' sectors of society, with whom, as we have seen, she may have unconsciously identified. She became a champion/parent for them, possibly as an expression of her own unconscious sense of not having being understood and championed by her own parents. Our choice of work can have both unconscious as well as conscious origins. In Helen's case, it went beyond a desire to help those in need and took the form of changing policy and improving the management of such patients. This is where we see her desire for impact (power) being expressed.

While her hospital manager focused on targets, she, the committed professional, focused on patient need. This is the way in which the NHS manages the dilemmas of balancing limited resources with actual patient needs, and often leads to unproductive conflict between managers and professionals, and an unhelpful splitting of 'we are the realistic/good people, they are the unrealistic/bad people'. One of the less conscious aspects of any public health service provider is its function on behalf of society as a rationing device: who shall receive priority and whose needs will be de-emphasised or even ignored. However, managing these dilemmas is a necessary and inevitable part of working in the NHS. While it can be handled usefully, and constructively engage both sides in a difficult decision-making process, it can deteriorate into personalised misunderstandings and unproductive conflict, with each side accusing the other of not understanding the problem. In reality, each side, in fact, only 'understands' half the problem – either management or adequate patient care – and accuses the other of being the impediment. It was good to see that in Helen's interactions with the second manager, the two sides seemed to have been able to communicate productively and find a way forward.

In her role as champion/parent for others, Helen took on ever-increasing responsibilities. Indeed, she seemed to thrive on this, satisfying her desire for impact and enjoying also the visibility and 'respect she was given by her peers'. Each of us has our own definition of what 'mattering' means; we are social animals with a concern about how we are seen by others. It also gives us a sense of achievement, however we define this, in both our work and personal lives. After stopping a full-time career, Helen, like many people, still needed to find a source of 'mattering', impact and achievement. This can often feel like a huge challenge. Despite agreeing with Tom that she should plan for this process, Helen, again like most people in such situations, just carried on even harder, fuelled by a defensive need to escape from the real issue of what to do next. Many are at risk of burnout at this phase of exiting. Helen, however, recognised this when she was just a year away from stopping. Her two contrasting fears – of leaving full-time employment on the one hand, and of leaving things too late on the other – could have resulted in her becoming frozen in a state of avoidance and indecision. Whichever way she turned, she was faced with either tackling the challenges of what to do next, or redoubling her current efforts but postponing decisions about the shape of her future life. This was further compounded by the fact that both her sources of 'mattering' – her work and her now grown-up children – would no longer provide the same sense of significance and being needed that they once had. Also, as is common, these two roles of worker and parent had occupied most of her time, giving her little or no chance to think about herself and her own desires, needs and pleasures. With so many things to consider, it would be easy to feel overwhelmed.

What Helen needs to do next is to identify, in a deeper sense, what it is that really matters to her about her work – what satisfactions it provides, and what about it gives her a sense of mattering and of significance – and then consider how she can achieve these outcomes through a different vehicle than that of being a doctor. This will be a challenge for her, because, following her parents' relative lack of understanding of her needs and what drives her, she herself did not develop a good understanding of these. This work, which was only partially done in her childhood, has to be reconsidered now. What might feel somewhat threatening may in fact be an opportunity to rework these questions. Just as the teenage years provide an opportunity to revisit, rework or readjust patterns of behaviour adopted during the generally socially conventional period of childhood (ages six to eleven), a change of gear provides an opportunity to re-examine existing solutions and adaptations. It is a chance to build a new identity and to rework issues, dilemmas and conflicts that have been put in the deep freeze of the unconscious, and now need to be taken out and examined in order to find new solutions to the perennial dilemmas of living and finding purpose and meaning in life. It is a time of life when one has the opportunity to re-examine and re-evaluate, although this is unlikely to feel entirely comfortable for most of us.

Embracing your true self

Discovering a new passion, or rediscovering an existing one – and with this a whole other sense of yourself – can be, on the one hand, wonderful and, on the other, a dilemma. Some hobbies can be weekend-only, but others might take on a greater importance, meaning a rethink of priorities and life plans. In theory, this can happen at any time, but as people begin to move towards their Third Life, or if they are able to make a sustainable change of gear early, then the chances of it actually happening become much higher.

The gentle way is to go part-time at work in order to create time for your passion. For those whose role can be changed to a part-time one and who are able to rethink their lives to make it affordable, it is an option that can be attractive from quite an early stage. However, making this choice involves trade-offs that have to be thought through carefully.

Dan's story is one of juggling a number of trade-offs. The decision he makes is ultimately relatively simple, but reaching this point was a long journey for Dan. Much of it was a good journey, but not all of it was easy. Dan's natural optimism and can-do approach to life has been a key factor in carrying him through to a happy place.

DAN'S STORY

A manager in financial services

Dan's parents moved to the UK when he was twelve. The move came out of the blue and, to Dan, was terrifying, daunting and exciting all at once. While he had a loving family, he was not really happy in small-town America, and had longed for his horizons to open up. He had struggled with the low-level racism he and his family experienced every day, and he had a growing feeling that he might be gay, which he could see would more than double the prejudice he experienced if he were to acknowledge this publicly at any point. He also knew that, if he did so, it would be very hard for his parents and, to a lesser extent, his siblings.

In some ways, the move to the UK could herald the new horizons he sought, but he had no sense of what he might encounter in a new country. His father had been offered a post in Liverpool, which at least would mean he would live in a city in contrast to his small hometown.

Happily, after a year or two, Dan felt less daunted and increasingly comfortable in his new environment. He still encountered some racism, but less than had been the case in America, and by and large, his family had been welcomed into their new community. When he was fifteen, he won a scholarship for the sixth form to a leading boarding school. Once again he felt terrified, daunted and excited. Academically, it would be great for him and, while he had enjoyed his local school, he was beginning to feel that he was not being stretched. He was also increasingly sure that he was gay. This was his one huge reservation: how would he cope in a boys-only school? When Dan got to his new school, he discovered there was a hidden but active group of gay boys. All the open banter was homophobic, but he soon learned that at night, once the lights were off, there was another reality. He did not know if the boys who participated were actually gay, or bisexual, or if they just had so much testosterone that, in the absence of a girl, a boy would do. It gave Dan the chance to experiment fairly safely with his own sexuality, and to learn that being gay might be a path for him. However, this was never discussed by the boys and so there was no pressure to come to any conclusions, and there was real safety in the unspoken pact of secrecy between the boys.

Once he left school he went on to study economics, and watched his former classmates embrace girls with a passion. So, he followed the norm and, on the surface, did the same. It was only once he started to work that he accepted that he was different to most of his classmates. He loved the girlfriends he had, in his way, but found himself longing for the feelings he had experienced with the boys at school. So, gradually, he embraced being gay, and, even more gradually, he brought his friends and finally his family into the loop. This did not always go smoothly. Although at times he found himself desperately disappointed by some people's reactions, his close friends and family were there to support him. He did not, however, tell his work colleagues, as he judged that this would be problematic. He worked in financial services and the culture in his office was quite macho. Not as much as he knew could be the case in investment banks, but it was definitely there, nonetheless.

Dan's career progressed really well and he enjoyed his work. So while he was not able to be the true Dan at work, he was actually pretty happy.

In his early forties, Dan met Nick and they moved in together. Over the next few years, Dan was as happy as he had ever been, and everyone could see that he was flourishing. Nick was much less conventional than Dan and introduced him to his dynamic, creative community of friends, which Dan loved. Gradually, Dan started to experiment with creative pursuits, and one of these experiments was a pottery class. To his delight, Dan discovered that, as well as loving ceramics, he had a real flair for it. His teacher could not have been more encouraging, and Dan found himself spending more and more time 'at the wheel'. One day, Nick suggested they turn the outhouse in their garden into a studio for Dan to make pottery. This turned out to be only the beginning.

Soon, Dan decided that he needed to rethink his life. Until now, although he had been his own person in many ways, he had never quite had the courage to be fully himself. Finally, he felt the need to be completely comfortable in his own skin. This meant facing who he was at work. Indeed, what did he want work to be for him? He was the breadwinner and he was not sure he wanted to throw either his own life – or Nick's life – up in the air, but he knew he had reached the point where he could not just carry on as he had been. After living in turmoil for the best part of a year, Dan took the opportunity of his annual appraisal to tell his boss that he wanted to leave. He did not know what would happen, but he did know he needed to move forward.

His boss proved to be amazing. He coaxed Dan into explaining why he wanted to leave, partly because he was a genuinely decent person, but also partly because the business relied on Dan and it was not going to be at all easy to replace him. During the next couple of weeks, Dan and his boss had a number of conversations that resulted in a huge win-win. They agreed that Dan would move to a flexible three-day week. This meant that, at busy times for Dan's department, he might work full-time, and that, at other times, he would not go into the office at all, overall working the equivalent of a three-day week. That still left Dan needing to tell his colleagues that he was gay and, after much agonising about how to do this, when he received the invitation to a company event with partners, he decided to take the bull by

CHANGING GEAR

the horns, and brought Nick with him. It caused a bit of gossip, but that died down pretty quickly and life soon moved on to Dan's 'new normal'.

This 'new normal' meant Dan was finally Dan, and it made him wonder why he had agonised so much and taken so long to get there.

Being yourself more, with skill

A psychological perspective on Dan's story

The idea of being yourself more, with skill, found in Rob Goffee and Gareth Jones's book *Why Should Anyone Be Led by You?*,[3] suggests that being yourself isn't quite as easy as some self-help books imply. Dan's story illustrates him not just being himself but becoming himself, arguably the task of a lifetime. As we will explore in Chapter 2, we have at least three selves: the self we think of ourselves as being (the autobiographical self); the self we present to others (the social self); and the self that other people actually experience (the experienced self). To manage one's way effectively through life is something of a balancing act between these different selves. Is any one of them more true or authentic than the others? Authenticity might not be so simple, either, particularly as we are shaped by different circumstances at different points in every day – at work, at home, with friends, in a library, at a night club.

Although this book focuses on the Third Life, we actually make transitions at each stage of our lives, often prompted by a 'crisis'. A crisis is a moment of danger, but also of opportunity, and people respond in very different ways. Dan seems to have responded positively to a whole series of crises. He made the transition from his country of origin to the UK without warning, a potential crisis that he turned into an opportunity, viewing it as a chance to get away from small-town America. In general, Dan seems to be opportunity-minded rather than threat-minded, an optimist rather than a pessimist. As we will explore later in the book, optimists typically find the uncertainties and anxieties of change and transition easier than pessimists. Experiencing crises early in one's life can make one stronger, though of course not always. Through a combination of his family's support, his partner's support, the relatively accepting environments of his school and his work, and his own inner strength, Dan seems to have been able to shape his sense of who he is in several ways through various potentially painful moments: being black in a white environment, being gay in a largely heterosexual world, having an artistic temperament in the quantitative world of finance. In each of these worlds, a member of a minority can feel defined by what they are not, rather than by what they are; an inevitably painful, confusing and alienating experience. He seems to have made the best of these challenges and turned potential crises into opportunities.

It can often seem easier to hide your true self, particularly when social conventions are not encouraging of who you feel yourself to be. Changing gear gives you an opportunity to reconfigure your outer, social self to be more in harmony with your inner, autobiographical self. But it requires a certain degree of resilience to withstand external expectations, whether from family, work or elsewhere. Those who are resilient typically demonstrate three features – sticking to their values, seeing crises as opportunities rather than threats, and focusing on influencing those things that they can, rather than trying to control the things they cannot.

Dan has probably learned a lot of this along the way, and maybe there will be opportunities to give back to others some of what he has learned through his personal experiences. As we mentioned at the outset, the coronavirus pandemic has given us all pause for thought, and although clearly a mortal threat, it is also an opportunity to reflect on the balance we have in our lives between the truly important and the apparently urgent.

Often, we partner up with somebody very different to ourselves, perhaps representing a shadow side of ourselves that we have not been able to develop. Through Nick, Dan discovers his artistic nature. This enables him both to shape clay into pottery 'at the wheel' and also to shape himself. In making this change of gear, both Dan and Nick had to face the choice between a more materially wealthy life if Dan were to continue full-time at work, and a less materially rewarding, but arguably more spiritually rewarding, life if he went part-time and pursued his passion.

Accepting the need to stop

Sometimes life does not deal us the hand we want. Sometimes, in fact, it deals us a hand we do not want. The acceptance of this can follow quite a complicated route. Human beings are well equipped with a selection of psychological mechanisms to avoid difficulty and pain; those most commonly employed are touched on in different ways throughout this book. However, there are times when the inevitable is – or, over time, becomes – undeniable and must be confronted. The acceptance of this is a form of transition in its own right, and, as with most transitions, there is inevitably loss, but also new opportunities and, potentially, a previously unimaginable alternative that is sometimes better.

In contrast to Dan's situation, where he was able to opt for his choice, Michelle found herself at a point where there was only one choice available to her – and, therefore, it was really a necessity, not a choice at all. Getting to that place was a painful process for Michelle, but once she had got there, the need to accept the only real choice available to her – namely stopping work much earlier in life than she had ever imagined she would – actually opened up a whole new set of opportunities and choices.

MICHELLE'S STORY
A PR executive

Michelle was a bundle of energy. Ever since she was a child, she had always bounced her way through life. She was warm and loving and fun to be with. She was at the centre of the social life at her school and university and, academically, she was comfortably in the middle of the pack. Her parents were also pretty sociable, and she was the third child of four, so from a young age she had learned to be relatively self-sufficient.

She met Mike when she was a trainee and they had an easy, happy relationship, embracing each other's friends and social lives. They both had jobs they enjoyed. Michelle's role in a PR company, while demanding of her time, was often also lots of fun. In their early thirties, they decided the time had come and they would like to have kids. For the sake of their parents, they decided to get married before they did so. In its way, deciding to have children of her own was the first 'grown-up' decision Michelle had made.

They had a wonderful wedding where all their family and friends celebrated both their marriage and their decision to have children. However, after trying unsuccessfully to get pregnant for a couple of years, Michelle came to wonder if there might be a problem. It then took a little time to cajole Mike into them both having tests. Once they had done so, they decided they would go down the IVF route.

Their rather perfect lives suddenly seemed rather less perfect. Because they had been so open about their plans to start a family, they both felt like they were in a goldfish bowl, and Michelle struggled to cope with all the very well-intentioned, but ultimately unwanted, advice from her family, friends and work colleagues. Being a grown-up definitely had its down sides.

Happily, after something of a struggle, they had a little girl. Then, as can sometimes happen after a struggle with IVF, Michelle soon found herself pregnant again. Her daughter had not been an easy baby, and although she was thrilled at the news, she was also daunted at the prospect of having another baby so soon. She had only just found her feet again at work and was loving being her old self again. By now, Mike's career had really taken off and he was busier than ever. Her second pregnancy was less straightforward and she prematurely gave birth to another little girl. However, they now had the family they wanted, and felt very blessed.

Life continued apace, juggling two children and two careers. There were stresses and strains, but they seemed to cope. However, gradually Michelle found herself feeling less and less happy, and less and less fulfilled. Their second daughter, who had not found the social side of school easy, began to struggle a bit more noticeably as she entered her teenage years, and Michelle's mother, who had always been such a role model for her, and who regularly helped out with the girls, also began to struggle with her health. Then, to make matters worse for Michelle, Mike was given a promotion. It was great for his career, but it meant he would have to travel a lot more, leaving her less supported at home.

It felt like the perfect storm. Michelle found it hard to maintain her 'bounce'. There was no one moment that tipped things over, but she felt there was a lot outside her work that needed more of her attention. She felt a far cry from her sociable, happy-go-lucky younger self.

So, in her mid-forties, Michelle found herself wondering where her life was going. She loved her work, she loved her children and her parents, and she could see how Mike was thriving, both professionally and financially. For a while, she just carried on, trying harder to get it right on all fronts, but increasingly she felt like she was climbing a mountain. Then, she came home from work one day to find her younger daughter sobbing. The source of these tears was a particular incident with a classmate, but Michelle knew this was symptomatic of a deeper problem: one which was not getting easier as her daughter found school increasingly challenging.

That weekend, she and Mike took the girls to stay with Michelle's parents, and then the two of them went off to a hotel they loved in the countryside where they could take some long walks. After some tough deliberations, Michelle found herself giving in to what she had resisted so far, accepting that she was exhausted and miserable and had lost her sense of self and *joie de vivre*. She hated the idea of giving up her job, but she also did not see how she could carry on as things were. Mike was now earning enough that, if they had to, they could live on his income. She also knew that there was not a part-time role at her company that she would want to do: what gave her pleasure was leading from the front.

Michelle could now see that her direction of travel was clear – but where would she travel to? To her surprise, there was a relief in reaching the realisation that things had to change, and the first thing that had to change was her situation. This led her to see that she needed to create time to understand and consider what support both her daughter and her parents needed. She also needed to devote some time to herself.

Resigning was incredibly hard, only helped by her certainty that it was the right thing to do. She could not continue as she had been, as before too long she now knew she would fall over and need help herself.

The first few weeks were the toughest. She found herself grieving for her 'work self', which had also come to embody her 'social self', because, after work and family, friends had become a distant third. However, within a couple of months, she was able to see what she needed to do for her daughter. She moved her to a different school, where she would be able to make a new start with less pressure and Michelle available to more proactively support her. As far as her parents were concerned, she had the time to organise more medical tests, which showed that her mother had the beginnings of Parkinson's. This meant persuading both them and her siblings that her parents should downsize sooner rather than later. All of this would take time, so Michelle decided to focus on her family for the next six months before she worried about herself.

During this time, she also had time to experience what she missed about work, and also to pay more attention to herself. She embarked upon a much-needed fitness programme and took up netball again with a vengeance, which helped her to indulge both her social and her competitive spirit!

Once she felt her daughter and her parents were on track, Michelle reconnected with her old colleagues and clients and went to see some headhunters. By now she was clear that she did want to work, but she wanted a role which gave her the ability to flex her time. Initially, most of them tried to persuade her to go back full-time now that her daughter and parents were more settled, but Michelle had come to the conclusion that she did not want to risk returning to a life that was potentially too unmanageable. Yes, by normal career definitions she was arguably too young to make this change, but now that she had taken stock of her own life, she was as certain as she could be that she had made the right choice for her. One that, now she had truly made it, felt very empowering.

Self-sacrifice and maturity; a courageous transition in midlife

A psychological perspective on Michelle's story

Although this book is primarily about changing gear for the third phase of life, this case illustrates how transitions can happen earlier. Being the third child of four is commonly either very difficult, since you are neither a novelty nor the youngest, or sometimes very simple, as your parents are less anxious, less rides upon your success and you are relatively free to find your own way. It sounds as if Michelle, with her relatively carefree childhood and early adulthood, was more a case of the latter. A lot probably depends on the child's temperament, optimism and tolerance for frustration in particular. But being noticed and getting attention as a third child may mean a good deal of doing what pleases others and going along with what others want to do, unless one goes for the alternative attention-getting device of full-on rebellion, which clearly Michelle did not!

The choice of PR for a career suggests a preference for promoting the interests of others rather than her own, albeit in a fun atmosphere that she clearly enjoyed. Issues around self-confidence are not uncommon in public relations and advertising, professions in which the focus is on promoting the work and products of others rather than oneself. Career choices can have unconscious as well as conscious reasons behind them: this doesn't make them bad or wrong choices, but being aware of these roots can be helpful.

Michelle and her husband did the conventional thing of getting married before having children 'for the sake of their parents': was this an example of her need to please others? Or perhaps it was just simply a caring thing to do? Was there a degree of naivety in Michelle and her husband's openness with their friends and families on the topic of IVF? Was being so open bound to stir up emotional responses and risk inviting ill-informed, unwanted advice? Her difficulty getting pregnant was certainly the first bump in the road in a so far essentially charmed life. After the arrival of their second child, we learn that they felt blessed, and all seemed to go well again for the family, despite some stresses and strains – until they were hit by the 'perfect storm' of their younger daughter's difficulties at school, Michelle's mother's deteriorating health and Mike being increasingly busy with his new promotion. The person who wasn't receiving attention was Michelle herself; while she was getting things right for others, she wasn't getting it right for herself. This is a common enough problem for working parents with a busy partner and small children, but compounded perhaps by Michelle's difficulty in finding ways of getting her own needs met. Her identity and sense of self received support and affirmation through her work, but if this was no longer so feasible, what was Michelle to do? Who would she be?

Although Michelle felt she had no choice but to resign, which felt like a breakdown in a life that seemed to be running pretty smoothly, perhaps it was, at the same time, a breakthrough. In acknowledging the difficulties her daughter was experiencing, Michelle matured. It would be interesting to know if Michelle now sees this as a turning point in her own development. Often, developmental moments aren't necessarily comfortable or even chosen, but out of this crucible moment of adversity, perhaps she grew and became more herself? And good for her that she was able to channel her energies into developing both her social self and finding an expression for her competitive spirit playing netball, becoming alive once more in her new life. When she decided to return to work, it took courage to recognise that it should be part-time, on the grounds that anything more would be unmanageable. But perhaps her maturity in a new-found self and sense of freedom was also speaking in this decision. She was able to resist the social convention of returning to work full-time, a decision that was in fact more empowering than a return to full-time working.

Caring too much and losing yourself

Is it possible to care too much? Those who are driven by a desire or need to help others place a high value on their ability to feel that they have helped in a tangible way. There are many ways in which this can be achieved, and it does not necessarily follow that not-for-profit cares and for-profit does not care. Such a distinction is far too simplistic. There are, of course, examples of commercial organisations where profit is the only motive, but, on the other hand, there are also examples of those in the overtly caring professions or working in charities who demonstrate behaviours that show scant regard for others in the name of 'doing good'. Making a positive contribution to society can be achieved in many different ways.

William took a very conscious decision to work for the 'good' of society. Clearly this was for the 'good' of William, too, as he took a great deal of personal satisfaction from his work, which enabled him to use his energy, drive and abilities in a way that lined up with his own sense of purpose and values. For much of his career, this was a successful strategy for him. However, he arrived at a place where his job stopped being 'good' for William. This forced him to accept what was happening to him and come to terms with having to make a change: one that precipitated him moving on in his life a little earlier than he had intended.

Acknowledging when things have become too much is especially hard when your sense of self is bound up in feeling that you have a duty to carry your colleagues and be the one they can rely on. This is not the usual definition of a work-aholic, but it does share many of the same components. The remedy is also similar, involving stepping back and taking a more objective view of the 'whole you': a view which may have been somewhat – or very – obscured.

WILLIAM'S STORY

A senior civil servant

William grew up in a family where caring and contributing to the greater good were front and centre. His father was a vicar and his mother was a social worker. From as young an age as he could remember, the family placed a high value and focus on helping others. As a teenager, he sometimes found this wearisome, and for a while swore he would never follow his parents into the caring professions. He studied geology at university, after which he decided he would have a life travelling the world, working for the big oil company who had just offered him a place on their graduate training scheme.

His first few years at work became increasingly unfulfilling, and he found the pull of his family values becoming stronger and stronger as he observed what he saw as the less-than-caring attitudes for the communities in which his company operated. William wondered if he had just joined the wrong company and if he would find working at a less single-mindedly commercial oil company less problematic. Over the next eighteen months, he explored several other options with different companies within the oil sector, but came to accept that his heart was just not in it. Gradually, the realisation that he was, after all, his parents' son took seed in his head, and ultimately became too hard to ignore.

This led him to have a rethink and he decided to apply to the civil service, where he hoped he could find a more values-based organisation and, at the same time, a stimulating environment in which to work. Happily he was asked to join, and he loved his first ten years. Over this time, he had a number of interesting and different roles, moving department and being promoted quickly enough to keep him feeling stretched. His first proper managerial role was in social services, which, he had to acknowledge, was unavoidably close to 'caring'. Needless to say, this made his mother very proud, but it also led to both his parents making sure that William knew just how hard they felt he needed to 'fight' on behalf of people who needed looking after.

Despite having never planned to be in the social services area, William now found himself increasingly driven by the same desire for social justice and support that had motivated both his parents over the years. He also found that he felt very comfortable in his own skin as he followed, closely if not literally, in his parents' footsteps. His wife was supportive of him too. She was a lawyer working in the court system, and she both understood and shared his drive to make a difference.

For William's next role, he was given an opportunity to review the policy in a particular area of his now 'home' department. His assessment of the changes that were needed included strengthening delivery at a regional level, and he recommended a change in the way this area should be led and managed. He had never considered becoming a manager on a larger scale, but seeing his policy being implemented, and the difference it was making, made him much more interested in management and the delivery of policy, rather than just developing policy from a distance.

His boss, who had seen William's interest evolving, then asked him if he would like to apply for a regional management job. This meant moving out of the central civil service and also relocating. After some agonising with his wife about changing their kids' schools, and checking she could move to a new job, William accepted the offer.

This was the start of what would become the rest of his career. It was not what he had planned, but it had evolved naturally and he felt increasingly fulfilled as he learned to manage what he could see was a much-needed service in need of a great deal of improvement.

He continued to be promoted, although the roles above were larger and the gaps between promotions became longer. William was a much-liked and respected colleague. People could see his natural empathy, as well as his ability to work out how to create a more efficient and effective organisation. When he was in his late forties, he was asked to take on the top regional leadership role in his area. He knew it would be very challenging, but he was up for that. What he did not know when he accepted the role was the extent of the cuts that were about to come.

Over the next few years, William battled to increase budgets and improve the delivery on the ground to those who needed most help and support. He had some wins, and the loyalty of a great team, but, as time went on, it was an increasingly hard slog. He did his very best not to let his own people know how tough he was finding it: only those very close to him in his leadership team knew and, although they felt the same, they were to an extent protected by him. William felt both responsible and powerless. He had the satisfaction of feeling he had tried as hard as he could. He knew he had not been perfect, but it was realistic to say that he had done pretty well, under the circumstances. 'The circumstances' being the main issue.

Then, after a particularly gruelling week when he had had to make some really difficult trade-offs in terms of the services his team would continue to deliver, William realised he was losing the will to fight on. This realisation came as a huge shock, as he had always put the importance of what he was trying to do above his own needs. His parents had 'trained' him well! When he spoke this out loud to his wife, she cried. She knew the toll it had been taking on him, and was so relieved he was able to see what was happening to him. He felt it sounded too self-congratulatory to say he had cared too much about caring, but it was the truth. What he had failed to see was that he had neglected caring for himself and his family, and that the last few years had been very hard for his wife in particular.

This led him to the sad but relieving conclusion that he needed to resign. William and his wife looked at their finances and concluded that he could take early retirement. While this would mean they would have less money for the future than they had expected to have, it also meant they would have their health and happiness, which was beginning to be something they could not take for granted.

In reality, once William had stood back and assessed his situation, it was a straightforward decision – but it wasn't an easy one. Telling his team, and accepting that he really did need to put himself ahead of others for a bit, was incredibly hard and there were days when he felt he had made a terrible mistake, chastising himself for giving in. Fortunately, the rational William knew he was doing the right thing – and, really, the only thing possible for him.

After a period of detox, the William of old emerged again. His wife had known, deep down, that this would happen, but at the same time she was incredibly relieved when it did. At first, he simply enjoyed having time to focus on his family. His parents were now quite old, and although they were in good health, he knew he could not take that, or them, for granted forever. His wife was still working, so William took over more of the domestic workload, which meant they had more time to relax and go out together. He could now see he had let slip more than he should have in his non-work world. This included his friendships in the village, and he was delighted when, after a few lessons and some hard practice, he was invited back into the tennis team!

With his personal life back intact, William turned his attention to a balance between his life and his work. Now, however, he was determined that the balance in his life in favour of non-work would stay. He planned to volunteer locally and to do things where he could help people on a personal level rather than by running an organisation. He knew that this would not be simple, as he was wired to see bigger ways to help. He told himself he would be a work in progress!

Contradictions and resolutions
A psychological perspective on William's story

We are told that William found his parents' high value for and focus on helping others wearisome as a teenager, and that his choice of geology at university was based on his belief that this would enable him to have a life travelling the world. Perhaps it was also, unconsciously, a way of travelling away from the somewhat burdensome nature of the value system he had inherited. Quite possibly, he had also seen the intractability of the multiple and sometimes irremediable consequences of human poverty. You can't get much further away from people than rocks! Rocks don't have feelings; they don't make demands and you can treat them any way you want – they certainly don't complain. Perhaps William was also not so ambitious as some, or at least not in an obvious way. After all, there is plenty of good work to be done influencing oil companies from within, but it is tough work when the shareholders have only a short time perspective, a situation which is changing. But making financial profit was probably never going to be William's thing.

We will discuss the psychological meaning of work in Chapter 4, and how work starts with something that is missing: an absence that has to be filled, something that is incomplete. The act of filling in or completing is the work. William describes his work in the company he joined as not fulfilling, and it sounds as if the work that William needed to do wasn't to be found in an oil company.

Although not materially ambitious, William seems to have inherited his parent's commitment to public service, rapidly and successfully moving up the hierarchy in the civil service. The change of career seemed to provide a way of channelling an interest in social justice, something that he shared with his wife. His model of leadership was perhaps of someone who fought the system and empowered the people. Sadly, as he was to discover, the higher up the system you go, the more you become part of it. You are now accountable, managing the inevitable disparity between needs and resources in any public organisation. For a number of years, however, William was able to find a role with direct people contact and to make an impact using his natural empathy in caring for people less advantaged than he was. William found fulfilment in a role that made the most of his ability to see how to create a more efficient and effective organisation, enabling him to provide the kind of leadership and empathy he may have learned from his parents. Being able to bring together strengths one has gained from both parents is a kind of fulfilment in itself. William had found work that also enabled him to fill an absence that was experienced by others.

William was, of course, battling a system under pressure, struggling to deal with the contradiction between the balance

CHANGING GEAR

of budgets and the desire to improve the quality of public services. Having a management role in such a system almost inevitably runs the risk of burnout, which William came close to. Was he right not to let the people who worked for him know how tough he was finding the work? After all, they were probably finding it equally tough. Could leadership in such a situation involve acknowledging these real difficulties, and deciding together as a team how to tackle them? Those drawn to the helping professions and helping roles tend to put their own needs second and just soldier on, but sometimes addressing their own needs is essential if they are to be a resilient resource to others. The military understand this, making sure that people are not on the front line for long periods of time. Sadly, but not unsurprisingly, it was only when the burdens of his responsibilities overwhelmed him that William was able to acknowledge this to himself.

After leaving the civil service, William was able to express his caring nature to those nearest and dearest to him, and to re-establish friendships that he had let slip. And he found a team to be part of that was fun rather than a hard slog. In his retirement, he was able to rediscover his desire to help people on a personal level, rather than by running an organisation which did so. Like many who have successfully changed gear, he was able to find a better balance in life for his particular personality. He may have learned the hard way, but he still learned, and he aims to continue to do so.

When work is life and life is work

Those who have achieved a degree of success in their careers have usually committed a significant amount of time to it, and, to some extent, are defined by it, either personally, or by others, or both. The issue in the context of changing gear is to what extent, and how much this matters as you move forward. The gift for all who find themselves in this position is the opportunity to look forward and be an active participant in shaping where your life goes next: an unfamiliar feeling for those who have been carried along on the wave of work!

Rose was carried along on the wave of not only her work, but also her life's passion. Perhaps because the two were both such strong drivers for her, and became so intertwined, it made it harder for Rose to see that she was a passive rather than an active participant in shaping her own life. Or perhaps she was just lucky that the two sat so comfortably together and made her life pretty easy and happy.

On page 213 we will explore the concept of 'flow' as the source of happiness. Perhaps Rose was carried along in the 'flow' of the wave. The question for Rose as she changes gear is how easily she can swim from the current she has been carried along in while working full-time, to another current that will take her in a new direction.

ROSE'S STORY

A leader in the arts

Rose was never in doubt about what she wanted to do. For as long as she can remember, she had loved the performing arts. As she grew up, she embraced dance, music and acting at school, and these continued to be the centre of her life at university. Her father was musical, but otherwise there was no history of performing in her family. However, her parents very regularly took Rose and her brother to the theatre and music events throughout their childhood. She grew up in a world full of theatre and concerts, and it was a world she loved.

Rose's enthusiasm and her engaging personality meant that she won parts in school and university productions. She was popular, hard-working and determined, and these traits continued to characterise her career. The first challenge to Rose's happy world came when she graduated. She applied to drama school, but was turned down. At first she thought she had just had a bad day or been unlucky, but her 'lack of luck' persisted. Could it be that she was not good enough, she finally wondered? Sadly for her, there is never a black-and-white answer to whether or not you are a good actor, but if there was, it seemed she didn't quite have what it takes. She picked herself up and, not stopping to think through which field to build a career in, she quickly decided to apply for jobs in the arts areas of television companies. This proved to be a good strategy, and she quickly joined one of the UK's major broadcasters.

Having accepted she was not a 'creative', Rose embarked upon a managerial career path and never looked back. Her whole life was drama, film and music – her work, rest and play! Rose had a number of relationships, but somehow never settled with any one person for long. Much of her time was spent working, and even when she wasn't working, she was with 'work' people.

She had never really minded this, because her job in the TV and performing arts world meant there were always fun first nights and screenings, awards dinners and events to go to, and fun people to be with. She adored being in the swim of her chosen world and felt she was really lucky. She had never paused for long enough to seriously wonder why she was alone, and she had never felt a burning desire to have a baby, so starting a family wasn't really a concern of hers.

Her hard work and dedication to her career paid off and, over time, she was able, within limits, to pick and choose her roles. Her popularity was something she rather took for granted. As she became increasingly senior, she was largely unaware of organisational politics, which from time to time tripped her up. Rose was sufficiently good at what she did that she found ways to overcome setbacks by working even harder. Although a number of her workmates started to move out of the city with their children, most of her peers and bosses prioritised work over the rest of their lives and commuted back into the city much of the time.

Her high profile made Rose a go-to person for charities in the sector. When she was asked to join the board of a charity that supported young performers from backgrounds who did not have the natural networks that benefited many of their peers, she was keen to become involved. She championed a scheme to help give young women in school opportunities to participate in theatre and dance. Over the next ten years, with Rose continuing to be its champion, the scheme proved to be a great success, and the number of students who benefited exceeded anyone's expectations. Rose was rightly recognised with an OBE, an honour she had not sought but was thrilled to receive.

As Rose became ever more senior, she, not unreasonably, took for granted that she was an 'industry figure' at the heart of her 'village'. What she had not really spotted is that it was her 'work village' not her 'home village' – but, in reality, she may not have been able to see this distinction. Looking back, if she were to criticise her career path, she would perhaps admit that she had never really spent time looking at where she was headed, or how her career would pan out as she became older. She knew that some people started to 'lose their touch' as they came towards the end of their careers, but it never occurred to her that she would. And, for a very long time, she didn't.

Eventually, though, Rose, like almost everyone else, proved not to be irreplaceable. There was no 'moment' where it suddenly became clear that she could not go on forever, but gradually she started to be sidelined by younger colleagues and consulted or included less. The CEO talked to her about retiring, but Rose was insistent that it was far too early. For a while, she kept her job, although her scope of responsibilities was reducing. Then, one day, quite out of the blue, she was gently – and as elegantly as possible – made redundant. It was a surprise to others within the organisation, but more of a surprise to Rose, and it came as a huge shock and a blow. Perhaps this was 'wilful blindness' on her part. Wilful, maybe – but definitely human.

For the first time, Rose was faced with the realisation that she had allowed her job to be her life. If she had ever thought about this, it was only to dismiss it. The 'wilful blindness' was long standing for Rose. She had the painful realisation that, along with her job, all the evening events that had kept her life full would go, too. At first, a few invitations continued to arrive, but these soon tailed off. At times, she was not sure which she missed the most: the job or the invitations that came with it. She felt like a 'non-person', something she found unbelievably tough to cope with. Of course, Rose knew that once you were not in a key role, you were taken off the list. She had been involved in the organisation of enough events herself to know that she had treated others, not unreasonably, in the way that she was now being treated – except that now she knew how hurtful it felt.

Who was she now? At first, Rose found herself clinging on to her past, finding herself saying 'I used to be . . .' or 'When I worked for . . .' or 'I was very . . .'

The one thing she did have left was her charity board and she tried to throw herself into this more. While she continued to make a difference, she found it far less satisfying without her executive responsibilities alongside it. It had been a haven to act in a non-executive mode in contrast to her extremely busy work responsibilities. Now there was no contrast to enjoy, she found herself enjoying being on the board less, and this became a tough reminder of what she had lost.

It took Rose the best part of a year to come to terms with just how much she had lost, and that she had lost it not because she had failed, but really just because she had grown older. It happened to everyone Rose knew, but she had failed to anticipate the inevitability of it happening to her, too. Rose began to see that her talent, dedication and hard work had enabled her to get this far without really having to answer the question she now felt to be looming large over her, namely 'Who am I now?' Which, of course, then called for the follow-up question: 'Who do I want to be next, if I am not who I was?' Reaching this point was a tough struggle, involving some very low moments, but once Rose started to really see her situation, she began to find the focus she needed to start thinking ahead.

The old, engaging Rose, with all her energy and a can-do attitude began to surface – not all at once, and certainly not every day, but gradually much more of the time. She began to accept her situation and work out what she wanted to do next. How would the Rose without the ready-made world of work spend her time? And, crucially, who did she want to be, as she built a life less dominated by work? The real change came when she started to look forwards and had the next realisation: there could be lots to look forwards to! It was up to her.

CHANGING GEAR

Contrary to her fears, it was not all bad. She had some friends who had also recently stopped working full-time, and they recreated some of the fun they had had together at work. One of these friends, who had had a similar experience to Rose, persuaded her to go and see a counsellor. It did not take long for Rose to recognise her situation: she was no fool, she just hadn't learned to look at herself from 'outside' herself. Naturally, this took some digesting, but the counsellor helped Rose to see that she was still 'alive and kicking' – she just needed to let go of the Rose that relied on being a mover and shaker in her old 'work village'. She needed to learn to validate herself rather than seeking validation from her job.

Having no line between her job and her life had arguably worked for Rose until she stopped work, but she paid a high personal price when her career came to an end, and she had to cope with feeling that she, too, had come to an end. The counsellor helped Rose to see that she needed to let go of the one-dimensional Rose and that, in doing so, she could start to find a new, ideally multi-dimensional, Rose.

Finding a new stage on which to perform

A psychological perspective on Rose's story

Unlike Christopher on page 83, Rose is definitely an extrovert! She gets energy from interacting with others and performing in the limelight. Her parents clearly had a strong interest in the theatre. Whether this was just stimulating to Rose or whether, in some ways, she was unconsciously shaped by them to fulfil passions they secretly held, we shall never know. Our career choice often – and, in the case of acting, almost certainly – has roots in early family experiences. It would be interesting to know more about Rose's role in her family: was she rewarded for 'performing' rather than being herself? She was turned down by drama school, but picked herself up and tried something else. If she were born to be an actor, perhaps she might have persisted a little longer at this ambition: some actors feel most real when they are on stage.

Rose is described as hard-working and determined, and it seems pretty sensible and realistic that she accepted she was not a true creative and instead chose a career in TV. She made her job her life, and perhaps shied away from the complications of an intimate, dependent relationship, preferring the more controllable world of work. A choice that she was, of course, perfectly entitled to make, and she doesn't seem to have any regrets on that front. She preferred the hustle and bustle of being in the swim of things, an environment to which she seemed completely suited, although apparently she was less suited to the inevitable politics of any large organisation. She didn't have a plan for her career, and perhaps she didn't need one, but the short-term attractions of popularity and the heady excitements of the television village distracted her from taking a more strategic approach to her career, as she herself came to recognise. Perhaps she spent too much time finding out about who other people were and what they liked in order to gain recognition from others, at the expense of getting to know herself, what she really needed and how her life was shaping up. Eventually, Rose discovered that she was not irreplaceable, a topic we will explore in Chapter 3. In choosing to ignore the advice of her CEO, was Rose perhaps wanting to retain her youthful energy and younger self, ignoring the facts of time passing?

Her experience of quickly becoming an outsider is one shared by most people who leave organisations: your place is quickly filled by another, and the wishful thinking that an organisation is somehow like a parent that 'always looks after its people' is rapidly dispelled. We might fantasise that our organisation is our family, but they just aren't designed for that purpose: they survive through a focus on efficiency and effectiveness, not a focus on human feelings.

Without her job, Rose feared that she would now be a 'non-person': how was she to focus her energy and drive without a work identity? This is a question that faces anyone at the end of a long and successful career. A period of depression is not uncommon, and Rose went through some dark and lonely times. She wisely worked with a counsellor, who helped her to let go of her identity as a mover and shaker in the television industry. We are not told where Rose went next, but it's likely she will have found a new role for herself; she is a survivor, after all. Hopefully she will have found that there are other worlds beyond the television industry, some perhaps even just as compelling and interesting. However, Rose will almost certainly have missed the buzz and will have sought out another stage on which to perform. Reflecting on herself as she is in situations other than the workplace might give her some clues as to aspects of herself that have lain dormant, but could now be developed: unlived lives that she now could bring to centre stage.

This is a story that ends with as many questions as answers. And that may be no bad thing. In *Letters to a Young Poet*, Rainer Maria Rilke provides some advice that might be useful to Rose:

> Be patient toward all that is unsolved in your heart and
> try to love the questions themselves like locked rooms
> and like books that are written in a very foreign tongue.
> Do not now seek the answers, which cannot be given you

because you would not be able to live them. And the point is, to live everything. Live the questions now. Perhaps you will then gradually, without noticing it, live along some distant day into the answer.

There are some big questions outstanding about who Rose really is without her work identity, and what she now wants. She can work on these with her counsellor. She may need to learn to love different aspects of herself and be less dependent on the regard of others as she begins to construct her next life.

2

The challenges in changing gear

The next four chapters are intended to help you think more deeply about what 'lies under your surface' and, in doing so, to be able to take a more holistic view of yourself. Moving to the Third Life, as we have said, gives us the gift of time, and it also offers the gift of having a new perspective from which to view this.

In this chapter, we will introduce some psychological frameworks to help shape how you might think about making your transition. These ideas show why making such a change when you are arguably already 'fully formed' is not straight-forward. Happily, they also show that change is very possible, if not easy.

'"Who are *you*?" said the Caterpillar.
. . . Alice replied, rather shyly, "I – I hardly know, sir, just at present – at least I know who I *was* when I got up this morning, but I think I must have changed several times since then."'
– Lewis Carroll, *Alice's Adventures in Wonderland*

'To exist is to change, to change is to mature, to mature is to go on creating oneself endlessly.'
– Henri Bergson, French philosopher

The rider and the elephant

The first of these frameworks to help you bring a different thought process to bear involves the rider and elephant concept we introduced on page 11.

We are all familiar with the experience of having the intention of doing something, but somehow not being able to do it. Why is this so?

One theory is that this is because we are really made up of two selves, the rider and the elephant. This metaphor can be helpful in distinguishing the conscious, deliberate, rational-reasoning self from the unconscious, emotional-reasoning self. (The 'elephant and rider' metaphor was first used by Jonathan Haidt in 2006 to contrast processes under our control with those that are automatic,[4] but we are using it somewhat differently here).

Some would argue that we are made up of many selves, and we will be exploring that idea later, but for the moment we will just stick to these two.

The idea of the divided self has been a subject of puzzlement throughout human history. Plato described it as a charioteer and two horses, one with good and the other with evil intentions; Freud distinguishes ego, id and superego, and the conscious and unconscious minds; Daniel Kahneman contrasts thinking slow with thinking fast; Iain McGilchrist speaks of the Master and the Emissary; Steven Peters talks of an inner chimp that our human brain struggles to manage.

The question of *how* the conscious, logical-thinking 'rider' tames the impulsive and emotional-thinking, often unconscious, 'elephant' is the subject of religions, moral philosophies and, most recently, neuroscience.

The 'elephant' consists of feelings, beliefs, impulses, attitudes, judgements, habits and preferences, which are built up as the result of experience and learning. It gets us through our day without having to think too much, or at all, making its perceptions based on past experience and responding on autopilot. The elephant operates by what Freud called the 'pleasure principle', seeking pleasure and avoiding pain. But if you are to change these programmed responses, your rather small 'rider' needs to direct your (much larger and more powerful) elephant of mindsets, behaviours and identity before you can act effectively. The rider attempts to manage the elephant using the reality principle to adjust the elephant's pleasure-seeking and pain-avoiding in accordance with the constraints of the actual external world and cultural norms. These are principles we learn from our parents and family of origin. In many situations, autopilot responses are just fine, but elephant thinking, based as it is on emotional thinking, is short-term, and its fundamental assumption that the present is like the past may not be helpful. The reasoning rider can see longer-term benefits because, from its perch atop the elephant, it has a wider perspective. But the rider also needs time to think and reflect, and to do so it must stop the elephant from immediately and impulsively reacting.

Changing gear requires the rider and the elephant to work together in a coalition of wills to shift entrenched habits of thought and behaviour, and to work towards longer-term objectives, such as creating a fulfilling life, rather than focusing on the short-term satisfactions that getting stuck back into work easily provide.

You can discover your inner elephant by the simple mindfulness exercise of shutting your eyes and concentrating on your breath as you breathe in and breathe out. Try this experiment and, very quickly, you will discover that this apparently simple instruction is actually very hard to follow: thoughts will intrude, your attention will be distracted and you may not even notice what has been happening to you for several minutes as the elephant mind takes over. By bringing your attention back to your pattern of breathing in and out, the rider can reassert control. The rider has a will, but so does the elephant and, because it is larger, it will generally win easily. How often have you wanted to listen to someone but found your attention drifting off, with the embarrassing realisation that you haven't heard some important things that were being said? That's your elephant-self, wandering off into a jungle thicket of half-formulated memories, associations, thoughts, opinions and feelings.

To expand the metaphor, Richard L. Daft suggests you can think of the elephant as having three aspects: a judge, who makes judgements about the self and others; a magician, who makes up fantasies it wants to believe; and a lawyer, who comes up with justifications for why both the judge and the magician should be allowed to do as they wish.[5] To tame your elephant, your rider will need to deal with all three: unwarranted, some-times harsh judgements; seductive but unrealistic fantasies; and endless convoluted justifications. Many high-achieving riders have already trained their ambitious, single-minded elephants to achieve remarkable individual successes, often at the expense of their health and their relationships. They then, not surpris-ingly, find it difficult to step away from a full-on career.

Despite the rider's best intentions, the elephant firmly carries on in its old, comfortingly familiar ways: for example, a senior partner who consciously wants to develop a junior colleague and can't resist 'improving' their emails before they are sent to the client. When human beings experience discomfort, they naturally look for familiar solutions to reduce this: familiar pat-terns of behaviour and ways of thinking that generate a feeling

CHANGING GEAR

of comfort. These produce short-term relief and pleasure, but also lead to long-term pain and disappointment when we don't achieve our desired change. As you go through the transition process, your rider will have its work cut out contending with the elephant's ingrained, habitual reactions. We will be helping you with this along the way.

The rider may be tempted to just tether their elephant, or to get off and make their way on foot, but without emotional reason, logical reason is unable to make up its mind. The rider needs to learn how to guide and discipline the elephant. However, just training the rider may not have much effect on actual behaviour. The elephant thinks as well: it just thinks in terms of emotions, impressions and experiences. It is guided by what Daft describes as a 'like-o-meter', attracted to pleasure and averse to pain, while the rider uses its logic-o-meter to devise rational principles, but has trouble persuading the elephant of their virtues. And the rider is prone to problems of its own: over-analysing; focusing on problems rather than solutions; and spending many happy hours planning and strategising, but not taking action, in a state of analysis paralysis.

Rather than fighting the elephant (a fight it has little chance of winning), the rider needs to learn to understand the elephant's motivations and shape the elephant's path in ways that it finds attractive, as explored by Chip and Dan Heath in their book *Switch: How to Change Things when Change is Hard*.[6] We will show you ways of doing this later.

While the rider needs a rationale for change, the elephant needs to feel change is worthwhile, because going through a transition process necessarily entails feelings of uncertainty, ambiguity, self-doubt, vulnerability, loss and grieving. In order to achieve a successful transition process, you must tune in to your feelings and become aware of unconscious patterns of behaviour, not just focus on the logical reasons for making a change.

Why is change so difficult?

Changing our behaviour is notoriously difficult. How often have you made resolutions that lasted only a few weeks, such as trying to maintain a diet or exercise programme? How many times have you set your alarm to get up early for fitness training, only to go straight back to sleep? Over the centuries, philosophers and psychologists have struggled to answer why this is so, and a multitude of reasons have been proposed: that somehow our lives are predestined and governed by fate; that we are determined by factors beyond our knowledge or control; that we lack willpower; or that our innate instincts and drives compel us to behave in certain ways which we find hard to restrain. Any or all of these theories may be true, and your preference for one or another will partly depend on the culture you come from and your own personal philosophy of life. None are absolutely right or wrong. Evidence can be amassed to support any of them; which explanation you choose is a matter for you to decide.

What is important is to reflect on what your predominant attitude to change is, and to be aware of it – it will have important implications, as we shall show you shortly. According to the Greek philosopher Epictetus, who lived in the 1st century CE, much about life is beyond our control, but the one thing we can choose is our attitude: to others, to events and to ourselves.

Change is difficult when we think about it in the wrong way. Transition and change are two different things. Change is about what you can see: the external behaviours that are observable, what happens on the outside. Transition is what happens on the inside: the emotional and personal adaptations required for sustained changed behaviour. Without transition, as William Bridges explained, change is likely to be superficial and transitory.[7]

The concept of change is mechanical, with an implication of linear cause-and-effect in which A follows B if we do C, based on manipulating objects in the physical world. But nature doesn't work in this way. Think of the Caterpillar at the beginning of the chapter, to whom Alice was explaining how she had changed several times already. The transition from caterpillar to butterfly begins with hatching from an egg. The caterpillar stuffs itself with leaves, growing plumper and longer through a series of moults in which it sheds its skin. One day, the caterpillar stops eating, hangs upside down from a twig or leaf and spins itself a silky cocoon. Within its protective casing, the caterpillar radically transforms its body, eventually emerging as a butterfly. Notice that the change from caterpillar to butterfly involves the all-important middle stage of transitioning in a cocoon: a safe space that it has built for itself. Real, lasting change for human beings happens in the same way. We must let go of an old identity and set of behaviours, and go through a process of upheaval before emerging into a new identity and new behaviours. A critical part of any transition is this upheaval, during which we go through a series of feelings: confusion, a sense of loss, or even of abandonment, feelings of helplessness and vulnerability. These are all part of the learning process that underpins the outward appearance of change. In order to go through this process, we need to feel a degree of safety or we will never dare to make the change.

Next, we will be introducing you to a framework that will help to put some shape around how you reflect on your experiences of change during your life. It explores how you have made transitions in the past.

The Transition Process

In his 1929 essay 'The State of Funk', D. H. Lawrence described social and political change in the early 20th century:

> The time of change is upon us. The need for change has taken hold of us. We are changing, we have got to change, and we can no more help it than leaves can help going yellow and coming loose in autumn, or than bulbs can help shoving their little green spikes out of the ground in spring. We are changing, we are in the throes of change, and the change will be a great one. Instinctively, we feel it. Intuitively, we know it. And we are frightened. Because change hurts. And also, in the periods of serious transition [notice Lawrence's use of the word here], everything is uncertain, and living things are most vulnerable. But what of it? Granted all the pains and dangers and uncertainties, there is no excuse for falling into a state of funk.[8]

Although he was writing about social and political change, this passage eloquently expresses the emotional challenges of transition at the start of the Third Life.

Each of these shifts from one stage to another can be viewed externally as changes take place, but internally they will involve varying degrees of emotional turmoil and upheaval. You will undoubtedly gain some real insights by taking time to reflect on how you have made transitions in the past: what has helped you, what hasn't helped you, and why you think this might be.

Life can be seen as a series of stages, from being a foetus in the womb, to being born as an infant, then moving into younger childhood, later childhood, early teenage years, later teenage years, early adult years, middle adult years, later adult years, early old age, middle old age and later old age. Each of these stages has distinct characteristics of personal and social upheaval. Our personal strengths and weaknesses affect how we negotiate each stage, and how well we manage to make the transition – or, in some cases, fail to make the transition at all, remaining stuck in one stage, unable to move on.

Social structures – whether parents, family, school, university, work organisations or broader society – provide tracks for us to follow that may or may not support us as we transition through different stages of psychological and social change and adaptation. Associated with each of these transitions are a variety of rites of passage.

The transition from later adult years to early old age has been conventionally described as 'retirement'. But this is a word that can conjure up ideas of retreat and passivity that some of us (probably including the people reading this book) no longer find attractive – added to which, society itself is in turmoil about how we can afford to have so many people alive but not working. Debates rage about the pension age and how care in old age will be paid for.

While you can make changes to things, you cannot *make* people change – unless under duress, and then any changes will only be temporary. For people to change, they need to do so with a sense of choice and come to see the change as for the better, otherwise it will only be superficial and transitory. Changes may be big or small, but in every case they involve an internal emotional process of transition as well as an external behavioural change. The rider needs to appreciate this and understand how difficult the elephant will find things at this time.

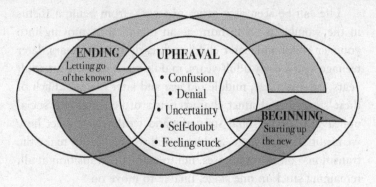

Figure 1: Transition process

Based on *Managing Transitions*, Bridges, W. (1991)

It is well documented that efforts to change both individuals and organisations frequently fail. Although we speak about managing change, more often than not, change just happens and we adjust to it – or fail to. Indeed, it could be said that change chooses us more often than the other way around. Transition is a more fluid, to-and-fro, evolving process characteristic of living things, with repetitive cycles of letting go and attempted new beginnings before the new identity and behaviours are integrated into the self. It involves the all-important in-between state of upheaval where we have left the safety of one bank of the river, but have yet to reach the other side. This has to be gone through if the change is to become permanent.

The word 'transition' implies a process that does not happen immediately, suggesting that we need to let go of old behaviours before we can take on new ones, and that we need to *choose* to do so if the change is to be long standing. As psychologist Kurt Lewin first observed, the process of change in humans involves an unfreezing of current behaviours and attitudes, an inevitable period of some turmoil in the unfrozen melted state, followed by a refreezing into new patterns of behaviours and attitudes. To make this passage, we have to feel sufficiently safe as we go through the process, like the caterpillar in the cocoon in our earlier example. Often we need reassurance and encouragement in order to adopt new behaviours. We need time to try out and test new behaviours and attitudes before we are able to make the transition. Our old habits and structures of thinking have to be unfrozen before they can be adapted to new circumstances. Most of all, we need a proper process that will lead to stable changed behaviours. Merely willing or wishing things to change is rarely sufficient: we need a series of steps, each of which needs to be achieved successfully before we get to the endpoint.

Although changes may be forced upon us – and getting older is certainly one of those – we still have the option of choosing how we respond to this. We go through a wide range of emotions during the internal transition process described above. There may be feelings of loss, or even abandonment, as we say goodbye to a familiar workplace or career. The phase of upheaval may well involve emotional volatility, feelings of uncertainty, and apparently overwhelming complexity and ambiguity. These are the very same conditions that the US Army identified as the conditions that it would need to operate in the 21st century, using the acronym VUCA.

The phase of upheaval at the centre of any transition process is what Plato describes as a 'liminal space'. This comes from the Latin *limen*, meaning a threshold of 'in-betweenness', a term used by anthropologists to describe a quality of ambiguity or disorientation that occurs in the middle phase of a rite of passage. For example, during the transition from childhood to adulthood, this 'in-betweenness' occurs when participants no longer hold the pre-ritual status and rights they held as a child, but do not yet have the status of young person they will hold when the rite is complete.

A transition process is, in reality, a series of multiple mini-transitions, each of which involves letting go, a degree of upheaval, and a new beginning. The process means acknowledging the good things you have achieved, but also accepting that some of your desired ambitions have not come to pass, although some of these might provide a focus for your future plans.

The first transitions we make in life provide the building blocks for how we approach change in the future. One of the earliest transitions we make is the move away from our attachment to our first parenting figure towards building attachments to others: other parenting figures and siblings, then friends and partners, then work colleagues. In order to do this, we need a background sense of safety. In this example, our first attachment relationship provides the safe holding environment or container (like the caterpillar's cocoon). Later in life, our work or career can also provide just such a holding environment, creating a holding frame of identity, as well as a sense of progress and 'reality'.

Work as a holding environment

'The fact is that, after I felt sure of myself as a welder, I felt sure of myself and everything, even the way I walked.'
— Primo Levi, *The Wrench*

'Two hours ago I could have said five words and been quoted in fifteen minutes in every capital of the world. Now, I could talk for two hours and nobody would give a damn.'
— US President Harry Truman, shortly after leaving office

The character in Primo Levi's novel felt like a somebody when he became a welder. President Truman felt he had gone from being a somebody to being a nobody as his presidency ended. As you approach your Third Life, how can you feel like the welder and not like a former President?

Our self-esteem is intimately related to our experience of work. Through our work, we get a sense of who we are, of what we are worth and of how effective we are. Work provides a structure to our lives and brings us into contact with the real world: it is a way of being present in the here-and-now of things, rather than getting bogged down in our internal worlds of memories from the past and dreams of the future.

But what do we mean by 'work'? Conventionally, it means paid work: the answer you give when you are asked 'What do you do?' But this is a very restrictive definition that excludes the work of bringing up children, the work of running a home and a family, and other work that doesn't result in financial rewards. Work starts with something that is missing, an absence that has to be filled, something that is incomplete. The act of filling in or completing is the work. This could be a simple task, such as cleaning a room, or a much more complex task, such as building a house. You may wish for your Third Life to have an element of paid work in it, but it is certainly not essential. What it must have, though, is some sense of work for a purpose: something that gives meaning, whether this be paid work, such as serving on a board or a committee, or gardening, writing a book, caring for grandchildren, career-mentoring younger people or helping those less fortunate than yourself. All these examples involve creating something that wasn't there before. What matters is clarifying what your 'work' will be.

Full-time employment has many functions beyond just economic returns: it regulates and structures the day; it provides an identity; it structures interpersonal relationships; and it provides a sense of value and self-worth. All of these things give you meaning and a sense of purpose. The impending loss of full-time employment raises the spectre of losing many of these, including the opportunity for relationships and participation in a shared endeavour, and sources of self-esteem in both work and social roles. In our society and culture, which places so much emphasis on effectiveness and productivity, a person's value and social worth is frequently solely determined by what they do at work. Of course, our work identity is but one of multiple identities – being a parent or a good citizen contributing to our community are just as, or arguably more, important. But social norms, in Western societies at least, prioritise paid work as providing the greater status – and being near the top helps, of course. Work has both intrinsic gratifications, derived directly from the work itself and the opportunities it provides for self-fulfilment, and extrinsic gratifications, derived from the social identity it provides.

The workplace is a setting in which the private world of emotions and meaning and the public world of fact and achievement come together. Sigmund Freud spoke of the two central achievements that define normality as being the capacity to love another person and the capacity to work. Both require the ability to reach beyond a private, self-centred world and engage with others. Work is a crucible in which the private and the public interact and give meaning to each other. It provides a regular shared setting for mature and realistic experiences with others and, through the evidence of the successes and shortcomings of one's own efforts, work provides the opportunity for a realistic relationship to the external world different from the intense intimacies of the family. Whether it is paid or not, work brings us into contact with goals and purposes greater than ourselves, with consequently broader satisfactions and achievements. It confers a status and identity in the world, a sense of self and personal agency through voluntary associations with others.

To have work of some kind is crucial. Loving and being loved is part of the foundation of our mental health; working and the relationships work provides is the other. Losing your job can be as traumatic an experience as losing a loved partner.

To be without work deals a double blow. For the unemployed person, there is not only the loss of being excluded from the wider world and the freedom that earning one's own living provides, but also of a basic opportunity for reassurance about one's worth. When the capacity to be effective in the world is removed, the results can be catastrophic. The consequence in many cases is depression. Aggression previously channelled outwards into society is then turned inwards against the self, a process that can even lead to self-harm and, in very rare cases, suicide. It is not uncommon for retirement to be followed quite quickly by serious illness and sometimes death. There can be a sense of impotence and depression at the obvious level of losing one's job, but also at the unconscious level of losing a medium for opportunities to create and repair, which help sustain a sense of internal worth and goodness. The loss of this means of psychological reparation can be even more catastrophic than the original external loss of job and colleagues. Little wonder that many high-achieving individuals regard the prospect of a life without full-time work with alarm.

The word career comes from the French *carrière*, meaning a road or path, and implies a more or less straight-on direction. Most careers are probably not that simple: we take diversions, get lost, return to a different main road. There may be periods of being out of work, whether by choice or not. Some people have a clear idea of their ideal career when they are teenagers; others take some time before they decide on a settled route and there may be changes along the way. You may have had several careers in different areas. The road may not have been straightforward if you have taken time off to care for children or relatives. Reviewing these experiences, and considering what you enjoyed, what you didn't, what you'd like to do more of, and what you'd like never to do again will be useful exercise in helping you decide how you want to spend the years of your Third Life. This exercise can be found on page 315. It enables you to make a list of your achievements, and also a list of some of your dreams that you have not yet achieved.

For adults, work can provide, at least at the best of times, a reasonably safe context in which we can transition from one role to another, moving from old behaviours that need to be changed to new ones, and from attitudes and ways of thinking that have become outmoded to fresh ones that are more adaptive. However, even when we go through apparently positive transitions at work, such as being promoted, we often do so with mixed feelings, sometimes holding on to our old patterns of behaviour even when they are outmoded.

An impending change of employment is a frequent cause of anxiety, especially to those who have not yet worked out what this new step might look like for them. They may be described as 'resistant to facing reality' by those around them. Underlying this resistance is really a sense of foreboding, uncertainty and even hopelessness about whether new behaviours and new ways of working are even going to be possible – particularly if the person feels that this 'reality' is being imposed on them. It is not so much change that is resisted as the anticipation of the uncomfortable but inevitable feelings entailed in the transition process, such as uncertainty and loss. As you have gone through your career, how have you reacted to imposed or even desired changes? Have you ever 'resisted' change, maintaining old habits of thought and behaviour even though you know they are now outmoded? You'd be unusual if you hadn't.

You will probably have found that you needed time to digest the implications of a change before feeling comfortable with new behaviours or a new role. The process of changing gear requires time to explore and investigate potential futures, ideally before leaving the mothership of the workplace. As human beings, we are often far more dependent on our holding environment than we care to acknowledge.

As we come near to the end of a full-time career, we approach an edge: a tipping point that requires crossing over a threshold into unfamiliar terrain. No wonder we so often find this so challenging!

If you're reading this book, you are likely to be someone who has a high drive to achieve, with a consequent fear of failure and thus a need to be in control. Going through the transition process will mean that these sources of competence will become sources of incompetence, stretching you in ways that will be uncomfortable and disconcerting. But remember that all learning necessarily involves not having the answer, even though, by now, you have become all too used to being the person who always expects – and is expected – to have the answer. During your transition, you will have to learn to 'live the questions', as the poet Rainer Maria Rilke puts it.

Even when we *choose* change, we will still have moments of loss and regret. Those who choose careers with leadership roles in organisations do so partly out of the desire for impact and influence, a sense of having power over events and people. Losing this can feel traumatic. When human beings are anxious, they often become angry as well (or instead) in an attempt to regain a sense of control.

When the time comes to move away from full-time work, adopting an attitude of somehow being a victim of circumstance is not uncommon. Focusing on an unreasonable retirement policy, 'ridiculous' and unnecessary new technology, or the unfairness of having an ageing body can feel preferable to a feeling of helplessness. And yet it is only through bearing this temporary helplessness that a new thought, behaviour or attitude can emerge. Those with successful careers anticipating the transition would do well to experiment and become more comfortable with feelings of uncertainty and confusion. You may want to consider some form of attention training, such as mindfulness or relaxation techniques, or more active methods, such as tai chi or martial arts, to help you practise focusing your attention and learning active quietness. Those who are more resilient in a process of transition stick to their values, view unexpected events and feelings as an opportunity and focus on the things they can control, not those they cannot, as they go through the process of change.

In order to transition, we may need to adapt some of our unconscious assumptions and ideas. These might include ideas such as:

— Good people have a successful career.
— Those not in full-time employment aren't doing any work or contributing.
— Your job is the true measure of your status and worth in the world.
— Retirement is really just another word for the exit lounge.

In order to make a change in your life you will need to decide what things you will leave behind, what things you will take with you, and what other things you will need to create or develop. The exercises in Chapter 8 will help you do this.

Self and self-renewal

'Whatever you wish to do, dream that you can, and
begin it;
Boldness has genius, power and magic in it.'
– Johann Wolfgang von Goethe

'This above all: to thine own self be true.'
– William Shakespeare, *Hamlet*

By the time you approach your Third Life, you will probably
have developed a fairly strong sense of who you think you are.
But what about who you are:

— in a relationship?

— at a particular time?

— in a particular place?

— with others?

Going through changes means a change in how we think of
ourselves and, as we have seen, even if the rider is keen to
change, the elephant often has other ideas. We hold on to old
ways of thinking and feeling about things, but change may
require some adaptation of these patterns.

Philosophers and psychologists have debated questions
about the self for millennia. Some, like the Buddhists, consider it an illusion; others distinguish a 'false self' – the self we

present to the world – from a 'true self', the self we really consider ourselves to be. Some consider the self a permanent thing albeit one that adjusts and develops over time; others see it as episodic, existing for a short period of time when we think about it, then disappearing for large stretches as we get on with our lives, before reappearing the next time we think about it again, with some similarities but significant differences. These people see the self as a temporary and transient thing. They would argue that the self you are now is very different to the self you were ten years ago. Some regard the self as a story we tell ourselves, with a history that colours and shapes all our conscious experiences. Others argue that you have multiple selves, that you are a different person in different situations: at work, at home and with your friends. Former Harvard Law School lecturer Erica Ariel Fox posits that the self consists of a group of selves in debate and dialogue with one another, and a successful life depends upon a continuous negotiation between these different selves. She describes them as:

- the warrior, who is led by willpower and excels at taking action
- the lover, who is led by emotion
- the thinker, who is led by reason
- the dreamer, who is led by intuition[9]

And there is a further complication: who you think you are is not who others think you are – their view of you might be similar to your own, but it will be different. In fact, it could be said that who you actually are isn't who you think you are at all, but the impact you have on others. You are, very simply, the effects that you have on other people and on the world. Or, to put it more accurately, you have two selves – the one you think you are, what some have called the 'autobiographical self', a story you tell yourself about yourself; and the self others think of you as, your 'social self'. This is important because having a satisfying Third Life will mean taking account of both selves: considering what you want but also what impact you want to have on other people and the world.

On top of this, on page 140, we introduced you to the idea that, within the elephant, there are three selves: the judge, the magician and the lawyer. So, one way or another, you're going to have your hands full managing all of this in order to create the life you want! Certainly, it would seem that the self-help instruction to just 'be yourself' isn't as simple as it sounds.

When thinking about your 'self', it may be helpful to consider the below.

You, the rider, are not your thoughts or your feelings. Most of the time, without your awareness, the elephant is busy generating thoughts, emotions and desires in a reactive way to whatever is going on, inside or outside. As we explained earlier, much of this is useful as it gets us through the day without having to do too much thinking, but it's important to be able to distance yourself from the elephant, to realise that just because you are feeling or desiring something doesn't mean you have to do anything about it. The rider can be intentional, choosing what to pay attention to and what to ignore. The better you are at this, the better you will be able to live the life you want – just don't ask 'But who's doing the wanting?' or you'll never make any progress!

The exercise 'Finding your best self' on page 309 is a helpful place to start this reflection.

Exploring, experimenting and playing

'We don't stop playing because we grow old; we grow old because we stop playing.'

– George Bernard Shaw

'Play is older than the culture, for culture, however inadequately defined, always presupposes human society, and animals have not waited for a man to teach them they are playing.'

– Johan Huizinga, Dutch historian

'When I was a child, I spoke as a child, I understood as a child, I thought as a child; but when I became a man, I put away childish things.'

– 1 Corinthians 13:11

'All work and no play makes Jack a dull boy.'

– Proverb

Many people feel uncomfortable with the word 'play'. It is associated with immaturity, unreality, whimsy, and even falseness – perhaps an expression of our ambivalence towards the idea. Work and play are contrasted as if one was serious and the other frivolous, associated with light-heartedness and fun-seeking, and unworthy of the serious businessperson. However, many such business-minded people take playing in the form of sports very seriously, while others go to see 'plays' at the theatre or the opera. The words 'creativity', 'innovation' and 'experimentation' are felt to be more grown-up and business-like, although all involve playing with the imagination.

Could this ambivalence towards the idea of play be partly based on a contempt for the child aspect of the self? Could it be the fear of ambiguity and uncertainty that threatens the feeling of competence upon which those with successful careers have placed such emphasis? Or perhaps it comes from a fear of losing control by throwing off constraint?

Despite this resistance, making a transition requires playing with possibilities, avoiding retreat into premature certainties, and being prepared to be lost before the answer is found. This entails a mental shift away from the self-aggrandising notion of Homo sapiens (the knowing species) to the idea of Homo ludens (the playful species), a concept put forward by the Dutch historian Johan Huizinga,[10] who defines play as the central activity in flourishing societies. Human development has been shaped as much by play as by the struggle to survive. Game theory underpins many of the most effective strategies in business and in politics. The use of sporting analogies and metaphors are much loved in business. All depend on the idea of a game as a set of rules within which spontaneity occurs. The analogies of playing as a team, playing cricket by the rules, and the distinction between a sprint and the marathon all rely on drawing a link between work and play.

Google and other companies have instituted play as part of their cultures, and give 'time off' for workers to spend on whatsoever they choose. To describe someone as a 'player' is to describe them as someone with power and status. In fact, some of the most successful people put aside time for play. This may be described as 'relaxation', but what is really being relaxed are the constraints imposed by the workplace.

The psychoanalyst Donald Winnicott described the 'play space' as a place in which we develop:[11] a space that is both real and unreal, involving the manipulation of real objects (like a cardboard box), which serve imaginary purposes (such as a castle). Children use the play space to vanquish their fears, to kill enemies and to be masters of the world.

Playing provides opportunities for reflection, creativity, increasing self-awareness and thinking in new and different ways. A play space, like a playground, is a container in which exploration and experimentation can be safely undertaken. Winnicott described it as a holding environment created by the mother so that the child can safely explore before returning to the secure base. Likewise, organisations need to provide a sufficiently containing environment in which the rivalries for resources between different functions can be fought out safely. When companies forget that their task is to create solutions to problems and instead focus only on the creation of profits, the organisation's culture and chances of long-term survival are likely to be damaged. Many mental health problems in later life have their origins in the child not having experienced a sense of safety in a holding environment in their early years. Without this, their anxieties have become overwhelming and uncontainable rather than bearable and time-limited. The structure of organisations provides an analogous function and, unfortunately, failures in this area can create similar problems.

If we are to play, we need a sense of safety. Playing requires a lowering of defences (and defensive attitudes) and a tolerance for uncertainty. The contempt often shown for play is a pejorative rationalisation: an attempt to justify the maintenance of defences against untidy feelings of uncertainty and unpredictability. Play is experienced as an unwanted challenge to a defensive mode of being. It can challenge ways of being that have served one well, or have even been the basis of one's success, such as the pursuit of achievement at all costs. It can also challenge the sense of self-importance derived from hierarchical status. Ways of being including the avoidance of failure, attraction to certainty and the denial of uncertainty and doubt are not given up lightly.

Playing changes your mindset, taking the focus from performance to an opportunity to explore. It allows other aspects of your nature to come to the fore, including what the psychoanalyst Carl Jung described as your 'shadow'. This part of yourself might have been suppressed during a busy career, but now needs to come forwards while you are contemplating your future in 'the forest' and exploring what the Stanford psychologist Hazel Markus calls your 'possible selves'.[12]

In Chapter 7, there are two exercises to help you explore this more: the 'Rebalancing how you spend your time' exercise on page 314 and the 'Lifeline exercise' on page 298.

HOW TO PLAY MORE

There are many obvious ways to set about playing more.

— Learn a new skill.

— Decide what 'fun' means for you – make a list of the things you enjoyed doing as a child and in your earlier life, followed by a list of what you enjoy doing now. Then highlight those that still appeal to you.

— Set the goal of playing more – you're allowed to play in the 'forest'. Set a 'fun minimum' – for example, two hours of fun, one day a week. Put it in your schedule and use it every week to play a game, whether it be tennis, bingo or bridge.

— Arrange 'play dates' with family or friends.

— Talk to fun people – ask them how they relax, be spontaneous and have more fun.

— Spend time with a child.

Dr Stuart Brown, head of the National Institute for Play, defines play as 'something done for its own sake. It's voluntary, it's pleasurable, it offers a sense of engagement, it takes you out of time. And the act itself is more important than the outcome.'[13]

Activities associated with pleasure and fun are learned more quickly and recalled more easily. Try new things, experiment, and experience the unexpected.

Making a change that sticks

So what do you actually do if you want to change? What is it you need to change, and how do you go about it? Often when we experience resistance to change, it is not so much the change itself that is resisted, but the uncomfortable feelings associated with it which have to be gone through: the feelings of upheaval. Going through the transition process will mean being prepared to tolerate some of this discomfort, otherwise you will remain exactly as you are.

Effective change happens at three levels: self (who you think you are), mindsets (how you think and feel), and behaviours (what you do). We have already explored the idea of self. Below, we will look at the other two in more detail.

MINDSETS

As we have seen, in order to make a change you need to go through a transition, an emotional and psychological adaptation that will involve a shift of role and identity, underpinned by a shift in mindset. Attempts to change habitual behaviours without addressing the underlying mindset rarely succeed.

Fixed and growth mindsets

Psychologist Carol Dweck argues that there are two fundamental mindsets that are relevant to change.[14] The first is the 'fixed mindset': the belief that characteristics such as intelligence or personality are primarily fixed by the time you are an adult, so that opportunities for change and development in behaviour and thinking are limited. This mindset values achievement within limitations, and success is defined by achieving more. The 'growth mindset', by contrast, believes that people are more fluid and that change and development is possible at any age. This mindset values learning over achievement, and measures success in terms of development. Both have value and validity, but both also have implications for how easy it will be to make changes.

Clearly, making changes to your life can be much more difficult if you adopt a fixed mindset that doesn't really believe in development or change. While some people may fall into one or other of these two types, many of us will be a mixture of the two.

What is your predominant attitude to change – the fixed mindset or the growth mindset? If you adopt the fixed view of things, you will find change far more difficult. Luckily, it is possible to change this attitude if you wish to. There is plenty of evidence from psychology and neuroscience that behaviour and brain changes are possible at any age. Remember what Epictetus said: while a lot of life may not be in your control, you can choose your attitude.

Changing behaviour is a matter of believing that change is possible, and then designing how to do it in a series of steps. First, you need to be aware of your assumptions about change, which by now may be largely unconscious. Next, you need to be prepared to challenge some of them. Having an idea of where you want to get to will help in this process. You will need to put routines in place to support the change you want, while also recognising that the inevitable upheavals of transition won't always be easy. You will need to talk to others about it and, importantly, be kind to yourself.

The best way to make a change is to have a positive visual picture of the desired future state in concrete terms. For example, rather than the abstract ambition of just 'losing weight', this objective is better achieved by creating a realistic picture of your desired outcome: perhaps you as you are currently, but with a flatter stomach and stronger abdominal muscles. Focusing on this positive outcome will give you a more positive attitude and, because it is concrete rather than abstract, it is more easily visualised and remembered. As you go through the transition process, it is important to have a positive visual picture of the sort of life you want for yourself in the future and to keep coming back to this. Sometimes change will feel impossible; it's important not to become too disheartened and to realise that oscillating between states of optimism and pessimism is part of the upheaval of transition.

Pessimistic and optimistic mindsets

The pessimistic and optimistic mindsets have been studied by psychologist Martin Seligman, who has demonstrated that behaviour change is far easier if you adopt an optimistic attitude. An optimistic and forgiving mindset helps you deal with the inevitable setbacks of change, regarding these as just a single event and part of the process, whereas a critical and rigid pessimistic mindset might assume setbacks are proof of the impossibility of change.

You can find out whether you are predominantly an optimist or a pessimist by thinking about how you react to setbacks. The optimistic mindset reacts to setbacks with an assumption of choice and personal power. Bad events are viewed as temporary setbacks that have happened because of bad luck, or are isolated to particular circumstances that can be overcome by effort and ability. The pessimistic mindset reacts differently, viewing setbacks with an attitude of fatality and helplessness, believing that somehow you, or someone or something else is to blame. Bad events are regarded as inevitable and long-lasting in their effects, undermining everything you want to do – even, it can seem, the whole of your life.

Seligman's suggested solution to the pessimistic mindset is a mental discipline he calls 'ABCDE'.

A = Adverse event or situation – for example, your car has a puncture.

B = Beliefs about that event – for example, this always happens to me, never to others; if only I bought the more expensive tyres, or not gone out in the car today, etc.

C = Consequences of those beliefs – generally a feeling of helplessness and not knowing what to do.

D = Disputation and Distraction – challenge the usefulness of your negative beliefs: how much evidence is there for them? Look for alternative explanations. For example, an optimist will take the view that punctures are simply chance events: you didn't cause the puncture and you weren't to know that you were going to get a puncture before you left home today. You can also distract your negative attitude by focusing on a more positive attitude, creating a sense of agency in yourself, rather than helplessness. For example, telling yourself 'I can get this puncture repaired and soon be on my way.'

E = Energisation – notice your energy levels, and how the pessimistic mindset de-energises you while the positive mindset re-energises you. Remember this the next time you face a problem that you find difficult to solve.

The pessimistic mindset is frequently driven by a wish to be in control, with the effect of making change even more difficult. To be in control, you must know the cause of things – and if you are the cause of things, then you are in control (albeit in a negative sense). Taking a pessimistic mindset and blaming yourself puts you back in charge, even if this is in a negative sense. It can be reassuring in its familiarity, like putting on an old coat and shoes.

The optimistic mindset requires hopefulness and a positive view of the future. This view cannot be certain or guaranteed, but requires a degree of faith. Optimism also requires a willingness to accept occasional obstacles or lapses in morale as temporary rather than giving up.

You have a choice about whether to see difficulties and adversities as permanent, pervasive and personal (in which case you are a pessimist) or as temporary, specific to these circumstances, and not your fault (in which case you are an optimist). And your choice of one or the other mindset has consequences. Seligman argues that optimism can be learned.

You can find out more about this and how to practise the optimistic mindset in his books, including *Learned Optimism* and *Flourish*.[15, 16]

You can probably see that these two approaches to mindsets have a lot in common. Optimism is a growth mindset that thrives on challenge and sees failure not as a personal matter but as something to be overcome by attitude and abilities. Pessimism is a fixed mindset that reacts to setbacks as simply more confirmatory evidence of the impossibility of change.

Coping with adversities and overcoming them is how we get stronger and develop self-confidence. Learning to notice your attitude to events and what you are paying attention to is key to this.

The pessimistic mindset is often underpinned by self-limiting beliefs that hamper your ability to make changes. Some of the most frequent ones are:

— All or nothing thinking – seeing things in only black-and-white terms.
— Jumping to conclusions – making assumptions about what people are thinking based on past experience or internal fears.
— Catastrophising – blowing things out of proportion.
— Minimising – discounting the importance of contradictory positive evidence.

BEHAVIOURS

'All our life, so far as it has definite form, is but a mass of habits – practical, emotional, and intellectual – systematically organised for our weal or woe, and bearing us irresistibly toward our destiny.'

– William James, American philosopher

'First say to yourself what you would be; and then do what you have to do.'

– Epictetus

The brain is governed by the pain–pleasure principle, which leads us to avoid pain and seek pleasure. When a behaviour is associated with pleasure or pain, the brain begins to form a habit accordingly. When we want to make a change, in order to have any hope of sustaining the change, we essentially need to change our brain's habits. Simple mental willpower is unlikely to be enough. The brain appears to have built-in biases, such as the negativity bias of paying more attention to negative events than positive ones. This means that things we have learned from threats and painful events are learned faster and are harder to change or inhibit than things learned from positive experiences. Negative experiences cling on like Velcro and are harder to dislodge than positive events, which slide away more easily, as if on Teflon. So to build habits effectively, we must minimise negative experiences associated with the desired behaviour and maximise positive ones. According to some research, the proportion should be about five positive experiences to every negative one. Taking one successful small step is better than endeavouring to take one huge (but likely to fail) large one.

Experiences of success are relatively weak when it comes to changing behaviour. If they weren't, we'd all be a lot more effective and confident a lot more of the time. One negative experience of failure and the whole house of cards can easily fall, hence the advice when learning to ride a bicycle to just get back on again. Setting goals and creating habits and routines that stick is an art.

Our level of willpower varies depending on how we are feeling in general, and also changes during the course of the day. In general, your willpower will be greater first thing in the morning than it will be in the afternoon. So that is the time to tackle difficult challenges, rather than falling into the temptation of postponing these in favour of behaviours that provide short-term feelings of success, such as answering unimportant emails. Any activity will reduce your energy levels and hence willpower. One way to overcome this is to set yourself three important challenges that you should deal with tomorrow. Write these down or, even better, put them in your calendar for tackling first thing in the morning. For more on this see the website www.themorningeffect.com.

In his book *The Power of Habit*, Charles Duhigg describes the three elements of a habit: cue, routine and reward.[17] First, there is a cue: a trigger that tells your brain to go into automatic mode and which habit to use. Then there is the routine: the behaviour that has been triggered by the cue, which can be physical, mental or emotional. Finally, there is a reward, which helps your brain figure out if this particular sequence is worth remembering for the future. Cues, routines and rewards can vary greatly, from simple to complex. If you look at your watch and see that it's 6 p.m., you may say to yourself: 'After all this hard work, it's time for a reward.' That might trigger you going to the fridge and reaching for a cold beer or glass of wine without any need for thinking about it. However, if you are wanting to reduce your alcohol consumption, then you need to be aware and conscious of this habit. You can change your behaviour by replacing the beer with an alternative, such as a soft drink that you enjoy and is good for you. And, of course, you could make things even easier by not buying the beer in the first place! If only life were always so simple.

Cues can be more complex. Getting to your desk in the morning may trigger you to go straight to your emails. To change a habit, you must insert a new routine, such as focusing on the three most important tasks you need to complete today, and make the cue of seeing your desk the trigger to tackling those tasks, rather than heading straight for your emails.

You can increase your willpower by strengthening your willpower 'muscle' in a defined area of your life, such as going to the gym. Completing your routines will leave you with a feeling of success and a positive mood, strengthening your willpower for whatever you have to do next. This makes it a good time to try something challenging. Or, to put it another way, if you need to face a tough challenge but don't feel ready for it quite yet, do something that you know will give you a feeling of success, and this will increase your willpower enough to help you tackle whatever it is that you have been avoiding.

In his book *Smarter Faster Better*, Charles Duhigg explains how motivating yourself is a skill you can learn and how to develop it.[18]

Currently, a lot of your habits will be focused on your work, such as the habit of going to work (or starting work at a home desk!) and the habit of how you structure your days, all of which will lead to a good day, leaving you with feelings of satisfaction and self-confidence. As you approach your Third Life, being without these work habits is going to be a challenge: these sources of satisfaction and wellbeing will need to be replaced by others. Don't be surprised, as you make your way through the woods of change, if you feel a little lost at times.

The helpful Epictetus has a useful contribution here, too: 'Nothing great is created suddenly, any more than a bunch of grapes or a fig. If you tell me that you desire a fig, I answer you that there must be time. Let it first blossom, then bear fruit, then ripen.'

SOME HELPFUL HABITS

— Focusing on the positive rather than the negative.
— Breaking problems up into smaller pieces that give a sense of achievement and reduce procrastination.
— Seeking help when you need it.
— Regarding mistakes and failures as opportunities for learning.
— Being flexible in your approach.

SOME UNHELPFUL HABITS

— Focusing on what went wrong.
— Being unforgiving of your mistakes.
— Not building positive experiences and confidence boosters into your routines.
— Fearing failure.
— Taking a rigid attitude.

3

The paradoxes of career success

'It is impossible to begin to learn that which one thinks one already knows.'

– Epictetus

This chapter explains some of the paradoxical psychological frameworks that can come into play for those changing gear from a full-on work life, for whatever reason. These frameworks may create feelings of some discomfort, but this is not the intended purpose of including them: the purpose is to help the reader to look at themselves from what might be new perspectives.

We will cover some of the things psychologists and coaches often work on with their clients. They are part of life's rich tapestry. For those who have experienced career success of some sort, it is possible, and even likely, that you will find a way to identify with some or indeed all of these to a greater or lesser extent. Some of them may be a challenge to your sense of self. The purpose of including these paradoxes is to enable you to explore to what extent they may apply to you. It might be useful to look at them in relation to who you are now, who you have become in recent years (especially at work), and who you might like to be in this next phase of your life.

If you've spent your life so far in a process of striving to achieve, of competing for the next role, goal, client assignment, or whatever, the very things that have led to your success can have paradoxical effects in your transition to the Third Life. Those who have been successful have often become so by developing one aspect of themselves, such as being knowledgeable, or a provider of solutions to others. But, as a consequence, they may have developed a fear of its opposite, a feeling of stupidity or incompetence. The paradox here is that, as you enter your Third Life, you will need to learn new skills. Placing a demand on yourself to always be knowledgeable and competent could impede your learning of new things. The paradoxes may take you back to some of your adolescent fears and doubts, and you could see a return of anxieties and concerns about self-worth that have been kept under wraps by outward demonstrations of success and achievement.

While you can take quiet satisfaction in having probably achieved far more than your twenty-year-old self ever expected, and possibly more than your parents expected either, the drivers that led you there may need some adjustment as you change gear. Unlike investments, where we are told that past performance does not necessarily predict future performance, human beings are different. We tend to suffer from strategic persistence – or, in other words, from carrying on with the same approaches to problem-solving that have been successful for us in the past. This is also seen in organisations. The paradox of success in business is that when a company is successful, it tends to persist with its existing strategies, and indeed there is a tendency to double down on these when the environment changes. Very recent examples include 'working from home is not going to be here any time soon' or 'the elderly will not embrace digital technology'. The state of lockdown we found ourselves in during the coronavirus pandemic has shown us we can adapt very fast when there is no alternative.

The point is whether or not we have the courage to notice and face the fact that some of our old ways of being or doing things are not working for us as well as they once did. Are we willing to adapt when the world changes, or have we become rigid, inflexible and stuck in our ways? If you have become too used to things coming easily to you at work, the upheavals of transition may come as a shock. A life of high achievement often overdevelops the ability to criticise, to think in a win/lose mindset, to seeing the detail, but not the bigger picture. You may have built up a series of habits that can have paradoxical effects and consequences as you transition into the Third Life.

THE PARADOX OF KNOWLEDGE
The fear of ignorance

If you have spent your life steadily becoming more knowledge-able and being the one who has all the answers, your Third Life will present the challenge of going back to a stage where you no longer have all the answers, and will need to stop feeling that not having them somehow makes you a 'failure'. The poet John Keats identified that creativity required us to be 'capable of being in uncertainties, mysteries, doubts, without any irritable reaching after fact and reason'.

Entering the Third Life means being prepared to open yourself up to new experiences and new learning, which inevitably brings with it feelings of incompetence: something to bear in mind when you're bobbing about on the sea of uncertainty as you go through the process of transition. In order to learn, you have to access your ignorance, not your competence.

THE PARADOX OF EXCELLENCE
The fear of incompetence

Striving for excellence is commendable, but it is frequently focused on the opinions of others. We do things because of the way others will view us. We wish to be seen as success-ful, which means that we dread getting things wrong. High achievement is driven by a positive desire to excel, but also a fear of being seen as a failure.

You cannot expect to excel at everything you try when you move into your Third Life. Learning new behaviours and skills necessarily involves feelings of incompetence: feelings that the high achiever has frequently learned to avoid.

THE PARADOX OF BUSY-NESS
The fear of stillness

The curse of high achievement can be a failure to distinguish the urgent from the important, driven by a high focus on getting things done. The rush that success provides can lead to a short-term perspective. Chris Argyris, who for many years was a professor of organisational behaviour at Harvard University, has a phrase for this: the 'underconfident over-achiever', trapped on a hamster wheel of continuous craving for positive feedback, concern with criticism and a failure to learn from mistakes, which are viewed as failures and blamed on colleagues or clients.

Those talking about retirement often speak of finding something to keep themselves 'busy', but why the hurry? Finding out what you want to do next may involve learning to slow down. Focusing on the quick hits of pleasure that each achievement provides can lead to an addiction to short-term success, and a failure to take a more strategic perspective on one's longer-term life goals.

Thinking of the first year after a full-on career as a detox from the habits of a high-achievement career is often helpful.

More often than not, it is not until a busy high achiever has actually stopped working that they will have the mental space to consider new options.

THE PARADOX OF INDISPENSABILITY
The fear of irrelevance

Often people find it hard – or even impossible – to contemplate what they will do after they stop working and put off the dreaded date, allowing themselves to be repeatedly drawn back into various work challenges for which they are told they are 'indispensable', as described by the LBS Business Professor Richard Jolly.[19] You may wish to consider that this might be simply a seductive ploy by your colleagues to solve a short-term problem by playing on your vanity! In fact, only very rarely is someone truly indispensable. Far more often than not, the loss of a particular person makes, if anything, only a small impact and often gives others the opportunity to rise to the new occasion. The longer you believe in your indispensability (a cunning defence of avoiding and postponing decisions about your Third Life), the harder you will find it to change gear. Even if you are one of the few who actually are pretty indispensable, the truth is that you are – until you are not!

Recognising the time to step away gracefully before others start wondering when you might take off your crown is one of life's great skills. Many think they will do this, and then fail to do so when the time comes. Even those who do take the decision to take their crown off in a timely manner still have to face the inevitable discomfort of transition. Doing so once the thought has taken root typically eases the extent and length of the personal upheaval. Once a transition is on the horizon, there is inevitably a limbo period, which, if too prolonged, is often damaging to both the individual and their organisation. Even if the rider knows this, the elephant is typically in denial!

THE PARADOX OF INVULNERABILITY
The fear of weakness

Success and the associated fear of failure often lead to a defensive denial of one's actual vulnerability. The paradox of vulnerability lies behind many 'accidents', such as the 2008 financial crisis, when people were too scared to admit to themselves and others that they had no clue how the financial products they were selling actually worked. Here, denial and fear of vulnerability led to the inevitable crash.

Successful men and women frequently see themselves as heroes who are generating wealth or other forms of 'capital' that protect their family from the vulnerabilities of life. But part of this heroic identity entails a denial of feelings of vulnerability in oneself that are then projected on to family members, who appear to be in need of you and, as a consequence, now seem to require your protection and occasional heroic acts of rescue even more. As part of this identity, we go to work with our armour on in an attitude of self-protection, putting on our 'successful face' and hiding self-doubt and fears.

Keeping busy can be a cover to obscure these realities. By trying to make the uncertain certain, you deprive yourself of opportunities for learning and development. The shadow side of maintaining the appearance of external confidence is an inner insecurity that has to be hidden and never shared.

Vulnerability is certainly a difficult experience, but is also the birthplace of love, creativity, joy and belonging. Being in touch with vulnerability might well be a skill for your Third Life.

THE PARADOX OF PERFECTIONISM
The fear of mistakes

A desire to be perfect may result in taking on only those things at which you are likely to be successful, locking yourself into work routines that generate not a sense of success but of dullness and boredom. A fear of failure can take the form of a spurious sense of 'guilt' when you don't work at the weekend. This is guilt in relation to failing to live up to your own standards, rather than to any actual need.

There are three types of perfectionists:

Strivers – Constantly struggling to live up to their high standards, and perpetual victims of their own self-criticism.

Zealots – Expecting perfection from others and, as a consequence, often harming their own relationships with colleagues and subordinates.

Idealists – Struggling to live up to an ideal they mistakenly believe others expect of them.

The workplace can be unhelpful in valuing and reinforcing these attitudes. The perfectionist mindset is an either/or mindset. There is no such thing as 'good enough'; things are either successes or failures. Small errors are stamped on as the individual sweats the detail, losing sight of the overall objective.

You can find out how much of a perfectionist you are by considering how much your achievements are driven by fear rather than risk; by a need to be right rather than an openness to being wrong; by a high need for control and a lack of spontaneity; by a focus on doubt rather than self-confidence; by criticising rather than encouraging yourself and others; and by micromanaging rather than delegating.

Perhaps you believe your perfectionism is the source of your success – and it may be – but bear in mind that perfectionism can also be self-obsessed, cutting you off from others and from an awareness of the bigger story of your life.

The only feedback that perfectionists want is acclaim and congratulation. Constructive critical feedback is heard as criticism only, and, rather than learning from others, they will redouble their efforts at polishing their output.

The exercise on page 306 on responding to failure may prove helpful.

THE PARADOX OF CONTROL

The fear of helplessness

A life of seeking control can be an albatross around your neck as you enter the inevitable upheaval of transition.

In an effort to maintain control, you may lose the opportunity to learn from new experiences and from others. By focusing only on what you can control, you run the risk of learning little that is new. The paradox of control in your Third Life may be that only by relinquishing control is it possible to have the new experiences necessary for learning. You might even enjoy letting go a bit!

THE PARADOX OF POWER

The fear of powerlessness

Having a powerful role at work can mean that you are used to getting your own way. The psychologist Dacher Keltner argues that those in power often lose their better qualities once they've made it, and some even completely lose touch with their better side. Being powerful is also stressful and can lead to a transactional mindset, with the blinkered view of others in which they are seen simply as a means to your ends. Relinquishing this power can be hard.

Success can feed the dark side: the desire to have power over others, and the need to be centre stage and viewed as more successful than others. These competition-driven behaviours and desires for power and impact will need some form of expression in your Third Life, but will need to be focused on new goals, for impact rather than power. Those used to being in powerful roles may struggle with feelings of helplessness during the upheaval of the transition.

The Third Life can be an opportunity to reacquaint yourself with your shadow (see page 162) to achieve a more genuine self-acceptance based on a fuller knowledge of who you are. Are you too focused on what you may lose, rather than what you would like to gain? Do you fear isolation and no longer being at the centre of things? If so, you may have fallen victim to the paradox of power in which an addiction to status and acclaim causes the very powerlessness that you fear in changing gear.

If you're a person driven by power and impact, consider replacing power 'over' – the ability of the powerful to affect the actions and thoughts of others – with other forms of power, such as:

— Power 'with' – the synergy of collective action, social mobilisation and alliance building.

— Power 'within' – a sense of dignity and self-awareness.

THE PARADOX OF CONFIDENCE
The fear of ineffectiveness

All work roles involve a degree of 'performance'. For example, the cabin crew on an aeroplane have to perform 'cheerfulness' whatever their private mood. It's part of the job description, and is described as 'emotional labour' by the sociologist Arlie Russell Hochschild in her book *The Managed Heart: Commercialization of Human Feeling*.

Being successful often requires putting on a performance of confidence in order to persuade others of your capabilities. Any professional may feel a pressure to give the impression that they understand their client's problem and will find a solution, even when they don't quite know what it is yet. Confessing confusion and a lack of understanding, albeit 'authentic', is not always a useful thing for clients to hear (although, sometimes, this honesty can be refreshing).

A desire for infallibility may have bred some unhelpful habits: a sharp mind can drift over into abrasiveness, dedication into workaholism, control into inflexibility, and perseverance into resistance to change. Those who have had leadership roles will have had to learn the performance of appearing confident even when they don't feel it. While the ability to tell 'a white lie' – for example, saying one has an answer even when one hasn't to reassure the client – is arguably part of the professional toolkit, it can reinforce underlying fears of being an impostor, which we'll look at next.

THE PARADOX OF EXPECTATION
Impostor syndrome

For some, their lives have seen them not meet the expectations placed on them by parents, teachers, friends – or sometimes even by themselves. However one of the arguably happy outcomes of a successful career might be the exceeding of expectations.

Having said that, all of us have felt, at one time or another, like a fraud. Somehow, we've achieved something, been selected for something, or been viewed positively by others in a way which we don't believe we deserve. You might feel that you are not really good enough for the role you are in, or that you are going to be 'found out' to be lacking.

Such a feeling can have a rational basis. In fact, the greater your success, the more likely it is that chance events will have played a part. After all, somebody has to be the most successful at any activity or skill, and being in the right place, at the right time, with the right connections – and, of course, the willingness to take up the opportunity – all play a significant part. As Nassim Nicholas Taleb puts it in his book *Fooled by Randomness*: 'Mild success can be explainable by skills and labour. Wild success is attributable to variance.'

We can all be prey to the feeling that our success or achievements are due to having worked out how to game the system, rather than being down to our innate ability. All the evidence would suggest that what consistently distinguishes the highest achievement is not simply ability, but also the willingness to practise – which, of course, means to work hard.

Many higher achievers feel their route to the top may have been in some ways illegitimate and, as a consequence, feel like an 'impostor'. 'Impostor syndrome' is a bucket term for a variety of experiences for a variety of reasons. The fundamental underlying cause is a sense that someone else should be in our place, that our reason for being there is somehow not genuine. It comes with a resulting fear that we are, at any minute, liable to be exposed as a fraud or somehow not good enough. It has its roots in both family and social dynamics. Generally, such feelings are transient and we recognise their irrationality. But, for many of us, they are a constant background noise in our heads. If this is true for you, clarifying the source of this 'background noise' may be helpful. There are a number of possible causes for this.

Being seen as less talented than a sibling

A child may have been viewed within their family (or viewed themselves) as somehow less talented than or inferior to a brother or sister. They may carry these views with them into their adult life, and so, when they do achieve success, it is experienced as somehow not in line with their own or their family's expectations, and therefore feels fraudulent.

Feeling guilt around jealousy of a sibling

A child may have experienced hostile or jealous feelings towards a brother or sister, causing a sense of guilt that leads them to view themselves as inferior and deserving of punishment. The individual may impose this punishment on

themselves by taking the view that they are somehow 'bad'.
Again, this is a view they may carry with them after they leave
home. It can result in the setting of unattainably high standards
and perfectionism.

Having learned by mimicry

A child may know that their apparent success stems from their
ability to copy the behaviours of others. This is the earliest
form of learning. We copy our parents or siblings, for example by stepping into Mummy or Daddy's shoes and walking
round the house, somehow believing oneself to have become
Mummy or Daddy in a more literal sense. This is a normal
stage of development and is usually met with amused approval
from other family members. Usually this form of learning is
largely replaced by more mature forms – what one might call
'real learning' – based on real effort and work, and trial and
error (for example, playing with physical objects and learning
about how to build and balance them). However, if the child
finds failure difficult, they may hold on to learning by mimicry,
copying the behaviours of others, since this is less painful and
obviates the sense of helplessness and failure that more mature
forms of learning entail. As an adult, and particularly one who
is intelligent and finds mimicking others easy, this provides a
fragile sense of achievement since the individual knows their
learning is not real but is simply superficial copying behaviour.
A clever child can progress successfully throughout the whole
of the education system in this way. Achievements are then
privately viewed as superficial and not solidly based.

Social norms

The sense of being an impostor can have its origins in social
norms, such as stereotypes based on gender or ethnicity, that

view certain behaviours, especially successful ones, as inappropriate for that person. For example, if the organisation or profession is predominantly white and male, despite a very welcome renewed and urgent focus on diversity, there is likely to be a bias in the culture of the organisation against promoting people who do not fit that specification. Members of minorities who do get promoted can consequently be made to feel they are somehow 'illegitimate'. Their promotion is countercultural and may be viewed with very mixed feelings by the dominant majority whom it threatens. The result is a toxic effect on the person's self-esteem and self-image, giving them a constant sense that their achievements are not recognised in their own right, and a feeling that any success is likely to be temporary and fragile. This results in a vicious cycle, undermining their self-confidence. The person tends to be viewed as the problem rather than the company culture, a view that, unfortunately, they may even adopt themselves (a form of defence that the psychoanalyst Anna Freud called 'identification with the aggressor').

Feeling separated from your roots

When a young person is the first in their family to go to university or join a profession, they may experience feelings of being an impostor for a different reason. Having risen up above one's roots and beyond expectations can evoke deep anxieties about separation from and loss of connection with the community that provided one's original sense of identity. They may unconsciously equate their success with a betrayal of their family, community or social class, or even having somehow overcome and defeated their parents, as Sigmund Freud describes with the Oedipus complex. Often the child may have outgrown their parents' understanding of their achievements at quite an early age, and their parents are therefore not able to provide a sense of the distinction between accidental and real, or even superior achievement, whether it is due to chance, privilege or real talent and effort. As a result, the young person may not be able to internalise an appropriate benchmark for themselves, or grasp the difference between ordinary achievement and exceptional ability. Hence they are at a loss when trying to make an accurately positive assessment of themselves, and feel at sea when explaining their successes. This can leave them prone to recurrent feelings of being not good enough or a fake.

Women and impostor syndrome

Some studies have suggested that women suffer more from impostor syndrome, due to their having little expectation of fair treatment in the workplace, and so questioning their success as perhaps simply luck or a mistake. They may feel they have to put on a false masculine front in a macho culture. Some women minimise their success in a 'man's world' to avoid fears of having 'too much' power, or being seen as somehow 'unfeminine'. Those from ethnic minorities can also suffer in a similar way, having to falsely adapt to a dominant culture.

Men and impostor syndrome

Men too can suffer impostor syndrome: they may feel they must uphold stereotypical masculine traits, such as being strong and unemotional, and suppressing their true thoughts and feelings in order to secure a 'man's job'. Some may feel a need to fall in with a macho culture, and avoid traditionally 'feminine' professions, such as nursing, teaching or social work. As a result, they may feel their more 'feminine' nature makes them somehow less acceptable, all of which results in a feeling of inauthenticity, while publicly complying with values that

CHANGING GEAR

they privately disagree with. Sometimes the only solution is to recognise this and move to a workplace that is more in line with your private values. However, that can be easier said than done when financial considerations come into play.

It is little surprise that so many of us suffer from impostor syndrome. Arguably, all of us suffer from it to some extent! You can find out more in *Love Your Imposter* by Rita Clifton, former CEO and chairperson at global brand consultancy Interbrand and now a portfolio board director.

4

Letting go – acknowledging loss and mourning

'To spare oneself from grief at all costs can be achieved only at the price of total detachment, which excludes the ability to experience happiness.'

– Erich Fromm, German psychoanalyst
who fled to the USA to escape the Nazis

Essential to moving on to the third stage of life is acknowledging that the full-on career that was a – or often, *the* – key part of the second stage, is likely to involve grieving for what has been lost. This is a totally natural part of life, and understanding and accepting this inevitable sense of loss is part of making a successful change of gear to the Third Life.

This transition will mean giving up some things that have been an integral part of your life, work being the most obvious. Work provides a sense of identity, a network of relationships and things to do during the day, all of which makes the prospect of losing it quite a scary idea. The transition can often be harder than people expect, even if it involves moving to new and exciting opportunities. Which only goes to show that insight (the rider) is one thing and emotion (the elephant) is another! Allowing for these difficulties as part of your Third Life planning might be a wise step.

Grief is a normal reaction to loss: it is the experience of the connection that has been broken. Like the pain of a wound, it is part of the healing process, and you can't rush it. It's important to allow this natural process the time needed to take its healing course. It can often take a year or more.

Loss triggers grief and mourning

THE STAGES OF GRIEF

The process of mourning can be described in a series of stages or phases. There is disagreement about the exact sequencing, and it would be oversimplifying to think of this in a purely linear way, but the sequence below roughly describes the normal course of events. In the case of the loss of a close relative, this may take place over up to two years, or it could be less depending on the suddenness of the event and the personality of the person suffering the loss. Adapting to the Third Life can take similar amounts of time.

Elisabeth Kübler-Ross originally described five stages of grief and mourning[20] and later, with David Kessler, added a sixth.[21] You may recognise these stages if you've ever attended a course on change management – and you may have seen them in others if you have ever had to fire anyone.

— **Denial** – Shock and disbelief that your career is coming
  to an end. A natural defence of refusing to accept
  painful facts and information.
— **Anger** – That the work that you loved doing has gone.
  This might be directed at the workplace or yourself.

- **Bargaining** – All the 'what if's and regrets. A rehearsal of unfinished business, but really an attempt to protest and put off recognising what has happened.
- **Low mood** – Sadness, regret, fear and uncertainty, as you let go of the old and look towards the new with trepidation.
- **Dialogue** – Reaching out to others to make sense of what has happened, and asking 'Who am I now?'.
- **Acceptance** – Acknowledging the reality of the loss, and adjusting to it as you begin to detach, beginning to achieve some distance and objectivity.
- **Moving on** – Finding a sense of purpose again and beginning to get involved in new activities.

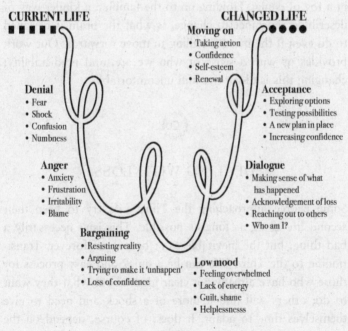

CURRENT LIFE

Denial
- Fear
- Shock
- Confusion
- Numbness

Anger
- Anxiety
- Frustration
- Irritability
- Blame

Bargaining
- Resisting reality
- Arguing
- Trying to make it 'unhappen'
- Loss of confidence

CHANGED LIFE

Moving on
- Taking action
- Confidence
- Self-esteem
- Renewal

Acceptance
- Exploring options
- Testing possibilities
- A new plan in place
- Increasing confidence

Dialogue
- Making sense of what has happened
- Acknowledgement of loss
- Reaching out to others
- Who am I?

Low mood
- Feeling overwhelmed
- Lack of energy
- Guilt, shame
- Helplessnesss

Figure 2: The stages of grief

Freud described the loss of his thirty-year-old daughter to Spanish flu as a seemingly endless withdrawing of all the points of attachment – his daughter's possessions and clothes, photographs, places visited and memories. As you age, it will become more likely that important people in your life will pass away, such as parents, teachers and colleagues. So living your Third Life means living with occasional experiences of loss. It's an inevitable part of having relationships and being alive. Freud described how, when some people suffer the loss of a partner, they attempt to cope with this by trying to keep everything the same, preserving their shared home just as it was when their partner died.

When life disrupts our accustomed sources of purpose and meaning, we need time to find new sources if we are not to sit in a fog of denial. Holding on to the familiar, a kinder way of describing resistance to change, is what the brain is designed to do even if the mind is willing to move forwards. Our work provides us with a sense of who we are, and predictability; changing this is disruptive and uncomfortable.

DEALING WITH LOSS

Some people approaching the Third Life try to keep their second life going as long as possible. This isn't necessarily a bad thing, but the inevitable can't be put off forever. Transitioning to the Third Life can be a quick and easy process for those who have already got clear ideas about what they want to do; others will find it more of a shock and need to give themselves time to adapt. It does, of course, depend on the nature of your Third Life.

It is not uncommon to experience a loss of self-esteem, doubt of one's worth and a sense of guilt at not having done better in your career, particularly when your sense of worth is heavily dependent on paid employment. These are all quite normal parts of the separation and mourning process. Leaving behind a full-on career can result in feelings of shock, numbness, disorientation and disorganisation that are all quite normal. You may feel out of sync, with nothing feeling 'right'; you may feel unsettled, confused and perhaps anxious or depressed. If you find yourself feeling like this, you will need to be kinder on yourself. You cannot expect yourself to always be in good spirits as you go through this process.

Talking these feelings through with a close friend can be helpful: after all, we have all experienced separations. Loss is something that we have only recently got better at dealing with in our Western culture. Talking things through is a way of recognising what has happened. If you are someone who thinks of yourself as a high achiever, acknowledging vulnerability may be hard. Explaining to those close to you what you are going through will help them better understand – and, in due course, accept – the changes they will notice in you. You will recover your normal spirits if you give yourself time to repair. Not giving yourself this time can mean you will remain stuck, and lacking energy and optimism, you may not find it easy to move on to new things. Allowing yourself to feel appropriately depressed is a life skill.

All loss provokes an anxious, intense and sometimes despairing search to recover a sense of meaning. We experience that search as grieving, and if it fails and stalls, grief may turn into a state resembling chronic depression, until new sources of purpose and meaning are found and consolidated. Without this, a chronic sense of worthlessness may develop, imposing a negative lens upon events and people. If allowed, nature will take its course and, with the passage of time, the healing will take place. So take care of yourself as you anticipate and go through the process of coming to the end of your main career.

Accepting a sense of unfinished business

Relationships almost always involve a degree of mixed feelings. Things are never perfect all the time, and most relationships are occasionally frustrating. An ending will bring both positive and negative feelings to the surface, and may potentially result in the re-emergence and expression of unresolved angers and frustrations. These can come out in unexpected, sometimes unconscious ways.

Moving on can mean uncomfortable feelings of disloyalty. When you decide to leave, you may feel you are letting your organisation down, or that it is letting you down. Once you announce your decision to leave your organisation, you may be surprised by the range of reaction from others. Some will be pleased for you, or even a little jealous of your courage; others will hardly appear to react at all; and, more commonly than you might think, your departure may be perceived by some as a kind of disloyalty on your part. After all, you are not the only one who is suffering a loss: so are your colleagues and your organisation, and they may also go through some of these grief reactions.

The weeks and months of mourning and adaptation to your new situation can reawaken old defences and old ways of managing. Old losses may be reactivated as you revert to old sources of meaning and value to provide structure and a sense of purpose, increasing the feeling of emptiness in the present. The loss of a valued career can reawaken doubts about competence, lovability and worth. When we are in the midst of loss, we may know that we have lost *something*, but not be quite clear what it is we have lost.

As we have seen, change entails loss, the moving from one settled state of affairs to another. Transition requires taking a leap of faith to an anticipated, but so far only imagined, future. Imagining the kind of future you want will give you ideas about what actions to take. In this chapter, we have tried to explore the kinds of emotions, questions and self-doubts someone making a transition away from their full-on career may encounter. We hope this has been helpful in explaining that these are a natural part of change and that you are not alone.

5

Strategies for flourishing in your new gear

Happiness and flourishing

'How to gain, how to keep, how to recover happiness, is in fact for most men at all times the secret motive of all they do, and of all they are willing to endure.'

– William James,
American philosopher and psychologist

'Happiness, in fact, is a condition that must be prepared for, cultivated and defended privately by each person.'

– Mihaly Csikszentmihalyi,
Flow – the Psychology of Optimal Experience

EUDAIMONIA

Aristotle used the term 'eudaimonia' to describe what he called the 'highest human good'. In Greek, *eu* means 'good' and *daimonian* means 'spirit'. Sometimes translated as 'happiness', it is really better described as 'human flourishing'. It is particular to each person, and different cultures and civilisations have different definitions of it (see *The Pursuit of Happiness* by Darrin McMahon[22]). It is about the connection between your actions and your gifts. It is linked to virtue, excellence and character. It is an activity rather than a state. In Aristotle's view, it is the ultimate purpose: the essence of a good life and living well, not as a means to anything else, but as an end in itself. One achieves eudaimonia not through quick actions, but through a lifetime of concentrating on one's character, morality, virtues and strengths in order to live meaningfully and fulfil one's particular potential in one's particular life. (For more on character strengths and virtues, visit www.viacharacter.org, where you can also complete a free online questionnaire.)

Eudaimonia can be contrasted with hedonia, which is a short-term state of pleasure, coming from external events. While there is nothing necessarily wrong with that, there is the risk of getting caught on the hedonic treadmill. This is caused by the inevitable accommodation to a recent pleasure. We become bored and restless, and then reach for the same pleasure for another 'rush'. It's called a treadmill because it doesn't lead anywhere: it is just the short-term pursuit of easy pleasures. Again, there is nothing necessarily wrong with that, unless you mistake it for a source of longer-term happiness. Hedonia is not the route to the sort of life Aristotle was advocating for us – but, of course, not everyone agrees with Aristotle!

For the British philosopher Jeremy Bentham, pleasure and pain were the ultimate drivers of all behaviour: 'Nature has placed mankind under the governance of two sovereign Masters, pain and pleasure. It is for them alone to point out what we ought to do, as well as to determine what we shall do . . . They govern us in all we do, in all we say, in all we think.'

Whether you place more emphasis on the external pleasures of hedonia or the inner satisfactions of eudaimonia is entirely up to you – a bit of both is probably the best answer!

CHANGING GEAR

OVERWORK AS A SOURCE OF SHORT-TERM PLEASURE

Overwork can be caused by relying on the short-term pleasures of meeting a goal, completing a task or winning a piece of work. These short-term hits of pleasure then recede and have to be sought again. If this is the basis of what guides your behaviour, you may find yourself seeking similar pleasures once again in your Third Life. Not having these pleasures may trigger a sense of failure. Workaholism is a thing and it is common enough in high-achieving individuals. So going 'cold turkey' and stopping paid work altogether may not work for you. If you have the choice, you need to gradually reduce the paid work habit and transfer your focus on to a different sort of work, something that will be a source of purpose and meaning for your Third Life. This is what is described in 'Work as a holding environment' on page 149.

A HAPPINESS FORMULA

Based on her research, the positive psychologist Sonja Lyubomirsky argues that fifty per cent of your happiness is genetic, ten per cent is based on life circumstance, and forty per cent is based on your actions.[23] This is captured in the formula:

$$\text{Happiness} = \frac{\text{Set}}{\text{point}} + \frac{\text{Conditions of}}{\text{your life}} + \frac{\text{Voluntary}}{\text{activities}}$$

In other words, human beings have a 'set point' of happiness, which is relatively fixed and possibly genetically determined and to which they return once the pleasurable or painful effects of a life event have receded. Lyubomirsky has studied the effects of unexpected pleasurable events, such as winning the lottery, or unexpected difficult events, such as losing a limb, on people's levels of happiness. Rather dramatic, perhaps, but her research shows that, despite ups and downs, we basically always return to our set point for happiness.

How would you rate your set point for happiness? Think of it as a number from one to ten. The idea is that we are all born with our own set point. Some people are naturally happy much of the time, others less so, and there's not much we can do about that. What we can do something about are the other two elements in the equation, our current conditions and voluntary activities, both of which Lyubomirsky's research shows can be used to improve happiness. Consider how to remove causes of unhappiness in your current circumstances, and how you could add activities that create happiness.

Expressing gratitude, providing a kindly service to a person, thinking positive thoughts before you fall asleep and focusing on what you are grateful for in your life have all been shown to have measurable effects on people's happiness. And perhaps it isn't a surprise that these behaviours are ones that most religions encourage. In that sense, our 'happiness depends upon ourselves', as Aristotle said. It's also worth remembering the view of Epictetus that, while we may not be able to influence events, we can influence the attitude we take to those events: 'Men are disturbed not by things, but by the view they take of them'.

While genetics and personality variables may largely explain your happiness set point, the goals you set yourself and what you choose to focus your attention on during your day play a role in your day-to-day happiness. In other words, you don't have to stay on the treadmill – you have some control!

As you plan for your Third Life, you will need to take account of both sorts of happiness, both short-term pleasures and longer-term satisfactions, and find ways to build both into your life.

A FRAMEWORK FOR FLOURISHING

The psychologist Martin Seligman provides a helpful framework for longer-term wellbeing and flourishing, which he calls PERMA:

P   Positive emotion – 'feeling good'.

E   Engagement – 'finding flow'.

R   Relationships – 'authentic connections'.

M   Meaning – 'purposeful existence'.

A   Achievement – 'sense of accomplishment'.[24]

He advocates creating a positive life by thinking of four aspects:

— Positive emotion: the Pleasant Life – a life with fun and pleasure in it.

— Positive character: the Engaged Life – a life with a sense of flow in it (see page 213).

— Positive institutions: the Meaningful Life – a life with meaning derived from being part of a wider community.

— Positive relationships: the Social Life – a life lived with others in nourishing relationships.

Reading through these lists may give you some thoughts on what you want your priorities to be in your Third Life.

YOUR HAPPINESS SCORE

To keep it really simple, we've created a formula that summarises research on what makes people happy. Happiness would seem to be the outcome of three elements. It cannot be sought in itself but will be produced by improving your scores on the following:

— State of your health (1–10)

— State of your relationships (1–10)

— Sense of meaning and purpose in your life (1–10)

Give a score to each of these, then add them up and divide the total by three:

$$H + R + P = \text{your current happiness score}$$

Typically, those with a full-on career will score lower on health and relationships. If you score eight or above overall you're doing well; six or less means you should pay attention to the areas which are lower – consider what you might do to increase your score.

Being in flow

'The best moments in our lives are not the passive, receptive, relaxing times . . . The best moments usually occur if a person's body or mind is stretched to its limits in a voluntary effort to accomplish something difficult and worthwhile.'

– Mihaly Csikszentmihalyi

The psychologist Mihaly Csikszentmihalyi called the state of finding deep satisfaction 'flow'.[25] In this state, you are completely absorbed in an activity, especially an activity that involves your talents and abilities. During this 'optimal experience' you feel 'strong, alert, in effortless control, unselfconscious, and at the peak of [your] abilities'. For Csikszentmihalyi, happiness does not simply happen. It must be prepared for and cultivated by each person, by setting challenges that are neither too demanding nor too simple for one's abilities.

The activity is meaningful or intrinsically rewarding by the very nature of doing it. While the end result might entitle you to a big outside reward, like a bonus, pay rise, or a high fee, the essential nature of the activity is so rewarding that you would do it at the same level, even without the extra motivation of some kind of external prize.

Which of your activities lead you into a flow state? Are these passions that you would like to pursue further in your Third Life?

According to Csikszentmihalyi, while the state of flow may occur across a wide spectrum of activities and be experienced differently by each person, there are certain shared elements that most often define this rapturous state. These include:

Working towards a clear goal with a well-defined process

The task, big or small, must be clearly defined and the steps needed to get there must be laid out in detail, or at least be highly delineated along the way. Getting there does not have to be easy, but you need to be able to see, even from a distance, where you are going.

Cultivating deep concentration

The nature of the job must require an intense sense of concentration. Examples would be a fast-moving game, like ping-pong, or an exercise routine. In a work setting, leading a high-stakes, face-to-face negotiation or drafting a complex document would qualify.

Lack of a sense of self-consciousness

You become so engaged in the nature of the work that you are no longer aware of yourself, but rather feel a sense of total absorption in the task.

Ongoing, direct feedback

You need regular enough feedback – either from other people or the testable nature of the task – to be able to constantly adapt, correct course, and make progress towards your goal. For example, when writing a computer programme, or writing a difficult report at work, you can constantly test and debug to ensure you are on the right track. During such activities, our sense of time is altered: it seems to either stand still or fly by in the blink of an eye.

The task needs to be highly challenging, but doable

The task must be hard enough to finish that it requires a significant investment of your attention, resources, and energy, leading to the sense of absorption. But it cannot be so hard as to allow you to believe that a solution is, in fact, impossible, or else you'd just give up. When the task doesn't really challenge us enough, it will become dull and boring. If it challenges us too much, we feel helpless and stressed. Balancing challenge and abilities in a way that leads to feelings of flow is part of the secret of a sense of flourishing in your Third Life.

While not every element needs to be present to effect a state of flow, the greater the number of elements, the deeper the state of flow you will find yourself in.

Needs and motivations

When we experience a need, we feel a tension between our current state and our desired state. There are many theories about potential 'drives' underpinning this felt need, but no one has ever seen a drive (and it is not clear what it would look like if you did) – a 'drive' is a hypothetical conjecture that we use to explain our behaviour. Theories of drives are essentially myths that cultures and civilisations use to explain themselves: myths that, it seems, we cannot do without. So, you can take it or leave it as far as drives are concerned, depending on your preference. What is unarguable is that we experience *needs*, and if these needs are not met, we feel frustration.

There are two basic types of needs.

Primal needs

The fundamental biological needs of physical existence, covering our basic material and physical needs for sufficient income, food, water and physical affection, as well as our need to feel reasonably safe and secure.

Social needs

The psychologist David McClelland proposed a framework of three fundamental social needs: the need to achieve, the need for relationships (which he termed 'affiliation') and the need for power. He argued that the importance of each of these needs varies from person to person.

When we feel our needs are being satisfied and our goals are being achieved, we obtain a sense of motivation. Our capacity to meet our needs depends on our situation: if the situation you are in does not allow for the satisfaction of what you need, you will become frustrated. As we develop through the various stages of life, the shape of our goals and needs change. When we achieve a goal, we have a feeling of satisfaction, and our sense of self-esteem and wellbeing increases. However, our goals need to be realistic, and we need to find contexts in which they can be achieved.

We are guided in our choice of goals and needs by the norms of society, as represented in the four lives model in Hindu philosophy (page 6). Each of these lives entails adjusting goals and the way that you meet your needs, moving from education to material wealth, seeking wisdom and contribution to the community, and finally to acceptance of death. Tenaciously holding on to earlier needs and goals when your life situation changes reduces the sense of being effective (self-efficacy), and affects your self-worth (self-esteem).

Alignment between an individual's abilities, needs and goals results in a feeling of flourishing: of relative harmony and self-worth. Misalignment causes disharmony and reduced self-worth. During the teenage years, if there is alignment between the individual's talents and the education system, self-worth improves. But when the individual does not obtain satisfaction (and hence self-worth) from educational tasks, they may rebel against the self-diminishing and constraining context of school. Delinquency and a refusal to conform to society's expectations are expressions of frustrated needs and are met by social disapproval, resulting in a vicious cycle of frustrations, disappointments and rejections. Similar patterns and reactions can be found in the workplace, and we know that less than fifty per cent of people find their work satisfying and meaningful. The same thing happens to some in their Third Life if they don't feel an alignment between their needs and the situation they find themselves in.

In planning your Third Life, you will need to take account of your various needs and how – and in what context – they will be met, in order to obtain a sense of satisfaction, self-esteem and motivation. If your work has been the source of much of this, then its loss will inevitably cause ups and downs as you proceed through the transition process and begin to think of alternative futures. You should look at your needs in terms of the five fundamental needs we introduced you to ear-lier: the two primal needs (our physical needs and a need for safety) and the three social needs (for achievement, relation-ships and power and influence). Not all of these needs can be met all of the time, but getting a reasonable balance will help you shape the sort of life you want next.

Living with a sense of purpose and values

'When a man does not know what harbour he is making for, no wind is the right wind.'

– Seneca

'Let yourself be silently drawn by the stronger pull of what you really love.'

– Rumi

If, as is likely, your work has been a significant determinant of your sense of purpose and meaning in life, then being without paid employment may leave you with a sense of lacking direction. Changing gear brings with it the opportunity to reflect on what you want your purpose – or purposes – to be in your Third Life.

A sense of purpose sits alongside a sense of your values and, together, they provide a sense of direction and meaning to your life. Research suggests that those who stick to their values are more resilient.

Business theorist Chris Argyris highlights a distinction between espoused values (what you *say* your values are) and values in action (the values *demonstrated by your behaviours*). It's easy enough to draw up a list of your espoused values – the question is, what are your values in action? How do you actually behave towards others? And, as you move into this next phase of life, are you comfortable with the values you have, either consciously or unconsciously, lived with and demonstrated to the world around you?

At the heart of being fulfilled in your Third Life is what really matters to you, and what sense of purpose and values you want to be guiding you. How you choose to behave going forwards is a very real choice, and one that deserves to be made consciously. Some will choose to focus on those people or things they love most; others might embrace a much wider focus, looking at how they can shape society and 'give back'; others still might concentrate on the activities they choose to undertake for whatever reason. There are no right and wrong answers to these existential questions of purpose and values, but, for each individual, some answers will be 'more right' – or 'more wrong' – than others.

One way to consider these overarching drivers is to take a look in the rear-view mirror. Bronnie Ware is a former palliative care nurse who worked for many years with dying patients. She has summarised from the top five regrets that her patients have expressed to her.

1. I wish I'd had the courage to live a life true to myself, not the life others expected of me.

2. I wish I hadn't worked so hard.

3. I wish I'd had the courage to express my feelings.

4. I wish I had stayed in touch with my friends.

5. I wish that I had let myself be happier.[26]

Her conclusion? 'Life is a choice. It is *your* life. Choose consciously, choose wisely, choose honestly. Choose happiness.'

You can use this idea to establish your own sense of purpose and values by completing these sentences. Write the answers down in your notebook.

- In my life so far I wish I had _____.

- I wish I hadn't _____.

- When I come to the end of my life, I want to make sure I have _____.

The exercises on purpose and values in Chapter 7 will help you get clearer about how to create a meaningful and purposeful Third Life.

6

The Eight-step Transition Process – how to find your new self

'It isn't normal to know what we want. It is a rare and difficult psychological achievement.'

– Abraham Maslow, American psychologist

So far, we have looked at a number of the most important considerations in changing gear. We have:

— introduced the concept of the Third Life, the stage those who have had a full-on career enter as they leave their second phase.

— shown why accepting you are heading towards (or already entering) your Third Life is one thing, but figuring out what to do and how to do it is quite another!

— explained that change and transition are different things, and that human beings aren't machines who can be modified in an instant. We need time to try things out, to move back and forth between the new and the unfamiliar, and to unlearn old habits as well as (or before) learning to do things differently.

The complete transition process involves eight phases and, as we've already said, takes longer than you may expect: one year to eighteen months is not uncommon, and up to three years may well be needed. The phases don't always happen in exactly the same sequence, and you will find yourself moving back and forth between different phases. Some will seem more relevant than others depending on the type of change you are faced with. As we have already shown, it is inevitably a time of lots of ups and downs.

Developing a transition mindset

Developing a transition mindset will give you the capacity to make the changes necessary to enable you to weather the process effectively. It involves recognising that existing ways of thinking and behaving – and perhaps feeling – have become outmoded; that old competence may have become incompetence; and that continuing to seek success through outmoded ways of reacting is now resulting in a failure to develop a new focus and new relationships, and thus requires a new definition of 'success' for yourself.

WHAT WAS COMPETENCE CAN START TO BECOME INCOMPETENCE

Much of what we do at work is a set of habits, behaviours and attitudes that we initially had to learn and internalise, acquiring them deliberately and consciously in the same way that we might learn to drive a car. However, with practice, this competence becomes unconscious, and we are able to skilfully manage our vehicle without having to be consciously aware of each action we are performing. When our circumstances change – for example, when we're driving in a foreign country on the other side of the road – what were unconscious habits have to be consciously managed and adapted. We have to be consciously deliberate in adapting our behaviour to new situations. Behaviours that were once successful could now easily cause an accident! Executives with one style of leadership frequently struggle to adapt and find new ways of operating in a new culture (whether that of a country or company) that is very different to their own.

Entering the Third Life can mean competences that were once effective can become less so. Gradually increasing incompetence may be all too obvious to others, but not necessarily to oneself, and those who have been trying to point this out can give up. As the world changes, what was competence can slowly become incompetence, as, while the world changes, one can remain stuck in a state of blissful ignorance.

Hopefully, however, we shift to becoming conscious that all is not well, accompanied by the uncomfortable sense of losing balance demonstrated in many of the stories in Chapter 1. Noticing this loss of balance can be a very unsettling but necessary phase to go through. Without this acceptance, however reluctant, it is not then possible to move towards finding a willingness to adapt by trying out new behaviours and habits. With deliberate practice, these new behaviours will develop into a new conscious competence that, in time, becomes an unconscious habitual competence – the new you.

In essence, what we mean by a transition mindset is one in which you are prepared to embrace the need for change, either in what you do or who you want to be, or both, and accepting that you are likely to need to learn new ways of behaving, thinking and being (and probably feeling) as you do so. The transition process can be exciting, but it can also have its more challenging moments. The diagram below shows how moving through the four 'competence modes' is a key part of the transition process.

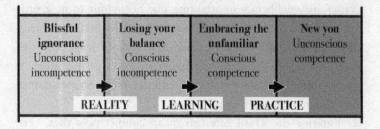

Blissful ignorance Unconscious incompetence	**Losing your balance** Conscious incompetence	**Embracing the unfamiliar** Conscious competence	**New you** Unconscious competence

REALITY   LEARNING   PRACTICE

Figure 3: Modes of competence

Unconscious incompetence

'I don't even know that I don't know what I don't know.'

Motivation to change = zero.

Conscious incompetence

'I know now where I want to be and what I want to be
    doing, but I don't know how to get myself there, or how
    to get myself to do it.'

Motivation to change = variable, depending on commitment
    to the new behaviour.

Conscious competence

'I know now how to make it happen, and I know I can do it
    (but I have to keep reminding myself to do it, and I fall
    off the wagon regularly).'

Motivation to change = difference between current and
    desired reality, and knowledge of how to bridge the gap.

Unconscious competence

'I just do it. I only think about it when I don't do it, and
    then I have to go and do it.'

Motivation to change = on cruise control now; minor
    adjustments only.

Understanding the Eight-step
Transition Process

The Eight-step Transition Process is designed to take you through the likely steps you will both need and experience as you change gear from your second to your third stage of life.

Although there are eight steps in total, they fall into four phases, as follows:

— First, becoming **AWARE** of the situation in which you find yourself.

— Second, exploring the **ALTERNATIVES** for your life going forwards.

— Third, taking **ACTIONS** which move you closer to the life you might have.

— Fourth, **ASSESSING** your new situation and learning for the future.

Awareness of your situation

STEP ONE

Losing your balance – and noticing

Change finds us as much as we find it. Change management is a subject about which a great deal has been spoken, written and debated in the world of business. Often, the change has already happened: the challenge is to recognise this and then figure out how best to respond. The idea that we can manage change in the sense of controlling it is often just a comforting illusion. How individuals lose their balance is obviously hugely important. It's often an event in the external world that kicks things off, and this event can determine the degree of pain (or at least discomfort) that is initially felt. However, as we have seen, this is just the very start of the transition process. Once a sense of change or an actual change has become, or will become, a reality, the disruption to the person can be equally daunting. As the saying goes 'stuff happens'. It's what you do next that matters. While managing change may be an illusion, we can certainly manage our responses to change, providing we have the self-awareness to do so.

What makes many of Henrik Ibsen's plays so compelling is the effect an unexpected visitor has on a previously stable situation. Topics that have lain dormant in a family or a marriage are brought centre stage, facing the characters with questions they thought they didn't need to face. At first, change is like this: a stranger in your midst.

The shape and structure of your life can be viewed as a series of responses to conscious and unconscious wishes, dreams and ambitions that you had at an earlier phase, combined with the solutions to the opportunities, obstacles, challenges and problems that life has thrown up along the way. When these dreams and ambitions have been achieved, even if only partially, they may no longer be so motivating. Similarly, the solutions you have found to previous situations may not be so relevant to what life is throwing at you now. This means that your familiar ways of responding to things may no longer be so effective. In other words, you may be blissfully carrying on, hoping nothing will change. Often changes happen around us – or within us – before we even notice. We are sometimes so busy living our life that we do not immediately realise when someone else – or something else – forces change upon us.

Our desire for consistency, continuity and a sense of control in our life can make us blind to what is going on around us. As a result, our first reaction to change may be denial. Noticing those initial responses to change, often expressed as disgruntlement or grumpiness, and taking them seriously, is the first step towards becoming skilled at transition.

Of course, as you may be thinking, change isn't always bad – it's often good. If change is going on in your life and you're enjoying it, wonderful! This book, however, is concerned with the changes that can be less enjoyable. Nevertheless, tracking where you are in the transition process is useful in identifying what you need to do next.

For some, this first step in the transition process feels like being afloat in the ocean at the mercy of the waves. One minute, you are happily bobbing in calm seas, with a relaxed sense of your life moving along as normal. The next, you are up on the crest of a wave, excited about the good things that change could bring. Then, suddenly, you are in a huge trough, struggling to stay afloat, lost in feelings of uncertainty and self-doubt about where you are heading.

For most people, it is not possible to avoid these feelings – and, indeed, we would argue strongly that it is not helpful, either. A useful skill to foster to help you deal with this time is that of multitasking between both your feelings and your thoughts, and learning to shift between the two – *what am I thinking, how am I feeling*. The concept of the rider and the elephant, which we explored earlier in the book, is a helpful way to understand how you might try to develop this new skill. Develop your awareness of how you are feeling and thinking, and try to use these feelings and thoughts to explore what you are uncomfortable about and why this might be. Use the rider – the more logical piece of your mind – to observe yourself as you are knocked around by the ocean waves, and be curious about what these feelings are telling you, albeit in a very messy, unsatisfactory and unstructured way!

Learning to both live with and learn from this phase is not something that happens in a few days. More often, there is a sense of a gradual clearing of the fog and moments of apparent lucidity where things feel like they are starting to make sense, and possible patterns and themes emerge in your mind. This might be followed by the fog rolling in again as your mind seeks to deny some of the strangeness, discomfort and discombobulation it is experiencing.

The two people below, Adrian and Meena, are examples of those who have experienced the sense of losing their balance and being in the fog.

ADRIAN

As a client director in a large advertising agency, I had felt very privileged. I had always worked in advertising and enjoyed the development of the agency's relationships with its clients. As an extrovert, I enjoyed the social aspects of my work, and many of my colleagues and clients also became friends.

In the latter stages of my career, new digital technologies meant the loss of some of the fun at work: relationships were more transactional and short-term and, increasingly, less happened face to face.

There was, of course, always a trade-off between my work and the rest of my life. I had not minded this, as I was broadly happy. Looking back, there were no deliberate decisions: life simply took its course and, gradually, 'my job became me'. I didn't really think about it all. I was busy doing what I was doing and, although I was probably more sociable than some, I was not very different to those around me at work.

I can't remember exactly when it happened, but I started to have a sense of not being right at the top of my game. Gradually, I realised that I might not go on forever at work. It wasn't a panicky feeling, more a slow, sinking feeling. This seemed to feed a lack of energy, and also a lessening of the enjoyment that had always been a big part of my work. Digital media had become reality, but I managed to hold on to the older ways for longer than most. Things had never been perfect, and I had always found some things irritating, but this feeling was more of a sense of disenfranchisement rather than frustration. I was clearly now the older generation and perceived as a bit out of touch – and that was new.

I had always thought it was other people who became old-fashioned. I had just been slow to grasp that this was now what was happening to me. It wasn't a question of would change happen – it was clearly already happening. It was simply a question of when and how, and who would initiate the next steps.

I could see the time to leave had come. I had to confront whether, on the one hand, I should show the world that I was in control and resign or, on the other hand, I should hold on tight for as long as I could to optimise my pension – and to put off making a decision that I was not sure I really wanted to make.

As I started to think things through, I began to see that I wasn't just leaving my job, but also much of my life as I knew it. I was not the first, and would not be the last, but knowing that didn't really make it feel any better for me. I wish, at the time, I'd had a better sense of how important it is not to fight inevitable change – and that I'd been able to acknowledge that I was treading a well-worn path for people like me in their mid to late fifties. When the HR director had tried to engage me in a chat about things, I just told her everything was fine.

My departure was a bit uncomfortable, and there were quite a few rows about the final package. I realise now I was angry at how the world had changed. I felt it had left me somewhat like a beached whale. I needed someone to blame, and felt like my organisation was rejecting what I had to offer. With the benefit of hindsight, I could have handled it with more grace. Sadly, I now see that this might have helped me to negotiate a better exit – both emotionally and financially. At least I am not too old to learn!

MEENA

I was the headteacher of an inner-city comprehensive school. As part of my role, I sat on various educational policy committees in the local authority and became a bit of a mover and shaker in the local community.

I loved my job and, although I am sure there were many things I could have done better, I was very proud of what I had achieved. I had always thought people should go when they were at the top of their game, not when they were pushed. So, I did not flinch when I had my sixtieth birthday and the moment arrived where I could see that now was the time to go.

I had built up a reasonable amount of savings and, because I had been in education, it was possible to retire early. We had always planned to move out of the city and live in the country once our careers came to an end. I said above that I did not flinch – but I did struggle! It was clear that now was the right time, but *thinking* that I would make the right decision when the time came and actually *making* it now that the time was here were two completely different things. However, I pressed on, as I had always promised myself I would.

What I had not realised was how hard it would be to let go in practice. If I had not loved my job, maybe it would have been easier. Deep inside, I wanted to be asked to stay on; part of me wanted to be told that no one else could possibly replace me. But I had made the case for going so convincing that this did not happen. So, pretty soon, I found myself on the edge of conversations about who should by my successor. I wanted to say that I knew best who it should be, but I knew I shouldn't.

This sense of losing control was in danger of making me lose control! I had always been one for wanting to influence events. Outwardly I kept my cool, but inwardly I was finding it so much harder than I could have imagined. I felt terrified: terrified about actually letting go, and terrified about what would become of *me*! I had thought about the good of the children in the school, the parents and the teachers, but I simply had not anticipated the need to really think about what would be good for me.

I should have been able to see that this was how I would react, but I was so busy doing my job and trying to do the right thing that I did not consider how I might cope – or, as it transpired, how I might not cope. For someone who had planned and exe-cuted so much over the course of their career, I found myself asking myself how I got the process of leaving so wrong for myself, especially when I was the one driving the change.

Maybe it was simple human denial, but I can see now that I could – and should – have taken more time to think things through. That is what I would have advised others to do. I think I had been 'in control' for so long that I had forgotten what it felt like *not* to be in control – or, worse still, to be out of control. It gave me a lot of sleepless nights. I wish I had been able to share my fears and concerns with others, but I was just too used to being the one who always coped.

In Chapter 7, you will find advice and exercises on how to heighten your awareness of this first stage in the Eight-step Transition Process.

STEP TWO

Taking stock – looking around you and
moving from alarm to curiosity

Becoming more conscious of thoughts and feelings

The psychiatrist Viktor Frankl, who spent time in a Nazi concentration camp, argued that, even in the most constrained situations, we have a choice over how we respond to them – and that this is our greatest freedom.

Psychoanalyst Karen Horney says that, when something new happens, we can broadly have three potential responses – towards, against or away. In other words, we can be drawn to and enjoy playing with novelty; we can oppose and resist change; or we can distract ourselves by shifting our attention elsewhere. All three reactions may be helpful or unhelpful, depending on the circumstances.

To be drawn to novelty might seem a good thing, but it can also become an addiction. Opposing change could be said to be bad but, of course, it depends on the situation. And allowing oneself to be distracted may seem like a bad idea, but sometimes it is the only way to manage the elephant described on page 11. Indeed, most meditation techniques involve a method of distracting the elephant by focusing on a word, an object, or the breath. People sometimes distract themselves by making external changes – like buying new things, moving house, taking on a new role or starting a new relationship – as a way of avoiding making a deeper transition to a new way of life. These 'substitute' changes or displacement activities distract, as they are unconsciously intended to do, and then can become obstacles in themselves.

An incredibly hard but helpful thing to do, once you have been through a period of listening to your thoughts and feelings as you 'bob around on the ocean', is to start to work out which things give you a sense of purpose and satisfaction – or simply enjoyment. These could be things you have done in the past, or things you are doing currently. Also, think about what things you have not been able to do which you believe would give you real pleasure if you could do them. Indeed, what is – or could be – real pleasure for you?

Are there things you currently do that you love and that you might want to adapt and do differently? Are there skills you have that you love and would like to hone further?

The exercises in Chapter 8 will help you think this through further.

Fantasy desires

Most of us have ideas about what we are going to do 'one day' – what you might call 'fantasy desires'. Sorting out your 'fantasy desires' from your real desires is tough, but it's an important thing to do. Are there things you say you would love to do, but somehow the time, conditions or people are never quite right? For example, have you always said you would love to play the piano, but rarely (if ever) placed your fingers on the piano keys? We all have these 'fantasy desires' that can sit happily in our heads; they just never seem to progress from there. Maybe they never will? This is fine, it is just helpful to know. These ideas are a part of the person we would like to be: our ideal self. Ideals can be useful if they provide a goal to action. If not, they may merely be an idealised version of yourself, used as a diversion from facing your limitations. It might be worth asking yourself what you hope to achieve by your fantasy desire: might there be a better, more achievable and practical way to accomplish this? Instead of wanting to play the piano but never getting round to it, for example, could you perhaps attend a course on music appreciation?

There is also the matter of not what you might want to do, but who you might want to be. You might be very happy with who you are and just want to express that same person differently. You might, however, want to shed some of the things your work (for whatever reason) made you become. People are very adept at adapting to their environments to survive. What at first may have seemed a less than perfect way to behave, may have become more hard-wired than you would wish. Or there may have been behaviours you used to have that you have lost and now want to re-establish. Again, the reason for having lost or gained these behaviours does not matter. What does matter is how you now move forward and discover (or rediscover) the person you would like to be.

Socratic understanding – knowing yourself, owning yourself and being yourself

Although nobody knows for sure (since he never wrote anything down!), Socrates supposedly said that the unexamined life was not worth living. Actually, there are plenty of people who are perfectly happy living unexamined lives, but if you're reading this book, you probably aren't one of them!

The advice to 'Know yourself' was inscribed in the forecourt of the Temple of Apollo at Delphi, where people went to seek counsel from the Oracle, and it has been the motto for many a philosophy since. However, equally important is to *own* yourself – in other words, to be prepared to be accountable for your behaviour and its effects on others (something that philosophers, intellectuals and artists are often less notice-ably attentive to!).

In fact, logically, you can only find out who you are in the reality of the world (rather than in the sometimes unduly positive, sometimes unduly negative, picture you paint of yourself) by asking others. It is impossible to accurately grasp how others see you without asking them, and the effect you have on others is, for all practical purposes, who you actually are. Your view of yourself is important, and will shape how you think and feel about yourself, and hence behave, but it's more of a framework than a fixed reality. A further complication is that the world is divided with regards to whether or not you have an enduring 'true' self or whether the self is constantly evolving. Being yourself is probably more of a modern than an ancient concern, where fate was more of a factor to contend with than our current preoccupation with authenticity.

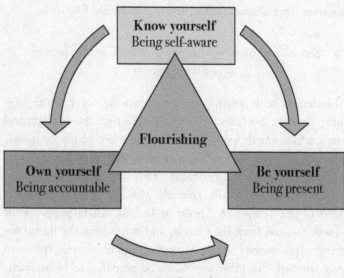

Figure 4: Flourishing

Below are the stories of two people trying to begin the task of changing gear and facing the prospect of thinking through who they might be. Crucially for each of them, they are also thinking about who they might want to be next and what they might want to do next, neither of which is a straightforward or easy question to answer.

ANGUS

I had longed to have more time for me. Work had been so time-consuming that I had not felt able to plan how I would spend my time when I stopped. (Although I can now see that I did not even try.) I am quite a focused person and my focus was work. I worked all week, and at the weekends I did all the things that needed doing at home, accepted the family and social invitations that came, and tried to do some exercise. I also worked much of Sunday. I did not think there was anything wrong with this, but I did know I was tired and wanted more time. Now I can see that was a fairly nebulous idea.

That first week at home was quite a shock. I had no need to put on the alarm and no structure for the week ahead. I had a holiday booked for a few weeks' time and my focus had been on that. But what would I do 'today'? It was an unanswered question. I found myself uncomfortable with doing nothing, so I started to plan activities. I organised some personal and home stuff, like getting financial advice, organising some maintenance work on the house and booking a doctor's appointment to ask about my aching shoulder, which I had steadfastly ignored in the past. I needed to get fitter, so I joined a local gym. I booked some theatre tickets and started to read film and TV reviews. I also reached out to my old work colleagues and contacts and arranged to meet up with them. But what was I really going to *do*?!

On the work front, I had been advised that I should take my time and not rush into anything. The truth was that I had nothing to rush into, and this now felt like very unhelpful advice as I wanted to feel less at sea and have an anchor.

Although I had wanted time for me and to feel less tired, I was not sleeping very well and, in fact, felt more tired! I was not sure how to feel. I was not on holiday and I was not busy with a new life. I knew it was very early days, but I felt lost.

Then it was time to go on my planned holiday. I knew how to do this! Or so I thought. This, too, felt different. I struggled with the idea that my emails were not stacking up for me to deal with when I woke up, so I decided to go for a walk before breakfast instead.

Over the next few weeks, away from home and normality, I began to relax and take the days one at a time. I found myself enjoying the 'me time' I had been wanting.

By the time I got home, I felt able to accept that I didn't know what I wanted to do. This felt scary, but also brought a sense of liberation and validation that I had made the right decision to step down. Now, I was actually ready to start to think about what might come next.

LANCE

Stopping full-time work was something that happened to old people, not to me. I was not old enough and certainly not ready to stop. I was a 'champion' – always had been and always would be! I had been a leader at work for a long time. That was who I was and what I did. I had not looked ahead to a time when this would not be the case. I was not asked to go, but I was put in a place where I might well have been asked if I had not taken the step myself.

I was furious and humiliated. How had I lost this battle? I knew how to lead an army, and yet I had been outmanoeuvred. It was partly an industry thing – the changing environment was not my fault. Indeed, without me, the organisation would have been in a much worse place and people knew that. What I hadn't realised was that they now thought someone else might be better at leading them to the next place.

Anyway, I would be fine – because I was a winner.

I set about filling my life straight away. I took on new physical challenges, signing up for an Iron Man event across the desert, which meant committing a huge amount of time to getting even fitter. I accepted invitations to give talks about how I had succeeded and gave advice to those who asked. I also had lots of meetings about what I might do next. I reassured my friends and family, as well as my old colleagues and associates, that I was fully occupied and in a great place.

Except that I wasn't.

It took me quite a while to discover that my life was going to change and, of course, it already had. What hadn't changed was me. I had seen other people, as their time came, hang grimly on to their jobs when it was clear to most around them that they should let go. But, like them, I had not had the same insight when it came to myself.

I did not anticipate having to go through a process of change. I was in shock and I dealt with this by carrying on as normal. All my 'normals' had changed, but I had not. I got very stuck and the dawning realisation that I needed to move on was extremely gradual. It was really hard on my family, who were watching me flailing around from the sidelines. However, they had experience of this, as I had never shared my work challenges with them in the past. I felt I was strong and did not need to share my difficulties – or, just maybe, I did not know how to do so.

But now I am getting there. The 'me' that is a champion and a winner is beginning to accept that I need to find new ways to use my energy and skills. I know I cannot become a totally different person – and I don't want to – but I am now starting to think about who is the best 'next me' I can be. I like the challenge of this and the energy it is beginning to bring.

While this has been a very tough period, I feel an optimism that there is more good to come!

There are a series of exercises in Chapter 7 that provide questions and frameworks to help you look at who you are. They will help you to explore the sense you had of who you were in your second phase of life, and how that might sit with your Third Life. Who you are, your 'self', is hard to pull apart from what motivates you and what you do. What is most helpful will differ for each person. Hopefully, embracing the breadth of the exercises will help you to find what resonates most with you and gives you the most valuable insights in to how you might move forward — and the new sense of self you might move towards.

Alternatives for your future

STEP THREE

Being open to the new – exploring and investigating fresh possibilities

Becoming conscious of potential desired competences

Travel with an open mind. As you go through your day and something sparks your interest or surprises you, take note and explore it a little further. As we discussed earlier in the book, all the organs in your body – your heart, lungs, kidneys and liver – serve to keep you alive; they work 'behind the scenes' while you get on with the business of living. Your brain is just the same; it, too, is built to ensure your survival. It does this by regulating your body in all sorts of ways that you are not conscious of, and, when you feel disturbed, it works to return you to a state of equilibrium. It also builds up habits based on what it finds rewarding or punishing. These habits 'work' in the sense that they are repeating patterns of approach or avoidance that provide you – largely unconsciously – with a sequence of behaviours that maintains control, predictability and, hence, survival. Making changes means coming up against some of these tried-and-tested routines. Don't expect success first time around! As we have explained, part of the brain's job is to keep us in a comfortable state.

Contemplating new possibilities can be overwhelming, even if it is also exciting. For many, it can just feel daunting to start with. The important thing is to be open to the new, and this means being open to exploring. Different people will be comfortable with different ways of doing this. There are no right answers, but there are approaches that are likely to be less successful. Trying to find 'the' answer at an early stage of transition is driven by the understandable desire to avoid uncertainty and ambiguity, but it is unlikely to succeed because, at this point, you are operating with existing knowledge.

The first task is exploration: not only exploring and investigating new possibilities, but also being open to new ways to explore and new places in which to do so.

One approach to this is to ignore, for the time being, whether or not something seems possible in order to open up your creative thinking. This also has the serious merit of avoiding closing down your options too early.

The real key to this phase is to be open and curious as to what the future might hold for you and note this down. Try mind-mapping the things that come to mind as you go.

Both Mary and Gloria, below, found it hard to open up to the new when they left behind the old. For both of them, it was a gradual process of accepting their loss of control and, once they had done this, of opening their eyes to new possibilities.

MARY

Here I was: the same me, but a new me. The 'same' because it was still me, but 'new' because I had the lost the me I used to be. When people asked me what I did, I saw the question as being about putting me in a box so they could decide if I was interesting to them. I found myself struggling with this and, yes, also admit that I had been guilty of asking this question in the same way for the same reason. I had been told that men sometimes dismissed women who said they did not work and I had not been very sympathetic, thinking the women's reaction was probably overly sensitive. Then I found it happening to me, and I wasn't just 'a bit' sensitive to it – I was massively sensitive, and found myself anticipating how the questioner would react to me!

In time, I began to play with what I said. I started off saying 'I used to be . . .', with a long explanation of how great my job had been and how I had decided to step away. However, this still left me feeling rather disempowered, which was not great. So I began to experiment, happily discovering that simply playing in my own head with what I would say was a helpful distraction. After a while, I hit upon answering, in a confident manner, 'I do nothing!'

Suddenly, I felt empowered and, to my surprise, I could also see that the people asking the question reacted more positively than they sometimes had to my long explanation. I think it was probably that they were asking out of politeness, and the confidence with which I answered mattered more than what I actually said. I also had the thought that maybe people meeting me for the first time were simply not all that concerned about who I was – or, more to the point, who I had been.

Gradually, this new-found confidence around experimenting and embracing new ways of being grew and I found myself approaching people and new activities with more of a spring in my step. I should add that the experimental 'springing' was a new skill and, metaphorically, I did keep tripping over and having to pick myself up!

Sometimes I could laugh at myself, but at other times it made me rather miserable. Some days went better than others, but I kept reminding myself that this was a period of readjustment. I had learned to see that I needed to encourage myself to keep experimenting, which meant rolling with the punches when they came, but equally it meant enjoying the fun that I was also having. Experimenting meant learning, and learning meant growing, and growing meant more interest and, ultimately, more satisfaction and a happier life. If I could keep myself on track, there was a positive feedback loop. On the days when this optimism eluded me – and they were not few in number – I shrugged and enjoyed an extra glass of wine!

GLORIA

I was never very gregarious. As my career developed, I always enjoyed being an expert. After I finished my degree, I went on to become a deep expert in statistical analysis and built a successful career around this. I was known as a bit of a geek, but I rather liked that. I took my position for granted and also the other things that came with it: the respect, the authority, the being needed, the teams I was a part of, the ability to get things done efficiently, the freedom to influence things and the intellectual stimulation.

How lucky I had been to be able to take my role and my company for granted in the way I did. However, it was not ideal preparation for what I was to face at the end of my career. I had completely failed to see that I had come to rely on the comfort of the environment in which I had been operating. So, confronting being on my own without any structures or support around me was very disconcerting.

My statistical analysis work was a precursor to what became the field of big data, and this meant that I had remained at the forefront of these changes. I believed that somehow I would continue to be useful and that people would carry on asking me to do other things, but I really was not confident enough of this to be sure, and I worried about whether I could I remain ahead of the curve – or at least on the curve – and stay up-to-date enough.

At a more practical level, who would want my expertise? How would they find me – or, indeed, how would I find them? I had always shunned networking, regarding it as somewhat self-centred and inauthentic, and I wondered with hindsight if this had been an altogether sensible strategy, but it was too late. I hadn't really built up a set of work relationships outside my organisation that I could call upon once I left. I had a vague idea I would set myself up as a consultant of some kind, but hadn't worked out at all what this would mean in practice.

At first, I was rather too brusque in my response after my 'retirement' when people reached out to me to offer a friendly shoulder or a sympathetic ear. I found it very difficult to take advice about a situation I was struggling to manage. For so long, I had been the one to give advice and be in control. The situation felt very unfamiliar and uncomfortable. I wish I had been able to tuck my fear away and been less defensive in those early conversations with others who were doing their best to help me.

Fortunately, my ego stopped getting in the way as I realised there was no (good) alternative, so I did swallow my pride and reach out to people. It was such a happy surprise. People genuinely tried to be helpful and, before long, I had a number of potential options to explore. It turned out that the hurdle had not been that there were no options out there, but that I did not have eyes to see them. All I had to do was open my eyes, which had proved easier said than done!

My realisation that opening up to others was the route to exploring new things gave me more confidence to think through for myself what I might want to do. Stepping out of the linear mindset that had become the norm in my approach to my work

was the real start of my transition. Now, with some more practice, I could begin to see that I had a whole world of possibilities
to explore!

Looking back at what did and didn't work for you in the past
can provide many clues about what kind of new things might
work for you now or in the future. The exercises in Chapter 7
provide a map to this treasure by getting you to explore what
'old' satisfactions will still need to be met in your Third Life,
although maybe in a different way, as well as helping you
rediscover the areas that you enjoyed but, for one reason or
another, didn't have room to pursue or develop.

STEP FOUR

Time to try out some new things – experimenting with
new behaviour, testing and learning

Developing and playing with new competences

As children, we learn new competences through play, like
building a brick castle and learning about balance and gravity.
However, when we become adults, we have a tendency to
dismiss play as 'childish' and lose the ability to use it. Play, in
reality, is a serious business: it means opening oneself up to
new possibilities, but requires being prepared to face uncertainty and vulnerability as part of the process of learning. The
attempt to be 'grown-up' at all times can lead to our cutting off

CHANGING GEAR

opportunities to learn through play – or, if play sounds too daunting, through new experiences! We explored the importance of play in 'Exploring, experimenting and playing' in Chapter 2.

There are many ways of understanding ourselves and who we are. Perhaps the simplest is the behaviourist view that we are simply a set of habits: routines that have been reinforced and repeated into something we call 'who I am'. We are what we do, and we do who we are. Changing those habits and routines is one method of helping yourself to make a transition. The management consultant Richard Pascale describes how 'adults are more likely to act their way into a new way of thinking than to think their way into a new way of acting'. But you can only do that if you (and possibly those around you) feel safe enough with tolerable levels of uncertainty.

Deliberately unbalancing oneself by playing with novel experiences forces us to play with new possibilities and helps to build the capability to explore. It can be something relatively minor, like wearing a new piece of clothing (it's amazing how stressful some of us find going to work without wearing a suit or make-up!), or it could be something more significant, such as embarking on a new friendship or attending an event we might otherwise not have bothered with.

We are only likely to experiment if we feel sufficiently safe to do so, and people vary enormously in this regard. Some seek novelty and risk, others seek to avoid it. However, trying to remain completely safe will cut off the possibility of new experiences. We talk of learning as an unequivocally good thing, but you can only learn if you acknowledge that you do not currently have the answer or know the solution, and this necessarily involves a degree of uncertainty and anxiety.

As quoted earlier in the book, the poet John Keats called this state of uncertainty 'remaining in mysteries and doubts without restless reaching after fact and reason', which he believed was the source of Shakespeare's creativity. Albert Einstein put it slightly differently; when asked how he was capable of coming up with such clever ideas, he explained that his technique was to stay with the problem longer than anyone else. Their issue, he explained, was that they kept coming up with answers prematurely and therefore cut themselves off from deeply understanding the problem.

Knowing that the best way to find the 'new' is to experiment, and also knowing that this is unlikely to happen quickly, should mean you can relax and play! In Chapter 2, we acknowledged that the idea of 'playing' can feel daunting, but trying to rush to an answer without giving yourself time to explore and experiment, with the expectation of some failure along the way, is to deny yourself the opportunity to be more different than you thought you could be! And anyway, the chances are you will not have the choice, because, as we keep saying, human beings take time to change – like it or not!

Who have I been? Who am I now? Who do I want to be next? These are the unavoidable questions that face people going through a transition. For almost all of us, they cannot be answered either quickly or easily. A person who has had a structured and demanding job or jobs for many years has not needed – or, indeed, had the spare capacity – to think about these questions, other than in the context of how to move forward along the path they are already on. Exploring, experimenting and playing are the ways to unblock and open up new possibilities. They are also ways to have some fun!

People are very different in their preparedness to enter their Third Lives. Some, like Suzanna below, have unfulfilled dreams or ideals to bring alive. Others, like Peter, have an intended purpose to fulfil. Others still face the daunting yet exciting prospect of a blank page. Everyone embarking upon changing gear has the opportunity, within whatever life or practical constraints they have, to experiment and explore the new in order to discover what might become their new normal.

SUZANNA

I had always promised myself that I would take up painting when I had time. I had loved drawing at school and was told I had a talent for it. Well, now was that time! It was a long while since I had been taught anything; I had become the teacher. With not a little trepidation, I searched for art classes I could attend. It was quite a shock to discover the talent my teachers had seen at school seemed to have left me somewhere along the way! It was even more of a shock to feel such a fish out of water in the classes.

Fortunately a really kind classmate took pity on me and suggested having a coffee. All my instincts were to reject the sympathy and nurse my uncomfortable feelings alone. Thank goodness for my manners, which, to my surprise, found me accepting. On the face of it, the classmate was not my kind of person, but when he confided that he had found the early classes a torture, I breathed a small sigh of relief. Then he went on to explain he took up art as a way to help provide some small measure of distraction from his son's cancer treatment. Suddenly, my discomfort zoomed into perspective. I was lucky: I had had a broadly happy career and my family life was really very good.

It was just the kick I needed to stop worrying about who I was going to become. This virtual stranger, who offered kindness to me when it was he who deserved the kindness, helped me to see I needed to grasp the opportunity in front of me. I had to embrace the new and welcome it with open – and also friendly

– arms! I needed to shake off the stuffy me and re-engage with the whole world, not try to cling on to the edge of the world I had inhabited for such a long time.

I asked my daughter to go shopping with me and help me choose some casual clothes that would make me feel a bit less of a fish out of water in my art class. She took up my challenge with gusto, and I feared I had bitten off more than I could chew, but I should have trusted her, because she showed such consideration and love that I felt very emotional. I am also now the proud owner of a rucksack and cannot imagine how I ever managed without one! The whole experience of reinventing my look has made me feel freer and more carefree, a feeling I had lost.

I have now also taken up archery, again something I had also loved when I was young. In doing so, I met another group of different but also good people, giving me the blinding insight that there are many great people out there for the finding!

PETER

Values had always mattered to me. I had championed a number of Corporate Social Responsibility initiatives, which led to some very good work being done by our people in the community. My role had been to champion and oversee this. I imagined that, when I gave up my full-time role, I would go on to sit on the boards of charities and help direct them.

Soon after I joined the ranks of the underemployed, I met the CEO of a very innovative charity who said she was looking for volunteers, not board members, which was not what I had expected!

My first instinct was to explain to her that I could add most value by taking a strategic perspective, but I could see this would not be a welcome response. Against my instincts, I found myself agreeing to commit a day a week. It was an open-ended commitment and I was clear that I soon expected to be too busy to do this for very long.

In the first few weeks, I kept sending her reports on what I thought the charity could do better overall, which she politely thanked me for, while always asking what I was learning personally about the specific volunteering activities I was undertaking. In turn, I politely ignored her questions!

Then, one day, I found myself in a situation that was quite distressing, and I found it hard to keep a distance. Suddenly I was not just looking intellectually at what the charity was set up to do; I became very emotionally involved in why it was needed.

At work, I had never been close enough to the front line to experience this or to see that it was essential for a charity of this kind to have a deep understanding of the 'customer interface' in order to make the best decisions and provide the best service. It was a light-bulb moment for me.

The next time I emailed the CEO, it was to tell her that I had now 'got it' and that this meant I wanted to continue my volunteering, and – no doubt to her relief – that I would stop trying to change the charity from the top down.

The experience also made me see other situations differently. It was not going to transform me overnight, but it helped me learn to make less one-dimensional decisions and to be more open to new possibilities going forwards. How grateful I was that the CEO had kept her faith in me and not written me off after our first meeting.

The exercises in Chapter 7 are primarily designed to help you reflect on the work you have done in your full-time career, but they could also be used to assess what you have enjoyed and what you might be good at as you explore new possibilities. Equally they might help you to see what may not work for you.

Actions for your progress

STEP FIVE

Letting go and endings – accepting the inevitable pain of loss and feeling naked

Confucius said: 'By three methods we may learn wisdom: first, by reflection, which is noblest; second, by imitation, which is easiest; and third by experience, which is the bitterest.'

Our attachments to ways of doing things and of thinking and behaving in certain ways are powerful, and letting them go always means a sense of loss – even for things and people we are pleased never to see again. Until you let go, you cannot move forward. Facing up to the necessary changes you want to make, or will need to make, requires making space for the new to emerge.

Our inherent drive to survive and to seek control and familiarity means that established behaviours, relationships and attitudes will be held on to even if they are no longer functional or adaptive. If we are to make a transition, then the anxieties associated with not changing (the imperative to survive) must be greater than the discomforts of transition (bobbing about on the ocean, losing face, feeling ineffective or threats to your identity).

As you begin to change who you are and who you might be, there is inevitably an analogous feeling of being somewhat stripped bare. Even if you are not bothered by power or status or appreciation of your expertise, or whatever you value in how others see you, this can still happen. When you are not quite sure what others will see, as you let go of the old, before you have a firm hold on the new, you are bound to feel a bit 'naked' at the very least. How you find yourself responding to this is, of course, very useful when it comes to building your understanding of what mattered to you – and will matter to you – as you go forwards.

The stress of change

Positive change can be exciting, but it can also trigger stress reactions. In fact, the body probably doesn't distinguish that well between change that is good and change that is bad. Either kind of change can result in difficulty in relaxing and even insomnia. Loss triggers pain reactions in the same part of the brain that is triggered by physical pain.

Pain is the body's way of alerting you that something is wrong. However, your mind can decide that the pain is actually good and choose to override the body's natural reaction to it: for example, when you're working out in the gym. When we say that pain can make you stronger, we do not mean that the pain itself makes you stronger, but that the rebuilding process, like building muscle strength, can make you more resilient. This means that pain only makes you stronger, if you also develop as a result of the experience. Just like in the gym, this means staying with the pain rather than avoiding it, denying it or dulling it. Mental pain is no less painful, and may be more so, than physical pain. The pain reaction itself is an instruction to the body to avoid the source of the pain, but sometimes the rider needs to step in and override the elephant's natural reactions. Staying with and pushing through the pain can result in psychological development and greater resilience.

Avoiding it, or using methods to dull the pain, will nullify any learning. The first days of school can be painful for many, but by going through that pain we learn that being separate from our mother or mother figure is not catastrophic – and, indeed, that becoming more independent has satisfactions of its own.

Research into the phases of loss over the past fifty years have established that there is a predictable sequence of reactions, as illustrated in the diagram on page 199. And even though you, the rider, may be overjoyed to be coming to the end of your career and starting out on a new phase of life, don't forget that the elephant may be sadder than you think to be leaving behind old ways. It is quite normal to go through a phase of depression after leaving a full-time career. Indeed, it is a time of stress and vulnerability, physically as well as mentally, as evidenced by a higher incidence of physical illness, even heart attacks at this time. According to the Holmes and Rahe Stress Scale, coming to the end of your career is one of the ten most stressful live events.

Some of those reading this book will have experienced deep loss and mourning due to the loss of someone they loved beyond measure. Although experiencing the loss of your career and mourning it does not typically have the same intensity, it is also very real. For those whose identity is largely defined by their job, it can be incredibly traumatic when this ceases to be the case.

The stories of Jonathan and Claire that follow illustrate very different situations, but both acknowledge the sense of loss and need for acceptance involved in leaving a job you have loved.

I had planned to leave in a very well-coordinated way to mini-mise the disruption to my clients and my people. The business model at our consulting firm relied upon continuity and excellent execution. But the best-laid plans have a habit of changing, and I found myself having to announce my departure ahead of the intended date. Initially I had mixed feelings. My main focus was on reassuring everyone that there were well thought-out plans to ensure no disruption when I did leave, but behind that, I also felt an initial quiet excitement that my new life was about to start and the period of limbo where confidentiality had been key was over. So I felt a mixture of deep concern and some relief.

However, very soon, another emotion emerged. Although I had no doubts about my decision, I was now face to face with the loss of what had been a hugely important part of my life. And, to make it harder, my competitors wasted little time in waving me goodbye – very prematurely, as it turned out, due to the best-laid plans having been unlaid!

To my shock, I found myself protesting too much that I was still a player. I knew I did not want to continue and would not do so, but letting go was so much tougher than I had anticipated, exacerbated by the timing glitch. However much my logical brain told me this was even better than I had planned, and as such a very good thing, my emotional brain was trying to repeat a pat-tern of many years and keep me doing and being what I had been.

I will never know if I would have felt differently under dif-ferent circumstances, but I suspect that planning to jump and taking the leap are unavoidably different things!

After some months of feeling very unsettled, I began to find a new sense of equilibrium and the excitement I'd been feeling about my next chapter started to return.

By the time I did come to say my goodbyes, I already had one emotional foot out of the door and, looking back, I can see that this made my actual leaving much easier than it probably would have been otherwise. So maybe what became the new best-laid plan was, in reality, better for me.

Over the next couple of years, my resolve was tested hard, and there were a couple of times when I came close to looking back. However, on both occasions, I had enough focus on my new future that I was able to let go of the old.

I still miss my old colleagues, especially all the laughter we shared, but I have no regrets.

CLAIRE

It took some time before my career settled. I had studied psychology and experimented in a number of related fields before settling on a very specialist area within the hospice movement. My unit developed some innovative and, over time, successful interventions to help families through some incredibly tough situations.

The work was deeply rewarding but it was also emotionally draining. Our organisation had been very insightful and together we developed support mechanisms to help all the patient-facing team members cope with the trauma they were witnessing. This was fundamental to the success we achieved and everyone felt huge emotional commitment and loyalty to the unit itself and the work we were doing within it. Personally, I was extremely proud of all we had achieved and felt a deep satisfaction in having pioneered some groundbreaking work.

Then a new director was appointed for the overall organisation, and my unit reported to her. This person had a managerial and administrative background and was not a qualified psychologist. She had little appreciation for the subtlety of our work or how hard-won our progress had been. In less than two years her organisational and management changes had impacted upon us in a seriously negative way. The morale in the unit was lower than I had ever seen it and we began to see some staff burnout, something I had known from the start would affect the results for our patients. I expressed my concerns to the director, but she prioritised other things over our unit. In the end, after what felt like a long fight, I was old enough to retire and I felt I had no choice but to go.

To arrive at the end of such a satisfying career in such an unsatisfying way was pretty devastating.

I struggled hard for the best part of two years, swinging between feeling relieved to be out, immense frustration at my helplessness to fight the changes the director made, and real anger at the loss for patients and their families. As a psychologist, I know about the grieving process, but going through it was still hard.

Eventually, time did give me perspective and I learned to accept that I had done all I could, despite it not being enough. Gradually, I started to let go of all my pent-up emotion and began to focus on all the good my unit had done when it was working at its best. I could then focus on myself and how I wanted my life to evolve.

There are no specific exercises related to this in Chapter 7, but in their own way, all the exercises are about helping yourself to move on. The main 'exercise' here is to allow time to take its course and to recognise that the sense of loss and mourning you feel for who you were, or who you felt you were, is a very real, reasonable and human thing. Another 'exercise' is to open up to this entirely normal state of affairs and to share your feelings with others. Such a well-worn phrase, but a problem shared is definitely a problem, if not halved, then at least reduced.

STEP SIX

Becoming your new self – practice makes (nearly) perfect

Building sustained, conscious competence

Hopefully, by now, you are buoyed by a sense of excitement for your new approaches and activities. For those who love learning, this should be energising and may be starting to give you confidence in your chosen path or paths. Depending on what you are doing and how you take your cues from the world, you should be able to feel others around you responding positively to you – at least some of the time!

Crucially, it is a time to be kind to yourself and to be your own champion. There will, inevitably, be moments or longer periods where you question what you are doing and why. Noticing what triggers this could be helpful in helping yourself not to be knocked off course. Even those closest to you are unlikely to 'have your back' all the time, as they, of course, will have their own needs.

Finding the right ways to build your own resilience may mean drawing on some of your coping mechanisms of old or developing new ones – whatever works best for you. Try to also focus on being your own best friend, looking out for yourself and doing things that make you feel good.

Just like being in the gym, practising takes both emotional and physical energy, so – without stretching the analogy too far – make sure you pay attention to your energy levels and ideally have your equivalent of a 'personal trainer', i.e. someone who is there at your side, encouraging you and giving advice. Also, work out what or who might serve as your sports massage therapist/physio when things don't go exactly to plan!

The key to sustained change is being intentional and deliberate. There is a considerable body of research to support the notion that practice that is purposeful, stretching and systematic is best for achieving long-term change. Practice that merely involves mindless repetition is not effective in the same way. Think back to your school days: how much did mindless repetition, whether this was in class, on the sports field, or in the music room, actually achieve? Practice that stretches and challenges (and, ideally, is tailored to the particular individual) produces lasting change. Design a process that will take you where you want to get to and concentrate on the process rather than the distant goal, which may simply be dispiriting as you focus on the distance yet to go. Having some metric, even as simple as an idea of where are you on a scale of one to ten, gives you a sense of how you're doing, where you're trying to get to and what the gap is. Setting milestones and celebrating your achievements will help you along your way. You, or at least the elephant you, must be motivated and exert effort to achieve a specified goal, otherwise you will just get lost in good intentions. To stress, this is about positive movement, not perfection!

Trying new stuff stretches and develops us, but, just like the gym, overdoing it may dishearten you and reinforce the status quo. If the discomforts of learning and the fears of failing are too great, then we shut down. We need to have a degree of confidence in our success; having someone to believe in and encourage us, whether a friend, a teacher or a coach, can be a valuable, even indispensable, support.

However, it won't all be plain sailing, there will be good days and weeks, and less good ones. Like the game of Snakes and Ladders (or Chutes and Ladders in the USA), you will have your ups and downs. The game was invented in India and encapsulates the Hindu philosophy of a life journey, contrasting *karma* and *kama*, destiny and desire, which, in Western terms, becomes snakes and ladders. The rational, ladder-climbing rider and the slippery, emotional elephant. This game is the origin of the phrase 'back to square one'. Ultimately, it is about acquiring the wisdom and acceptance that, although on occasion you might feel you have taken one step forwards and two or more backwards, your overall trajectory is still forwards. This helps when you feel dispirited.

There are those who take some time to feel they are, on balance, moving up more ladders and not encountering as many snakes, and life is not always fair or easy. But, given time, effort and persistence, together with a little faith, hopefully there is a way forwards for every reader. Iain and Philip below have had different but relatively gentle experiences as they have embarked upon changing gear and moving into their Third Life.

IAIN

Family has always been enormously important to me, but my business grew faster than I had ever expected and while, in the end, it has brought some financial reward, I have some sense of lost time with my family.

My wife has always had a fantastic eye for interior design and, over the years, all our neighbours and friends have been amazed at how she has made our houses look so good – never more so than in the early days of our marriage, when we had very little money.

Our daughter was always a self-starter and has a successful career in the music industry. Our son, however, is severely dyslexic and has not found life as easy. He has my commercial nous and his mother's sense of style and design, but struggled to find his niche. The area where he had spent most time was working for an estate agent. So, when I sold my business and found myself at something of a loose end, with some money in the bank, I suggested to him that the three of us went into partnership and experiment with buying some property and doing it up to sell.

Our new business is nearly two years old now. It is still early days and the property market is not great where we live, but the early signs are encouraging. We are all learning – not only what to buy and what will make it sell best, but also how to work together.

My wife and I are determined this should be led by our son, supported by us, and not the other way round. So far, the ups have outweighed the downs. Ably assisted by my wife, I have learned to ask, not tell! My son is learning to trust his own judgement and it is wonderful to watch his confidence grow.

Of the three of us, I have had the most to learn. I missed my business terribly at the start and, of course, I missed being the boss. I had not expected that early period to be so emotionally tough. My business was in manufacturing and I knew it inside out. We owned our own building, but apart from that, there was not much in terms of transferrable skills other than basic commercial understanding. However, knowing I needed to do my best to get it right for our family has made my commitment to trying unwavering.

I do not know yet how successful this new business will be, and on my darker days I do worry about that. However, I also know I am delighted I took the risk and tried. Yes, we are incredibly fortunate to be able to do this, but our retirement funds will be a lot smaller if we fail, so it is not at all risk-free for us. Not trying, though, would have been a risk too – and that was a risk we decided not to take.

PHILIP

Having spent my career as a lawyer, I wanted to use what I had learned in a different way. I was happy to discover there were a number of ways in which I could do this. None of them were at all prestigious, but after wrestling with giving up my status as a high-flying lawyer, this was not my priority. I wanted to do something where I could see it would make a difference.

After trying a few things, I settled on two areas: coaching young lawyers and working as a 'buddy' to prisoners for the Prison Reform Trust. Both required training and I discovered that, not only could I learn new tricks, I could also enjoy doing so.

The contrast between the two pursuits was huge and this made each more enjoyable for me.

After a couple of years, I really felt comfortable in my new skin. I could see the difference I was able to make to the individuals I helped and could also see myself becoming more effective over time. I was invigorated by almost every one of my clients and, although the idea was that I was helping them, I felt they were helping me, too. I was becoming a more emotionally alive and empathetic person, traits that would not have been easily attributed to me in the past. Not that I was unkind or unfeeling, but I can see now that I was somewhat detached.

Much as I had in my early years as a lawyer, I could now see many happy years ahead of me, honing my skills and deepening my expertise.

There were two key differences this time in comparison to when I first became a lawyer. First, I felt much more emotionally connected to my work and involved at a very individual level, something which gave me increasing satisfaction. It felt as if the more I gave, the more I got back. Secondly, I had a whole new hinterland in my life. I spent three days a week in my new 'work', but I had won back the other two days for myself.

Not only had I been able to find a new and satisfying kind of 'work', I had also been experimenting in the rest of my life. I had always loved being taken sailing by friends, so I signed up for a dinghy sailing course and, during the summer months, plan to indulge my more competitive nature by racing. It has to be admitted that my skill as a sailor is rather mixed, and I shall not be troubling the upper levels of the dinghy racing scene any time soon! But I find it huge fun just trying.

When I think back, I know that, in fact, it was not all plain sailing: it just feels like that now. In the early days of letting go and not being sure about what I was going to do, and be, the water felt pretty choppy!

The exercises in Chapter 7 can be used to revisit areas where you get comfortable less quickly, or as a benchmark against which to think about your progress and maybe revise or evolve some of the things you are doing.

Assessing your situation

STEP SEVEN
Enjoying a new sense of poise and balance

Conscious competence becoming unconscious competence

As you start to feel you are 'swimming in new waters' with renewed energy, you will become more comfortable with who you are becoming or have become, feeling that your personal values, behaviours and attitudes are more in harmony.

By now, you are beyond moving into your Third Life and actually living it. It should be a chance to relax and feel good about the 'new you' or your new way of being. If this is the case, hooray! This phase is the 'new normal'! However, we all know that life means good and bad days and we might have to remind ourselves of this and take a compassionate attitude when one falls short of the ideal.

More specific to being in the early phases of your Third Life, maintaining change requires strategies for dealing with falling back into old patterns, and being compassionate towards ourselves when we inevitably fail to maintain a change as well as we might wish.

This is the danger zone in the transition process, and most failures to make sustained change happen here. The pull of the certainties of the old and the safety of the comfort zone beckon when uncertainties and fears of the unknown come to the fore.

For Martin and Caroline, becoming unconsciously competent at living their new lives took some adjustment, but both found their own way to be at peace with the new them.

MARTIN

Making the move from being an executive to becoming a non-executive was one I had always expected to make. When I took on my last role, I said I would not stay for more than six years. In the event, I stayed for seven years in order to complete an acquisition that put my company in a much stronger position for the future.

In preparation for this, I had taken on a non-executive board role and a charity trustee role. I thought this would prepare me for the future, and I was very happy that I had done it. I watched my fellow directors and trustees and tried to learn from their experiences. I could see how over-contributing was very frustrating for the CEO and other board members, and equally how too narrow a contribution was not adding enough value. In addition, I was surprised at how some were too focused on their own interests or agendas and not those of the company. Being a good non-executive contributor was something that needed to be learned.

When my seven years were finally up, I was keen to have secured enough non-executive roles to move to. Like many others leaving a demanding leadership role, I feared having nothing to do and being "label-less". I also wanted to feel a sense of purpose and belonging, both of which had been important to me in my executive career.

I realise now that I failed to think about what I might explore and enjoy outside work. It was not on my radar.

CHANGING GEAR

I was offered lots of advice about not taking the first thing that came along and taking a breather before committing. *You will feel different when you have stopped*, I was reliably assured. I did not believe this, or that just because something came along quickly meant that it would automatically be wrong. Anyway, I was in a hurry and, despite being reassured that I would receive lots of approaches, underneath I was scared that it might not happen. In making decisions for my business, I could be objective and un-emotional, but when it came to launching myself into the world for the first time since I did the 'milk round', my judgement seemed to become more emotional and lose objectivity. I now know this is a well-trodden path – or should I say trap? Given my time again, I would have sought more well-informed input and advice and taken a more rational perspective – at least, I think I would!

Scared to wait, I joined the boards of two companies and retained the two non-executive roles I already had. This was not the worst decision, but it was not the best, either. One of the two new roles was a reasonably good decision, but the other was not. I had not done enough homework on either the company or myself. I learned that I needed to really think about what made the right fit for me, and to consider what my longer-term goal was. I also needed to think about what I wanted from the rest of my life. I was simply in too much of a hurry – and, secretly, too insecure – to put myself in what I perceived to be a risky position.

These were invaluable lessons and I was relieved to discover I had a 'guardian angel'. The company whose board I felt I'd made a mistake by joining was taken over, leaving me home free. This gave me time and space, which I then took to think through how I wanted my portfolio to develop and also, crucially, how I wanted my life as a whole to develop.

Once I was ready, I began looking for other roles. Now I have a complementary mix of non-executive roles that build on my experience but which also help to build new experience and expertise in operating in a non-executive capacity. These days, I know I need to make time to reflect on how well I am contributing, but also on how well the board is contributing to my own development and sense of wellbeing.

Outside of my new 'work' roles, I am expanding my horizons. A chance encounter has led to me volunteering at a local museum and rediscovering my long-lost passion for architecture. I am currently considering working towards becoming a city guide, which is something I would never have considered until very recently. I am determined to keep opening up my horizons rather than keeping them narrow or, worse still, closing them down.

CAROLINE

I would not have recognised myself today even five years ago! I feel like a different person and, in almost every way, I am. I have gone from full-on to full-off!

Once I had entertained the thought, my decision to retire came quite quickly, if not easily. I had been lucky enough to have an amazing career as a top banker and adviser. I loved what I did and loved the pleasure of being able to give great advice as much as the thrill of a deal.

Between us both having full-on jobs, my first marriage, which produced my wonderful children, ended in a fairly amicable split. My second husband was also very driven, but we met understanding what we each were rather than growing to discover we were not compatible.

My dream was to swap work for home and family. Beyond that, I had not spent much time planning how it would work, as I was too busy to do so. Everyone I talked to told me I would find it very hard, and when I protested that I would be fine, they said 'Just wait and see'. My family were equally sceptical!

However, I not only proved them wrong – I proved myself wrong, too. I swapped work not just for my family, but also for my friends and myself. I threw myself into my non-work life with my usual energy and gusto and expected it to work well.

If anything, it worked too well and, before I knew it, I was as busy as I had been when I was working. I realised that I did need to prioritise, and that meant deciding what mattered to me most. It was not as easy as I thought it would be, because I had spent so long working hard I did not really know what I would enjoy the most and how to do less.

I started with my family, principally my husband and my daughter, who lived close by and whose children were still at school locally. My daughter did not know what to expect and was careful not to be too demanding, but I found that unhelpful. After a few months, I sat her down and said, 'I want to help you with your children, what would be most useful to you?' To my delight, she said that me collecting her youngest from school and giving her tea on the days she worked would be ideal. Seeing much more of my favourite grandchild was no hardship and I readily agreed, with the caveat that I would sometimes take holidays in term time! This also gave me an anchor for my week.

I then asked my husband what he would like us to do together. We both had a love of music and this prompted us to plan further in advance and to be much more discerning and organised about what concerts we wanted to go and see.

Once these priorities were clear, I then planned some more 'me' time with friends. Of course, I was still 'running my diary'!

Over time, I have settled into a much more relaxed way of being and hardly recognise myself. I really do feel like a new 'me' and one which I love just as much as I loved the work me, possibly even more!

How lucky I have been to have found a wonderful new life that is such a contrast to my old one but, in its own way, in its own time, equally fulfilling for me as a person.

The last exercise in Chapter Seven uses the metaphor of being your own CEO as a perspective from which to view your new life. It also highlights the value of having a team around you to help you.

STEP EIGHT
Reviewing your progress

The final step of the transition process is to now review the progress you have made. It is an opportunity to review and reflect on how far you've come and what you have learned about yourself. Throughout, the book has drawn attention to the process of transition as being one of to-and-fro. Some stages may begin before others have yet to finish, and there may be overlaps. You may notice that there are stages that you haven't been through: if that's the case, it may be worth revisiting those.

Below, a series of questions are used to take a look at each stage in turn.

It may be helpful for you take some notes for yourself as you answer some or all of these questions.

Becoming AWARE of the situation you find yourself in

— Change finds us as much as we find it. Was that your experience?

— Did change creep up on you slowly before you realised it?

— Were you in any way trying to push back the tides of history?

— Was there a moment when you realised that your old career was over?

— Were you able to use your feelings as well as your thoughts as you started out on the process of transition?

— Did you have any concerns? What were they?

— How do you feel about those concerns now?

Reviewing step one:
Losing your balance – and noticing

— In retrospect, when did you first lose your balance and notice that you needed to make some changes?

— What indications were there?

— How were you thinking and feeling about embarking on the transition process?

— Was transition to your Third Life something you relished and looked forward to, or perhaps not?

— Was your work becoming a little repetitive and dull, if the truth were known? Or was it full-on and exciting right up to the end?

— Were you somewhat in denial of the need to change, or were you looking forward to creating a new life for yourself?

— What were some specific moments or events that made you realise you needed to look at your life afresh?

— What feelings did you notice yourself having?
— If you were in a bit of a fog, when did this begin to clear?

Reviewing step two:
Taking stock – looking around you and moving from alarm to curiosity

— Hopefully, you began to feel you had some choices – what did you feel they were at the time?
— Did they change over time?
— Did you explore some fantasy desires that, on reflection, turned out to be just that: unrealistic or not things you really wanted to actually do?
— Did you reflect on what you wanted to keep the same and what you wanted to change?
— How well were you able to tolerate not knowing what the future would look and feel like?
— Would you now say that you have become better at staying with the unknown?
— What patterns do you notice in yourself when faced with uncertainty?
— Have you learned to tolerate that feeling a little better?

Exploring the ALTERNATIVES for your life going forwards

— What are some of the alternatives you looked at?
— Are there some worth investigating further and reconsidering?
— Should you do some more exploring?
— Did your picture of yourself change in some way as you thought about yourself without a full-on career?
— Have you become more comfortable with that?

Reviewing step three:
Being open to the new – exploring and investigating
fresh possibilities

— Did you find time to play and explore?
— How easy did you find it to give yourself permission to do so?
— Did you discover some ambitions from an earlier phase of your life yet to be fulfilled that your Third Life might give some opportunity for?
— Are there are more opportunities to do this now?
— Did you give yourself some new experiences?
— What did you learn from them?
— How did you find being in the unknown?
— Were you able to live with the questions?
— How did you find it not having the answers?

Reviewing step four:
Time to try out some new things – experimenting with
new behaviour, testing and learning

— Did you find opportunities to explore and play with some new behaviours and try out some new skills?
— Did you find ways of using existing skills in new situations?
— Are there some more skills that you want to learn?
— Did you deliberately provide yourself with some novel experiences to explore what might or might not suit you?
— Did you experiment with new situations that you might find stimulating or challenging?
— Which seem to fit with your new life?
— What did you learn about what didn't suit you?
— There are three questions which it might be worth

asking again: Who have I been? Who am I now? Who do I want to be next?

— Did you explore some alternatives which turned out to be blind alleys, and if so, what made them so?

Taking ACTIONS which move you closer to the life you might have

— Were there some elements of your old life that you wished to continue with, albeit in the new context?
— What were those elements?
— Have you managed to find forms of expression for those elements?
— Are there others that still need to find expression?
— Did you identify some new skills you wanted to learn and develop?

Reviewing step five: Letting go and endings – accepting the inevitable pain of loss and feeling naked

— How did the ending go?
— Did you experience feelings of loss as you exited your old career?
— What form did they take?
— Were there things you knew you would miss?
— Were there regrets about some things you didn't achieve in your full-on career?
— How have you dealt with these?
— Is there still some work to be done in letting go of them?
— Are there opportunities to achieve these things in a new context?
— Perhaps there are some things you thought you would leave behind but realise you don't want to?

— Have you found avenues for their expression?
— If you had a position of leadership, were you content with leaving that behind, or did you want to continue in a leadership role?
— If so, have you found a setting in which to do that?
— Leaving familiar situations and people you may have known for years can be a cause of stress – what was your experience of this?
— How did you deal with that?

Reviewing step six: Becoming your new self – practice makes (nearly) perfect

— Have you had the experience of a somewhat different self emerging out of the cocoon of the transition process?
— How would you describe the changes in yourself?
— Are there changes that you need to make sure you practise and sustain, or are you out the other side already?
— Did you experience a sense of 'Snakes and Ladders', with some ups and some downs?
— Would you say your character has changed in any way?
— Have others noticed changes in you?
— Have you asked them?

ASSESSING your new situation and learning for the future

— Did you find yourself feeling a new sense of poise and balance?
— Was your sense of your personal values and ethics a help?

— It's now all about maintaining changes that you have made and not slipping back into old habits – have you built in ways of keeping yourself on the forward path?

Reviewing step seven: Enjoying a new sense of poise and balance

— Did you notice yourself feeling more skilful with your new ways of life?
— Do you feel you are now 'swimming in new waters'?
— Should you venture forth more than you already have done?
— What and who will support you as you take the risk of swimming in different parts of the sea?
— Looking back on it all, did you manage to be compassionate with yourself when things were not easy?
— Are there patterns of self-doubt and self-criticism that you could usefully ditch?
— Have you found yourself being drawn back to the comfort zone of familiar people and activities when really what you need to do might be to move on?
— How far have you been able to discuss your transition process with those closest to you?
— How have they reacted?
— Have they found it difficult at times as well?
— Are there some more conversations that it would be worth having?
— Have you developed strategies for coping with the inevitable setbacks and failures in your experiments? There could be useful lessons in that for your future.

If the transition process has made sense to you, remember that there will be future transitions ahead of you. The notes you have made now about what you have learned about yourself in managing this transition will probably be useful in the future.

Hopefully, you have enjoyed changing gear and found that, as you progressed through the stages, you learned some things about the differences between external changes and internal transition. It's likely that there is still some work to do. Using the eight steps of the transition process will hopefully help you on the next phase of your explorations and development. Transition is an iterative process, a repeated cycling between the different steps, more or less in the order we've laid out, but not always. Returning to and repeating steps – or parts of steps – is all part of the process. Trust your gut as well as using your head as you continue on your journey to make best use of your experiences.

7

A toolkit for changing gear – exercises for you to do

This chapter provides you with a toolkit of questions to ask yourself, and exercises for reviewing your life so far, both at work and beyond. These can help you identify some principles for creating the life you want to lead in the future.

While the exercises can be done sequentially, there is no need to do this if you would rather pick and choose those that seem most relevant.

Some people enjoy completing exercises like these, others are a bit ho-hum about the whole idea – but encouraging yourself to at least have a go could lead you to a happy surprise full of insights and ideas. Answering a series of structured questions is often a good way to get a bit deeper into the issues you will need to consider, and can create a renewed sense of purpose and meaning in your new life.

There are some things about your current life that you will want to continue with, finding new ways and opportunities to express these things after a full-on career. There are other things that you will want to let go of – although remember that letting go, as we've explained throughout this book, is not always so easy. It can be hard, for example, to let go the things you don't enjoy but are good at, and so nevertheless give you a temporary hit of accomplishment. At the same time, though, there are things that you do enjoy but are not so good at that you now may want to spend some time developing.

Rather than taking a 'me at work' versus 'me at home' perspective, try to view yourself as a whole person with a range of current activities expressed both in work and beyond that give you a sense of enjoyment and flourishing. Changing gear provides an opportunity to review which values are most important to you and what principles you wish to live by going forwards.

These exercises will help you to develop a clearer picture in your mind of the life you would like to be leading in the future.

In the introduction of the book, we talked about how the reality of changing gear necessarily raises many questions, including:

— Who am I now?
— What would I like to define me in the future?
— What might my options and choices be?
— How will I get from here to there?
— What will the impact be on those around me?
— How can I be the 'best me' in this next phase of my life?

This chapter will help you to begin to answer these questions.

Things to help you in each step of the transition process

Here are some ideas to try, using the Eight-step Transition Process as a framework. You can work through them or pick and choose what grabs your interest.

FOR STEP ONE

Things you can do to develop awareness

Notice – The desire to make a transition is often a secondary reaction to changes that have already taken place in yourself, in your family, your workplace or in your environment: a disruption to the status quo. So, the first step is to notice disruption in the form of the unusual, the strange, the unexpected or unfamiliar, whether in yourself, in others or in the world. Has anything or anybody surprised you recently?

Scan – Cultivate a sense of curiosity and interest in what is going on and emerging, whether within you or outside you. Developing the habit of scanning yourself, those who matter to you, and your environment, means you are more likely to notice the early indicators of disruption. As a result, you are more likely to notice things sooner rather than later. If you allow yourself to be aware and to notice a change, you can then choose how to respond. What are you finding your attention is being drawn to currently?

Open up – Often the need to deal with change is more evident to others than to ourselves. Allowing yourself to open up, even a little, to those you trust most is arguably essential, but at the very least extremely helpful. Talk out loud to others about what is going on in your head. By trying to explain the jumble of thoughts you are having, you might find yourself making a bit more sense of what is going on for you. Obviously, this conversation needs to be with a trusted person who is a good listener and will bring empathy, can avoid judgement and will provide gentle and ideally insightful challenges. The more you open up to those family and friends you trust (within reason, if you are already a talker!), the more you are likely to learn. How honest are you being with others about your feelings?

Journalling – Keep a journal in which you write down what's happened each day or week to help focus your mind on your experiences. Try not to be too judgemental in what you write, but remember nobody else will read it! So, perfectionists (i.e., most of the people reading this book!) be warned: this is not an opportunity to write your magnum opus for posterity. It's not intended for anyone else's benefit but your own!

Attention training – You will probably have heard of mindfulness, a method of focusing your attention in order to manage the continuous stream of distracting ideas and thoughts that spontaneously come into your mind. It is used by sportspeople to help them be in the present and focus on performing at their best. There are plenty of other methods, such as tai chi and relaxation techniques. If you haven't tried one of these, we suggest you experiment with one to help you learn to focus more effectively.

FOR STEP TWO

Things you can do to help you take stock

The first step is to be interested in – rather than rejecting – your experiences of what is happening to you.

Know yourself – You can learn more about yourself through various instruments, such as personality tests, learning styles inventories and strengths and values questionnaires. Exercises and tests to better understand yourself can be very helpful. Sometimes they shed new light on the hidden you in a useful way. They can also help you understand the ways in which other people are very different to you and may need a different approach. (And sometimes, they serve to demonstrate that the tests can be wrong and that you know yourself better than they do!) Some of these tests can be downloaded online at relatively low cost; for others, you may want to book some time with an expert psychologist or coach in order to get the most benefit.

Own yourself – Collect feedback on how others see you. This might feel high risk, but taking a deep breath and being brave enough to ask those whose views you would like to have can be hugely valuable data for you. They have these thoughts anyway, so all you are doing is opening the cupboard to see what is inside! A word of caution, however: make sure that you treat this feedback with respect and do not jump to setting the other person straight on why they are wrong! Take a deep breath, thank them, maybe ask questions for genuine clarification, and then reflect on whether they might possibly be right or how their feedback could be helpful to you in some way.

Be yourself – Be present. 'Being present' is a much-used phrase these days. In this context, it means paying attention to how you are interacting with what is happening in your head and in the environment around you

Explore your unlived life (or lives) – Think about what these might have looked like and use examples, e.g. 'As a child, I wanted to be a vet and I think I could have had a lovely life doing this. With a different set-up for my life, I would love to have more animals in it!'

Do a self-audit – Ask yourself:

— What in my life energises me, what depletes me?

— What do I want to keep the same, and what do I want to get rid of?

— What makes me feel happy, valued and secure?

— What really matters to me?

— How do I respond to people, to activities, to events, to specific things?

Notice how your answers fit with 'you': both the 'you' that you are and the 'you' that you would like to be.

FOR STEP THREE

Things you can do to help you to be open to the new

Talk – Talk to others who have been through a transition from a long-standing career. Ask them about how they went about this, how it felt at the time and whether there was anything they found useful during this process.

Play – Play with new attitudes. Deliberately spend time with people living in a different way to yourself. Ask them about the things they enjoy and the satisfactions they find in life.

Reflect – Think of other times in your life when you have been faced with change: how did you react then? This could include going to school or leaving school, heading to university, job or career changes and relationship changes. How do you typically manage transitions?

Explore – Explore new ideas, films, theatre, fiction, non-fiction – what have you always said you must read or find out about? Read novels which transport you to new and emotionally different places. This is all part of giving your brain new avenues to trigger new thoughts about where you have been and where you are right now.

Observe – Pay attention to what you see others doing or what others have done that you could learn from or even emulate. Go and ask them what they have learned. People are pretty much always happy to talk about their experiences and share advice.

Keep a list – Create a list of your ideas, dreams, fantasies and aspirations. Keep the list going and see how it evolves.

FOR STEP FOUR

Things you can do to try out some new things
and experiment

Surprise yourself – Deliberately give yourself new experiences. You will quickly learn that you can survive after possibly experiencing some initial discomfort or slight humiliation, and the sense of achievement in taking yourself out of your comfort zone should be a reward itself. You might even find something new to enjoy! Or – also helpful – you might learn what you do *not* want to do!

Confront a fear – Confronting a long-standing fear, such as heights, improves your confidence in facing other fears.

Be intentionally different – Try out some new behaviours. For example, if you are a natural extrovert and tend to dominate conversations, try holding back and listening and asking questions rather than giving your views. Practise being more introverted! Likewise, if you tend to hold back, try to engage more actively and be more extroverted. If you are able to multitask while doing so, observe how people react to your different approach, and also how it feels for you. What did you learn?

FOR STEP FIVE

Things you can do to help with endings and letting go

Draw up a balance sheet – What have you gained – or what do you think you will gain – from the plans you have made, and who you plan to be in your third phase? What might you have lost from your life to date? What might you still have to let go of?

Make 'gratitude visits' – Visit someone who has had a big impact on you, but whom you have never thanked. Closing this chapter will help you to move on.

Reflect on what matters to you – Decide for yourself what you really care about. Maybe shake off some old prejudices or stop doing things that take time away from the things that matter most to you. Think about who really matters to you. Does who you spend your time with match who you most care about or enjoy being with? This requires thought, resolve and politeness!

Self-care and compassion – Don't ignore common sense. Talk things through with your partner, family and friends. Watch your diet, use relaxation techniques – and be gentle on yourself.

Time for an MOT – If you experience ongoing stress – or even if you don't – consider seeking some form of professional help, such as a counsellor, coach or psychotherapist.

FOR STEP SIX

Becoming your new self

Set your own goals – Lay out what you plan to try to do over the next year or two. State your goal, then what will help you achieve it, along with some milestones that you can review.

Work with a 'change buddy' – If possible, find someone else who is also going through the same stage of life as you. Meet up to compare notes and encourage and support each other.

Keep journalling – Identify two things at the end of each day that have made you happy or given you energy and made you feel good about yourself or what you are doing. Identify one thing at the end of each day that you felt could have gone better, was not helpful or did not feel great. Reflect on what you might do differently.

Treat yourself – Managing the rider and the elephant is helped by building in some personal 'treats' when, after a bit of hard work, you make progress. Treat yourself with things you know will give you pleasure as a reward when you make progress.

Self-care – Throughout this phase, keep supporting yourself health-wise. Try to build new diet and exercise habits if you haven't already. Find the people who can be there for you to offer advice, be a shoulder to cry on and act helpfully as cheerleader for you! Having someone you are accountable to will help you stick to your programme and achieve your objectives.

Self-coaching – Many professional coaches use a simple format called the GROW model (Goal, Realities, Options, Will), which was first devised by McKinsey consultant Max Landsberg. Use this model to identify your next Goal; then explore the current Realities of where you currently are and where you wish to get to; and next consider some Options for your next steps, including their pros and cons, before making a decision on your next step. Before finishing, rate your Will to achieve your goal, on a scale of one to ten. If you rate yourself seven or below, you're less likely to achieve it. What would make it into an eight? Think about how you will manage the times when you will inevitably fall short of what you wanted to achieve, just as a professional sportsperson does.

FOR STEP SEVEN

Things you can do to build your new poise and balance, and review your progress

Keep on being kind to yourself – Remember that you need to be – or at least try to be – your own best friend. Be compassionate as well as objective. Consider what supportive things you would say to a friend or someone you love. Find those words for yourself.

Have a plan for disappointments and failure – Strive for good enough, not perfect! Go back to the goals you set yourself and make sure they were, or still are, the right fit for you.

Continue to learn, review, reflect and renew – Keep asking yourself, 'Who am I now?' Once you have crossed the transition river, it is essential to embrace this final stage of reflection. When you are established in your new life, and new behaviours, attitudes and habits are being maintained, taking time out to review and reflect on how you went through the transition to the third stage of life is a valuable thing to do. On days that are less than great for the 'new you', this gives you a framework in which to think about and reflect on what is happening, or why you might not be feeling on top of things (or, indeed, on top of the world!). Life will always continue to be a journey and we never stay completely still, but hopefully the big transition to your Third Life will be one with some significant longevity.

Be your new self with skill – Continue to develop and maintain your transition mindset. Without this, learning for your next bump in the road or next transition does not take place. Reviewing what lessons can be learned for future transitions helps to reinforce your transition mindset, which can therefore be brought to bear when you need it next. Realising that transition can be rewarding – and, for some, even fun and stimulating – should hopefully provide a source of motivation when the going gets tough the next time around, especially as you know now that you can rely on adopting the transition mindset to help you through.

List your new ways – What are the key features of your new self and life? How well are you maintaining these? Are you perhaps slipping back into some old habits and behaviours? If so, what are they?

Continue journalling – Maybe once a month, just to take stock of where you are and how you are feeling.

'External' care – Keep talking to others, both those who helped you on your 'transition journey', and those who you feel it would be good to share things with. Go back to those who gave you feedback at the beginning of your transition process and who are still close to you, and ask them for feedback again. Check in with your change buddy. Regular feedback is one of life's great gifts!

Reward yourself – Keep taking time for things that give you pleasure, and seek out new things as you grow and change. Be comfortable again, but not complacent. Keep challenging yourself as to whether you are maintaining the changes you wanted to maintain.

The lifeline exercise

This exercise will help you to identify the high points in your life: times when you have felt energised and in 'flow', as well as some of the low points, when things have been difficult and you have perhaps felt a little 'lost'.

Think of your life as a line from the day you were born right up until today, a line that goes up at times when you were feeling good about life, and down at times when you were feeling less good. Take a look at the lifeline diagram below. On the vertical axis, there is a scale from high (+5) to low (-5), with zero representing 'chugging along just fine'. Along the horizontal axis, the years of your life are broken up into five-year chunks. The purpose of this exercise is to remember as many 'high points' in your life as you can up to the present time. High points are those times you remember with some satisfaction, pride or gratitude that you were there. They are times when there was something special in terms of what you were doing and how you were involved. Include all your high points, both inside and outside work.

Concentrate on the high points rather than low points, because they tell us where our energy lies. When we look back at high points, they often occur at times when more than one or two things were going well in our lives. The reason for including low points at all is so that you can look at them in relation to the high points. The key when looking at them is to help you reflect on how you worked through them, and to think about what events triggered more positive feelings.

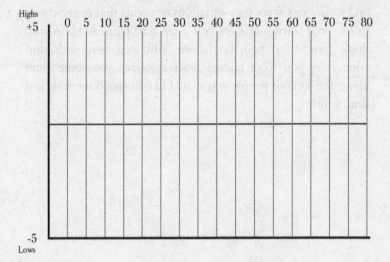

Figure 5: Lifeline

Looking at your lifeline, you can often see reoccurring positive themes in your life, and you can also see the sorts of negative events you want to avoid.

Once you have done the exercise, look at the high points and low points and ask yourself:

— What was the situation?
— Who else was there?
— How was I feeling?
— What was I doing?
— What talents was I using?
— What role was I taking?

Looking across all the high points, do any common themes emerge? Similarly, looking across all the low points, what are the themes there? What does this say about the situations you find satisfying? Were they situations or events that enabled you to use your talents or gave you a sense of flourishing? Again, think about what you were doing, who you were with, and what roles you were taking. Does this give you some clues about the sorts of people you would like to spend more or less time with?

Life and career review

Cast your mind back over your life and career and answer the following questions.

— What have I most enjoyed during my life and career?

— What have I least enjoyed during my life and career?

— What is in my 'bucket list' of things to do over the next five to ten years?

— Where have I got my sense of identity from?

— Where will I get my sense of identity from in the future?

— What communities do I currently belong to?

— What communities do I wish to belong to in the future?

— When did I feel most challenged and learn the most in my life and career?

— What challenges and learning do I want to undertake in the future?

Make a note of any reflections you have had while completing this exercise.

THE ACTIVITIES YOU HAVE PREFERRED
IN YOUR CAREER

Getting work done involves taking on a variety of different roles. Which of the following have you tended to take up during your career? There may be several, but see if you can find the primary one in order to help you think about the activities you would like to explore in your Third Life. Some roles are more task-focused, while others have a more social focus.

The Specialist – Someone who enjoys being the technical expert in a particular area.

The Creator – Someone who likes developing new ideas and approaches.

The Shaper – Someone who enjoys having impact and leading change.

The Planner – A methodical person who prefers to think before acting.

The Warrior – Someone who enjoys the fight and beating the enemy.

The Influencer – Someone who enjoys having impact through persuading others.

The Stimulator – A person who enjoys challenging the status quo, sometimes perceived as a maverick.

The Participator – The quintessential team player who prefers working with others to working alone.

The Developer – Someone who enjoys supporting others.

The Coordinator – Someone who enjoys bringing people together to achieve things.

The Assurer – Someone who enjoys working alone to check the details.

The Implementer – Someone who enjoys putting plans into action.

WHAT DID YOU DO AT WORK AND WHY?

This exercise will help you get at some of the deeper motivations behind what you have enjoyed doing in your work. It consists of a series of questions. Firstly, what exactly did you do at work? What did you spend your time on? Secondly, how did you go about that? Then, thirdly, why are these things important to you? Digging into this third question will identify the deeper motivational themes that made your work fulfilling. We have given you some examples to get you started. When you have completed the whole exercise, think about how you can fulfil these underlying motivations in the future.

How to complete this exercise

In your notebook, draw a table with headings like the one on the next page. Begin with the first question: 'What did I do at work?' Briefly note your answers in the top box of the left-hand column. Use short phrases, for example 'advised clients', 'prepared reports', or 'organised my staff'. Answer quickly, without a lot of thought. Don't be afraid to repeat yourself, but try to dig deeper as you do so.

Next, ask yourself, 'How did I do that?' For example, 'by understanding what they needed', 'by analysing the nature of the problem', or 'by helping them synchronise their activities'. Briefly note your answer in the second box in the left-hand column.

Now, ask yourself, 'And how did I do that?' For example, 'by listening and asking questions', 'by using root cause analysis', 'by resolving conflict between them'. Briefly note your answers in the third box in the left-hand column.

Finally, ask yourself once again, 'And how did I do that?'. For example, 'by tuning into what's important to them', 'by

What did I do at work?	Why is that important to me?
• *Advised clients*	• *I enjoy complex problems*
•	•
•	•
•	•

How did I do that?	And why is that important to me?
• *By understanding the problem*	• *To understand root causes*
•	•
•	•
•	•

And how did I do that?	And why is that important to me?
• *By listening and asking questions*	• *It plays to my strengths*
•	•
•	•
•	

And how did I do that?	And why is that important to me?
• *By understanding what's important to them*	• *It made my client successful*
•	•
•	•
•	•

And how did I do that?	And why is that important to me?
• *Being of practical relevance to people*	• *Helping people achieve their aspirations*
•	•
•	•
•	•

understanding the fundamental issues', 'by helping people communicate better with each other'. Write your answers in the final box in the left-hand column. This last 'how' may be difficult to answer, but try it in order to get at the deeper motivations for your work.

The left side of the chart now contains a short description of what you did, followed by your three 'How did I do that?' responses. Before you move on, read it over and look for patterns in what you have written. Note any themes that have emerged.

Now go back to your answer to the first question: 'What did I do at work?'. Turn to the right-hand column and ask yourself, 'Why is that important to me?' Note your brief response in the top box in the right-hand column. Do this quickly. Notice any feelings it evokes.

Now look at what you have written in the second box of the left-hand column. Again, ask yourself, 'Why is that important to me?' Note your response in the second box of the right-hand column.

Do the same for what you have written in the third and final boxes, writing your answers in the right-hand column.

Now take a look at what you have written on the right-hand side of the page. Do you see any patterns? Note any themes that have emerged. Did you have any strong feelings while doing this? If so, what were they?

Now try a comparison. How did all that you wrote, thought, and felt for the 'why' questions compare to your responses to the 'how' questions? The 'hows' tend towards the methodologies, the practices, the tasks involved in getting work done. The 'whys' more often lead to the *reasons* for work, its deeper meaning, the aspirations that lie behind it. This can give us an idea of the underlying purposes of our lives. Most people find the 'hows' easier to think about and talk about with others; the 'whys' seem to lead in a more personal direction. The 'hows' tend to take us deeper into the present and past; the 'whys' move us towards the future.

HOW DO YOU RESPOND TO FAILURE?

First, think of a past failure. How did you respond to it? Did you ask for help? Could you have? Were you overly concerned about what other people might think?

Now reflect on how these attitudes might be getting in the way and causing a fear of failure when it comes to the new challenges of the Third Life.

Instead of responding in your habitual ways, what could you do differently this time? Be compassionate towards yourself. Allow yourself to ask for help, rather than worrying about what other people might think. In fact, *ask* them what they think – it's rarely what you anticipate and generally they will be more generous and understanding of you than you are of yourself.

COLLECT FEEDBACK ON YOURSELF

Although this is a rather scary idea, finding out how others see you can help you identify activities that you are good at. And as we have explained, as far as the rest of the world is concerned, you are simply the impact you have on others.

Identify the six to eight people you respect the most and ask them to answer these two questions. You will probably need to give them some forewarning by sending these questions in advance. You can either do this face to face or by email.

1. How would you describe me to someone who didn't know me?

2. What are two of my strengths, and what is one thing I could get better at?

You will almost certainly be surprised by some of the things they say: hopefully positively, but not always! Review all the material you have gathered and use it to identify some themes that you could work on.

THE WHEEL OF LIFE EXERCISE

Use the Wheel of Life exercise to review the current balance of your activities and those that you wish to increase or decrease.

The idea of this exercise is to visually represent your level of satisfaction/dissatisfaction in different areas of your life. We have suggested eight areas below, but you may want to remove or add areas to fit your own circumstances. The centre of the wheel is zero and the outer rim is ten. Draw your own version of the wheel and rank your level of satisfaction with each area of your life on a scale of zero to ten, marking this in the relevant place, and then connect these up, as shown in the diagram below. You should do this exercise twice: first, showing how you would score your life currently, then secondly, how you would like your life to be. Think about how you might reduce

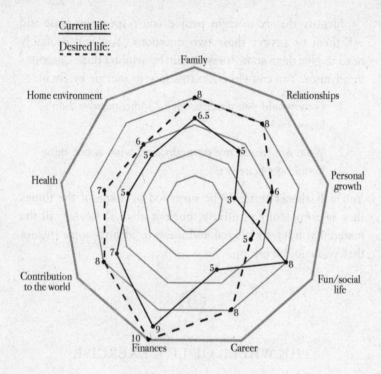

Current life: ─────
Desired life: ─ ─ ─ ─

Family
Relationships
Home environment
Personal growth
Health
Fun/social life
Contribution to the world
Career
Finances

8
6.5
6
5
8
5
6
7
5
3
7
8
5
5
8
5
9
10
8

Figure 6: The wheel of life

the gaps in the scores where they are significant. The idea isn't to score ten out of ten on everything – some areas will be relatively less important than others – but to identify areas where you want to concentrate on making some adjustments as you change gear.

IDENTIFYING YOUR STRENGTHS
AND BEST SELF

Finding your best self

Sometimes we are at our best; other times, not so much. This exercise aims to get you to describe characteristics of yourself when you are at your best. Firstly, think of some occasions when you have been at your best. Choose different periods of your life: from your childhood, teenage years, young adulthood and more recently. Think of particular incidents, and think about who was there, what was happening and what you did. Pick a range of situations: at home, at work, with friends, and perhaps when you were on your own. They need not all have been entirely positive, but they should be situations where you were at your best.

These might be times when:

— Your best qualities emerged.

— You felt fully alive, engaged, effective and free.

— You achieved more than you expected to.

What stands out for you about these experiences? Think about the attributes, qualities, strengths and talents that you showed at these times. How might you put these attributes, qualities, strengths and talents to best use?

Finding your strengths

In your notebook, write down a brief story about each of those times. What are the qualities that you found within yourself that you used to create a positive impact? Once you have completed three to four stories, identify what the theme of each story was, such as bringing people together, celebrating somebody's success, winning against the odds, taking a brave step, etc. Then identify the qualities or strengths that you were using, such as empathy, generosity or courage. Keep doing this for a while, looking at different periods of your life, until you have a list of at least seven or eight personal strengths. Finally, rank these in terms of their importance to you in order to produce your top three strengths.

Now think about these strengths in more detail.

— How could you use these strengths in your future life?

— Where might they find expression, and how could they be used to achieve some of your future goals?

— What sorts of situations bring out the best in you?

— And what kind of situations block you from using your strengths? These may be situations you will want to avoid in the future.

If you're feeling adventurous, you could try this exercise with others, by asking them to write brief stories about when they have seen you at your best on a number of occasions.

YOUR NEEDS AND MOTIVATIONS

On page 216, we talked about primal needs and social needs, and David McClelland's proposed framework of three fundamental social needs: the need to achieve, the need for relationships, and the need for power. As we explained, he argued that the importance of these needs varies from person to person.

To discover how important each of these social needs are for you, ask yourself the questions below, assigning yourself a score from one (not at all) to ten (extremely).

— **The need for achievement** – How much am I driven by the desire to do something better or more efficiently than before? This might present itself as a concern with excellence and problem-solving.

— **The need for relationships** – How much am I driven by the desire to establish and maintain close relationships, to get along with others, and to be in a group with other people?

— **The need for power and influence** – How much am I driven by the desire to have impact and be influential – to affect others, the organisations to which I belong and the world?

Is there one need for which you have recorded a higher score? That will be your fundamental need, the one that needs to be met in order for you to have a good day. Making sure there are opportunities to satisfy this need should be a significant factor in how you structure your life. If your fundamental need (or needs, as you may have more than one high-scoring need) are not met, it is likely that you will feel a lack of purpose in your life. Our desires for recognition, approval and status are shaped by these three social needs.

DISCOVERING PURPOSE AND MEANING
IN YOUR FUTURE LIFE

Consider these questions:

— 'What is my life purpose?'
— 'What sense of purpose is important to me?'

In your notebook, write down all the thoughts that pop into your mind. For each thought, ask yourself, 'What is my purpose in that?'

Keep doing this until you reach an answer that moves you deeply.

Some examples of what you might write include: helping others to grow and achieve their aspirations; creating a better world of fairness and justice; aiming for happier people in a more loving world.

At first, your answers may seem banal, but keep going. Keep asking the question 'why' until you get to a deeper level. Generally, asking 'why' five times about an activity will get you to its core purpose for you.

For example, if your first answer was 'to see more of my grandchildren', asking yourself why might deliver the answer 'to deepen my relationship with my children'. Asking 'why' again might lead you to 'to help my children and grandchildren develop their lives'. Digging still deeper, asking why once more might produce 'to create happier lives for others after I am gone'. If this statement touches you, then you have reached one possible definition of your life purpose for the next stage of your life. You may want to generalise it into 'Make the world a better place for future generations'. Write your statement down in a place where you can refer to it easily. It will provide a lodestar for decisions you will be making.

You could also try asking yourself about a time in your life when you felt lacking in purpose and meaning. What caused that? What lessons are there for you in those experiences? Does that help you to identify what to avoid in the future?

YOUR CORE VALUES

A good way to identify your core values is to reflect on your life and identify times when you have made mistakes or somehow violated an important value of yours. Another way is to give yourself the exercise of listening to and observing others, and noticing when they clearly demonstrate or express a value that is of central importance to you. A third way is to ask yourself who do you want to be of service to? Who are you living for? In other words, think about who are the most important people in your life, and consider your values in action in your relationships with them. A fourth option is to ask yourself who has taught you the most in your life. Think of the people you have known personally who have inspired you. Then think about three or four values which they have expressed in their life.

You can also get a sense of your values, and what you value, from things you admire as well as people. These could be buildings, special objects of personal relevance to you, plays, books, movies, poems or pictures. You may want to reacquaint yourself with some of the things that you value, and even spend some time learning more about them and why they are important to you.

What do you wish to achieve and be accountable for in the way you live your Third Life? What are the values that will support this?

Another way to identify your key values is to pick a time in your life when things were tough. You might even pick several of these from your childhood and teenage years, and also from your adult life. Write down what happened, including what led up to the situation and how it evolved. You might write about your parents separating when you were a child, or an important person dying, or a valued relationship ending, or a much-desired career ambition that was not achieved. Reflect on how you dealt with the situation and try to identify the key strengths that helped you get through it; these may well be the foundations of your key values in life.

When you're ready, try sharing some of your thinking with people close to you, and ask them whether there are things you've missed out.

REBALANCING HOW YOU SPEND YOUR TIME

There are things we do that we enjoy and are good at, but there are also things we are good at that we don't enjoy. We do them out of a sense of duty or habit, or just because they are unavoidable. But there are also things that we enjoy but that we are *not* so good at. This exercise is aimed at identifying some of these activities: things that you enjoy doing, and which you now have the opportunity to improve your skill at, and perhaps get deeper satisfaction from.

Look at the diagram opposite and draw your own version in your notebook. Start by listing things that you are good at and enjoy in the top right-hand box. These are the sorts of things you would do anyway, even if you weren't paid to do them: things that give you a sense of inherent satisfaction and joy. Then, in the top left-hand box, list those things that you are good at but don't enjoy. These are the things you do out of a sense of duty or habit, or perhaps because others rely upon you to do them, even though ideally you wouldn't. Create a 'not to-do list' and put these things on it. Now, in the bottom

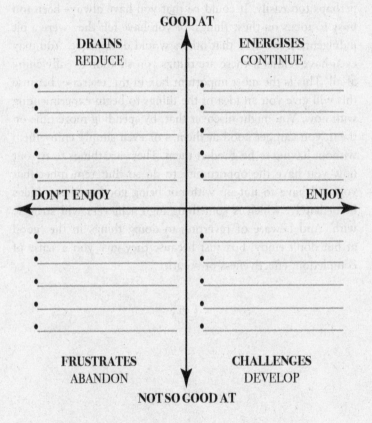

Figure 7: Rebalancing how you spend your time

left-hand box, list the things you don't enjoy and are *not* good at, but that somehow you still keep doing. Again, this might be out of a sense of duty, or a feeling that you ought to or should. These are things you should also seriously consider adding to your 'not to-do list'!

Finally, and most importantly, list the things that you enjoy but are not good at in the bottom right-hand box. These are things you have perhaps tinkered with, but never really had the time to get good at; things you might have tried but given up, perhaps too easily. It could be that you have always been too busy to focus on these things, or you have felt they were a bit indulgent, or worried that others would disapprove. You may even have felt as if these are things you shouldn't really enjoy at all. This is the most important box in this exercise, because this will give you an idea of the things to begin experimenting with now. You might discover that, by spending more time on them, you can get good at them – or even simply enjoy them without having to be good at them. These are things to try out now you have the opportunity to do so. But remember that you will have to put up with not being good at these things immediately, which is something high achievers will struggle with. And beware of reverting to doing things in the 'good at but don't enjoy' box just because they give you a sense of completion, effectiveness or security.

LIFE IN PERSPECTIVE – DEVELOPING YOUR THREE-, FIVE-, TEN- AND EVEN TWENTY-YEAR PLANS

Choose a date in the future. Pick a date that seems right to you. It should be at least three years away. Then visualise and describe how your life will be: who you will be with, what you will be spending your time doing, where you will be. If you have a partner, it's generally best for them to do the same exercise and then to compare notes; the future has to be meaningful and fulfilling for both of you.

Then work backwards towards the current date, dividing the time by about half each time. So, if your first date was in five years' time, the next date should be three years from now, then eighteen months, then nine months, four months, two months, one month, two weeks, one week, and finally today! Serious change efforts need to start today, even if in only a small way, such as doing some research about something, or having a conversation. If you don't make a start today, no matter how small, it leads to procrastination. Now you need to put the end date you have selected in your calendar; the brain doesn't take much account of the mind's intentions, but it does pay attention to actions. Most of us have developed the habit of more or less obeying our Outlook calendar: if you put the date in there, it becomes 'out there' in the real world, and the brain tends to take notice. If it's a work diary, you might want to disguise the dates with a suitable word or phrase. If you make it a positive phrase, like 'Hooray!', you're more likely to do it!

This exercise is designed to help you to develop a concrete picture in your mind of the life you would like to be leading in ten years' time. Having a clear picture of what something would look like but also what it would feel like is a well-known principle used in leading change in organisations, but this time, you are leading yourself! Having a clear picture of the future you want – what it will be like, who you will be with, what you will be doing and where – will help you to achieve it.

FORCE FIELD ANALYSIS

In making your transition to your Third Life, there will be forces driving you to make change, but also restraining forces that will resist you. They may be either within or outside yourself. When you find yourself stuck and not making as many changes as you would like, this exercise will help you to analyse the various factors pushing you forwards or pulling you back.

Take a look at the diagram on the following page and draw your own version in your notebook. Now follow the steps below.

First, state the objective you wish to achieve.

On the left-hand side of the line, identify the *driving forces*: those forces that are pushing you in the direction you want to go in. Above the arrow, write what the force is.

On the right-hand side, identify the forces that oppose the direction of change you desire: the *restraining forces*.

Now examine the force field and ask yourself which forces can be altered to 'unfreeze' the system – to cause a disequilibrium that will create motivation to change. You will discover that you have three basic options:

— Increase one or more of the driving forces.

— Decrease one or more of the restraining forces.

— Do both.

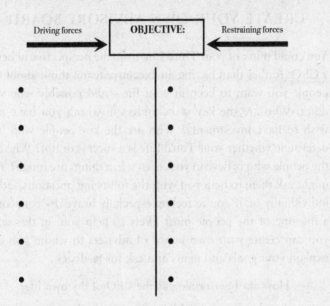

Driving forces | **OBJECTIVE:** | Restraining forces

Figure 8: Driving forces and restraining forces

Increasing driving forces is generally easier, because you are likely to have more access to them than to the restraining forces. However, if increasing the driving forces also increases comparable restraining forces, all you have accomplished is an increase in the total tension in the system. In this case, decreasing restraining forces is more likely to work, because there are already driving forces in the system, but such forces are often more difficult to manage.

CREATE YOUR OWN ADVISORY BOARD

You could think of your Third Life from the perspective of being a CEO. Rather than having an executive team, think about the people you want to keep in your life – and possibly who you don't. Who are the key stakeholders in whom you have and wish to have investments? Who are the key people who will determine whether your Third Life is a success or not? Who are the people who believe in you, even when things are tough? You might ask them to help you with the following questions, either individually or, if you're feeling especially brave, by convening a meeting of the people most likely to help you. In this way, you can create your own board of advisers to whom you can explain your goals and plans and ask for feedback.

- How am I performing as the CEO of my own life?
- To what extent am I living my purpose?
- What might I need to say yes or no to?
- How am I balancing the important and unimportant, and the urgent and not urgent in my life?
- What other activities might I consider?

Don't worry if you find this difficult. It's hard work finding the answers to these questions, and it will take time. You don't need to have sorted all this out before you begin the transition process. Your sense of purpose will gradually develop and emerge, and some of the details will get filled in. But having an initial idea of what happiness and flourishing mean to you, which activities get you into a state of flow, what your needs are, what gives your life a sense of purpose and meaning, and what your key values are, along with some strategies to achieve these, will help you to identify what will be a purposeful and meaningful Third Life.

8

The practicalities – managing the realistic consequences

In parallel with thinking about how you would like to change gear, it is absolutely key to consider what is practically doable and what needs doing in order to support your future plans.

This, too, is an essential part of deciding how you want to move forwards. You will need to consider the realistic consequences of the options you have in mind.

Most obviously, your current and future financial situation will have a critical bearing on the choices you make – and, indeed, on the choices you *can* make. However, there are many other practical and personal issues that need to be thought about.

This book is not intended to cover these areas in any detail, other than to flag how important they are. There are a number of expert organisations and people far better qualified to assist you in this.

Listed below are some of the areas you will potentially need to address, but it is by no means an exhaustive list. Obviously, these things will be different for everyone, depending on their circumstances.

Financial position and future financial demands

It should go without saying that it is essential to take an in-depth look at your finances for the future. Think about your pension(s), investments and savings, together with any future income, and also your known, and as yet unknown, outgoings in the short, medium and long term. Creating future scenarios for how these might or might not meet your needs can help to either reassure you, or to let you know that you need to reassess things.

It can come as a shock to discover the obvious, but somehow strangely emotional, reality when your income and capital start to decline after many years of increasing, or at least remaining relatively constant. The logical rider knows this will happen, but the emotional elephant can find it rather panic-inducing! Panic not. Instead, engage your logical brain and know that your emotional brain is simply trying to take you back to what has been your normality for so long.

The impact on those close to you

We have talked about the importance of thinking through how your relationships with those you care about will evolve in your Third Life. While it is your transition, it is not *only* yours. It may well have a big impact on others, especially those who you live with. This impact may be incredibly positive, and, of course, the hope is that this will be the case; however it is, at the very least, wise to test your assumptions with those close to you.

This is true at an emotional level, but also at a practical level. The very old adage 'for better, for worse, but never for lunch', while now outdated does serve to highlight the new 'rules' that will most likely need to be navigated and possibly negotiated with those around you. Failure to do this in a considerate and thoughtful way might have very unwelcome consequences, which could potentially have been avoided with forethought and sensitivity on your part.

Tech skills and support

If you are tech savvy and already control your own use of technology, you may not find this to be a big issue, but it can be a challenge for many people, especially those who have been supported by their organisations in this area, meaning they have been able to avoid engaging with learning any tech skills. Learning to deal with your own technology can be a serious challenge, and one that is potentially seriously time-consuming, frustrating and very possibly quite scary! Many who have been through the process will tell you this was one of the hardest parts of changing gear. However, these skills have become as essential to life as reading or driving – or arguably more so. Learning or relearning these skills can be very challenging, but the rewards and utility they provide are well worth it. A crucial lesson for some is the art of perseverance and discovering that, if you keep trying, eventually you will figure out some of it, if not all.

Our advice is to forward plan as far as possible. If part of your 'digital life' is entwined with your work, it is very helpful to unscramble this in advance of leaving your organisation. You are more likely to get sympathetic and constructive support this way. The humiliation of your children rolling their eyes at your incompetence should be reserved until you have no choice!

Office set-up and logistics

Not everyone will want an office (or a study/garden shed/shepherd's hut!), but for those who have been office-bound, having a physical or even a virtual space for yourself is likely to be important. Work out what you need and also what is possible within the constraints of your home or budget. Finding a space where you will be happy matters. The smallest room in a dark corner of the house might seem fine to others, but if it's not fine for you, you may need to re-establish that this is your home, too, and open up a conversation about other options.

For those readers who have had some kind of assistant, it can be a shock to lose not only tech support but also all the other support that makes life easier, such as travel and diary management. Again, thinking this through before leaving can be the best strategy, but knowing what you do need is often hard in advance. If you are continuing to work, there are part-time assistants who work virtually and could match your less-than-full-time needs. Using your network to find these assistants is often a good starting point, as is asking others in advance about what their experiences of this part of their transition have been. Some will no doubt say it came as the biggest shock!

Coaching and counselling

If you have read your way through the whole book, you will now have a sense of how challenging you think your transition may be or already has been. This is a road well-trodden, and there are coaches and counsellors out there who might be really helpful at the right moment. Obviously, no two people's journey is the same, so there are no right and wrong answers about if and when to find someone to help you along the way.

Although not at all true, you may still harbour the prejudice that only the weak need coaching or counselling and that this is definitely 'not for me'. This may well be an occasion to take yourself out of your comfort zone and experiment. Here, too, asking around your network about who others have used may be a good starting point. Your organisation may offer you this help as you leave, or be able to suggest individuals you might like to check out.

Health and wellbeing

You would have to have been living in a cave recently not to know that looking after your health is essential for your wellbeing. There is no secret recipe: being healthy involves exercising, eating moderately, maintaining a healthy BMI, and sleeping well. We are all being encouraged to take personal responsibility for this, both for our own good and for the good of society. Finding the right way for you to develop your habits is covered earlier in the book, and entering the Third Life is a great time to either perpetuate existing good habits in your new circumstances, or to create new ones to take you through the next – hopefully long – stage of your life.

These days, there is so much more of a public conversation about mental health. If this is something either troubling you or sitting at the back of your mind, then now is a good time to face into it. It may be that a counsellor could be a useful support, but exploring psychotherapy or psychiatric support are also options you should consider. There is so much support available for people seeking or accepting help, together with genuine respect for those that do so.

Colleagues and networks

Old colleagues often become closer after they have left. Any old rivalries or 'positioning behaviours' may melt away and it can be a time in which friendships flourish. This is another opportunity to take yourself out of your comfort zone and be open to the new. Do not be afraid to 'make the first move', all you have to lose is the contact with a person you would have lost contact with anyway! Many find a whole new social life emerging from connecting in a new way with old colleagues.

We have already talked about the importance of your networks and old colleagues. Although it is perfectly possible to get back in touch or retrace some of your steps after you stop your full-time role, there is real merit in doing so before you leave. There are some things you have more licence to do when you are still in a particular role. However, if you are reading this having already left, don't worry: just focus on how best to reconnect.

Updating (or writing) your will – and the all-important Power of Attorney

Even the most hard-working of people neglect their personal finances and personal affairs (and, arguably, the most hard-working of people are often also the most guilty of this). Writing a will is often something people mean to get round to, but somehow fail to actually do. And as life moves on, wills need updating. Entering your Third Life is a very good time to either make or update your will. The experience is a helpful one, as it is another mechanism for focusing on who and what really matters to you and how you want to support them.

As more and more people are exposed to the dementia diseases, there is a growing understanding of just how important it is to have your affairs in order in the event that you either die or become physically or mentally incapacitated. Dementia is terrible, not only for the sufferer, but also for their close family and friends. If you prove to be unlucky enough to develop one of the dementia diseases, of which Alzheimer's is the most common, having the right powers of attorney already in place can protect those you care about. Making arrangements so that you are prepared for such unforeseen circumstances is an act of love – and, arguably, not doing so is an act of neglect.

In conclusion

Being the best self you can be is arguably a bit of a cliché, but nonetheless, it is a worthy goal.

We hope that this book will help you to make a smoother transition to your Third Life, and that it will serve as a guide along the way: one that helps to open up your thinking, and metaphorically holds your hand through the tougher times you are likely to experience (unless you are a very lucky person!).

Donald Winnicott, whose work we looked at on page 161, once said that being a perfect parent is too much to strive for, and that being 'good enough' is just fine.

With that in mind, our hope is that you are able to change gear and find a Third Life that is long and, at the very least, good enough for you: one that, at least much of the time, enables you to be your best self – and, most importantly of all, a happy self.

Acknowledgements

Jan would like to thank all her colleagues and clients over the years who have been such an amazing source of inspiration, learning and fun. Also, an enormous thank you goes to her wonderful assistant, Nicola James.

Jon would like to thank Fay Ballard for her contribution to his thinking, and support, encouragement and wise counsel over many years. Also his clients, and his colleagues at the Tavistock Clinic, Said Business School, Meyler Campbell and his business partner Richard Jolly, for many years of enriching collaboration. Huge thanks also to Sophie Kazandjian, his personal assistant.

Thanks also to our wonderful agent Martin Redfern for all his support, to Lindsey Evans, our publisher, for believing in the project, and to Rufus Olins, who played a major part in the development of the early stages of the book.

Further reading

Happier by Tal Ben-Shahar. Based on the Harvard University course on happiness.

Managing Transitions by William Bridges. How people and organisations make transitions.

Extra Time by Camilla Cavendish. Ten lessons for an ageing world.

How To Grow Old by Marcus Cicero. Ancient wisdom for the second half of life.

Love Your Impostor by Rita Clifton. A practical guide to dealing with this common fear.

The Happiness Hypothesis by Jonathan Haidt. Why some people find happiness while others do not.

On Grief and Grieving: Finding the Meaning of Grief Through the Five Stages of Loss by Elisabeth Kübler-Ross & David Kessler. The classic view of the grief process.

The Pursuit of Happiness by Darrin McMahon. A history of the pursuit of happiness.

The New Long Life by Andrew Scott and Lynda Gratton. A framework for flourishing in a changing world.

Flourish by Martin Seligman. A psychologist's view of wellbeing.

Playing and Reality by Donald Winicott. A psychoanalyst's view of creativity and transition.

You can find out more about the virtues and your character strengths using a simple free questionnaire here: www.viacharacter.org

References

1 Bridges, William. *Transitions: Making Sense of Life's Changes* (40th Anniversary Edition), Da Capo Lifelong Books, 2020.

2 Heffernan, Margaret. *Wilful Blindness: Why We Ignore the Obvious*, Simon & Schuster, 2011.

3 Goffee, Rob, and Jones, Gareth. *Why Should Anyone be Led by You? What it Takes to be an Authentic Leader*, Harvard Business Review Press, 2019.

4 Haidt, Jonathan. *The Happiness Hypothesis: Putting Ancient Wisdom to the Test of Modern Science*, Arrow, 2007.

5 Daft, Richard L. *The Executive and the Elephant: A Leader's Guide for Building Inner Excellence*, Jossey-Bass, 2010.

6 Heath, Chip and Dan. *Switch: How to Change Things When Change is Hard*, Random House Business, 2011.

7 Bridges, 2020.

8 Lawrence, D. H. 'The State of Funk', 1929. *Late Essays and Articles*, Cambridge University Press, 2004.

9 Fox, Erica Ariel. *Winning from Within*, Harper Business, 2013.

10 Huizinga, Johan. *Homo Ludens: A Study of the Play-Element in Culture*, Angelico Press, 2016.

11 Winnicott, Donald. *Playing and Reality*, 2nd Edition, Routledge, 2005.

12 Markus, Hazel, and Nurius, Paula. 'Possible Selves'. *American Psychologist*, 41 (9), 1986, pages 954–969.

13 Brown, Stuart. 'Play is more than just fun' [video talk]. Retrieved from https://www.ted.com/talks/stuart_brown_play_is_more_than_just_fun, 2008.

14 Dweck, Carole. *Mindset: the New Psychology of Success*, Random House Publishing Group, 2006.

15 Seligman, Martin. *Learned Optimism: How to Change Your Mind and Your Life*, Nicholas Brealey Publishing, 2018.

16 Seligman, Martin. *Flourish: A New Understanding of Happiness and Well-being – and How to Achieve Them*, Nicholas Brealey Publishing, 2011.

17 Duhigg, Charles. *The Power of Habit: Why we do what we do and how to change*, Random House Books, 2013.

18 Duhigg, Charles. *Smarter, Better, Faster: The Secrets of Being Productive*, Random House, 2017.

19 Jolly, Richard. 'The Paradox of Indispensability', *Business Strategy Review*, 2011.

20 Kübler-Ross, Elisabeth. *On Death and Dying: What the Dying Have to Teach Doctors, Nurses, Clergy & Their Own Families*, 50th Anniversary Edition, Scribner Book Company, 2014.

21 Kübler-Ross, Elisabeth and Kessler, David. *On Grief and Grieving: Finding the Meaning of Grief Through the Five Stages of Loss*, Simon & Schuster UK, 2014.

22 McMahon, Darrin. *The Pursuit of Happiness: A History from the Greeks to the Present*, Penguin, 2007.

23 Lyubomirsky, Sonja. *The How of Happiness: A Practical Guide to Getting the Life You Want*, Piatkus, 2010.

24 Seligman, 2011.

25 Csikszentmihalyi, Mihaly. *Flow: The Psychology of Optimal Experience*, Harper Perennial Modern Classics, 2008.

26 Ware, Bronnie. *The Top Five Regrets of the Dying: A Life Transformed by the Dearly Departed*, Hay House UK, 2019.

Index

CHANGING GEAR

A NOTE ON THE AUTHORS

JAN HALL

Jan has been a successful entrepreneur and business leader. She is now an adviser to CEOs and chairmen. Overall, she spent 20 years as a head-hunter, founding JCA Group in 2005, which became a leading global CEO and board search firm. Jan and her partners sold the business in 2016. Previously, she was a senior partner at Spencer Stuart, the European CEO of a mid-sized PLC and the CEO of a successful private company, having started her career as a brand manager for a global business. She has over 30 years' experience of being a non-executive director and is also a qualified executive coach. She was awarded an OBE in 1996 for her work with government, has regularly been a speaker on leadership and boards and is the author of *Dementia Essentials*, a guide for loved ones who find themselves becoming carers. She has an MA in Biochemistry from the University of Oxford.

JON STOKES

Jon is a clinical psychologist, psychotherapist and leadership coach. He trained and worked at the Tavistock Clinic, where he was chair of the Adult Department and the founder of Tavistock Consulting. He taught for many years at Said Business School at the University of Oxford, where he was a Senior Fellow, and is a member of St Antony's College. He is a Director of Stokes & Jolly, a leadership advisory firm. He has advised and coached many leaders from a wide range of businesses and organisations, both in the UK and abroad, with a particular interest in the creative industries and professional service firms. Among his recent publications are 'Defences against Anxiety in the Law' in Social Defences Against Anxiety (Karnac, 2015), 'The New Landscape of Leadership: Living in Radical Uncertainty' in *The Tavistock Century: 2020 Vision*, (Phoenix, 2020) and 'From Ego to Eco: Leadership for the 4th Industrial Revolution' (Said Business School, 2020).

For more information and to download the materials for the exercises, please visit: www.changing-gear.com